Sixty Trends in Sixty Minutes

Sixty Trends in Sixty Minutes

Sam Hill

A BRANDWEEK BOOK

John Wiley
& Sons, Inc.

To my brother, Michael, and the memories
of my sister, Marian, and mother, Martha

Published by John Wiley & Sons, Inc., Hoboken, New Jersey
Published simultaneously in Canada.

This publication is designed to provide accurate and authoritative
information in regard to the subject matter covered. It is sold with the
understanding that the publisher is not engaged in rendering professional
services. If professional advice or other expert assistance is required, the
services of a competent professional person should be sought.

Wiley also publishes its books in a variety of electronic formats. Some content
that appears in print may not be available in electronic books.

ISBN 0-471-22580-0

Printed in the United States of America.

10 9 8 7 6 5 4 3 2 1

CONTENTS

CHAPTER 1

Is Purple the Next Black?

I hope to make you think—and then to do something with that thinking to improve your business or maybe even your life. To do that, I'm going to introduce you to the art and science of *trend analysis*. It's the same process my team uses with Fortune 500 companies to generate new business ventures, the same one that takes us to major speaking fora in a dozen countries each year, the same one that has gotten us published in everything from *Harvard Business Review* to the *Wall Street Journal* to *Fortune* magazine to the *Los Angeles Times*.

Sorry, but I felt I had to sell a little. Here's why.

You may well be a little cynical about the whole subject of trends. After all, sometimes it seems like we are all trend experts. We have little choice—the daily paper and the evening news are full of them, adding up to more than 100,000 articles and broadcast pieces each year. If you assume that adults get a 30-minute dose of trends each day from the media, that means a 37-year-old MBA has already inadvertently spent more time reading and hearing about trends than she or he spent studying for her or his professional degree. Isn't that enough to make her or him (and us) experts?

I don't think so. There's a big difference between observation and understanding. We all observe thousands of trends each year, but we don't really invest the time to understand them. However, if you want to change careers, invest money, start a business, design a new product, write ad copy, make an acquisition, or sell off a corporate division based on trends, you need more than casual observation. You need understanding—real understanding.

Let me illustrate the difference between understanding and observing with a small, personal example. My niece, Kristine, recently married. At the wedding, I noticed that every woman of a certain age seemed to be wearing purple. When I pointed this out to my wife, she replied, "Oh, sure. That's the fall trend." Actually, it's not. It is a *fashion,* which, as I will explain later, is something else entirely.

Whatever it was, it was in full bloom. Now, the point is that I hadn't *foreseen* that purple would become the next black. (My wife tells me purple is actually the next brown, and that gray is the next black.) If I had known about this ahead of time, presumably, I could have profited from it (e.g., by investing in purple fabric options). But I didn't, I just observed it.

More important, even once I spotted this profusion of purple, I still didn't really understand it. At least, I didn't understand it at any sort of useful level. As a result, I have no idea if it will stick around for awhile, how big it will be, or who will follow it. I didn't know if it is a Louisville or Midwest fashion or some global color wave fresh from the runways of Paris. I will never know. What I did in that church was simply observation—trendspotting—which is what most of us do when we read a trend article in the newspaper. We glance at it curiously for a moment or two, then we shrug and turn both the page and our attention to something else.

Trend analysis means something else entirely. It requires systematically dismantling a trend to understand what's behind it, why it is or isn't important, how it will manifest itself in the day-to-day world, and when it will break into the mainstream. That final element is what Malcolm Gladwell called the *tipping point.* (Malcolm's book of the same name is one of the two best books ever written on the subject of trends.) What? Why? How? When? Every one of these elements is important if you want to do more than just observe.

To drive home the point about the value created by really understanding trends, let's take a stroll through my Trendmeister Hall of Fame. Please don't add this museum to your list of places to visit in Chicago. You'll be disappointed. It's not a building at all, but a black file cabinet in my factory cum office in Skokie. Also, you won't find any busts of Faith Popcorn or John Naisbitt or other trend experts, either. Instead, I devote every square inch of space in the Hall to those who turned trends into real businesses.

Were it really a physical space, the Hall of Fame would have two wings. One side of the building would be devoted to serial trendmeisters, the professionals who have built huge careers off correctly reading trend after trend after trend, and building business after business around them. That list would include people like Ian Schrager, Madonna, Steve Jobs, Richard Branson, Bill Ziff, and Jerome Lemelson.

The other wing, however, would be devoted to an even more intriguing group: one-time trendmeisters. These are more or less ordinary people who spotted a trend, took the time to really understand it, and then turned that understanding into a fortune. Hanging on the walls there would be portraits of people like Ed Kaplan of Zebra Technologies, Sir Martin Sorrell of WPP, Clay Mathile of Iams, Mike Egan of Alamo Rent a Car, and Howard Schultz of Starbucks. Their stories are even more fascinating than those of the pros.

Both groups are worth getting to know a little better.

CHAPTER 2

The Trendmeister Hall of Fame

Of course, you've heard of Steve Jobs, Madonna, and Richard Branson. But you may not know who Jerome Lemelson is. Here's a hint: Thomas Edison has 562 patents, Jerome Lemelson has 558.

> **Trendmeister.** Jerome Lemelson (1923–1997)
> **Trend.** Numerous, including machine vision and bar-code scanning
> **Pivotal moment.** 1953, when he received his first patent for an improved version of the beanie with a propeller on top

Over 750 companies license Lemelson patents, including Alcoa, IBM, Ford, Cisco, Boeing, and Dow Chemical. So far, license fees have brought Lemelson, his attorneys, and the Lemelson estate nearly $1.5 billion. If you own a Sony Walkman or a Mattel Hot Wheels, you have contributed a tiny portion of that amount. Lemelson may well be the best-paid inventor in history.

Fans call him a modern-day Edison, a da Vinci, a Jules Verne—a visionary who had a genius for seeing the future direction of technology. Critics argue that Lemelson wasn't a real inventor, because he patented his ideas but never created working models. Both groups agree, however, on his ability to analyze technological trends, to "figure out where an industry was headed, and then put a patent directly in its path."[1] There's also no doubt that Jerry did this not by happenstance, but by employing a very deliberate and disciplined approach to analyzing technological trends.

Here's how he did it. Jerry scoured technical and trade journals looking for early signs of technological trends. Once he'd worked out the likely trajectory of the technology, he'd file broad patent applications on ideas that he thought would one day be invented, continually updating the applications as technology moved along. After the technology became commercially available, he'd sue to enforce his patent rights. Voilà. This simple business model ginned out so much money that even his lawyer owns his own mountainside in Aspen.

At the heart of his success is the following process, which he used to analyze tech trends:

1. He dug in technical journals and obscure publications outside the mainstream. That's important. By the time a trend appears in the *Wall Street Journal* or the *Washington Post,* it may well already be so far along that it's too late to climb aboard.

2. He read a broad cross section of media, subscribing to more than 40 technical journals. He concentrated not on the information in each article, but instead searched for potential synergies and cross-connections.

3. He took the time to document in careful detail, after he'd noodled on it for a bit, what he thought the implications would be. An excellent draftsman, he filled pads with sketches of inventions of over-the-horizon devices. Then he could track the trend as it evolved, updating both the trend and his estimate of the time when it might break as the technology came closer and closer to market.

Obviously, Jerry was a technical whiz. He graduated in the early 1950s from NYU with three engineering degrees. Lots of people have technical degrees; however, not all of them become billionaires. The difference was that Jerry had a process that enabled him to know what was going to happen before it happened.

Let's continue on our tour of the Hall of Fame. Quickly, we come to Madonna, Richard Branson, Steve Jobs, and Ian Schrager. They don't have 500 patents each, but they are no less impressive.

Consider Ian Schrager, for instance. Studio 54, the nightclub he founded, was the intersection of the seminal fashions and cultural currents that defined the decade of the 1980s. Ian is also the man who invented the concept of boutique hotels, and who built New York City's Hudson, Morgans, Paramount, and the Royalton. Now the large hotel conglomerates are following his lead: Starwood's, the owner of the Westin and Sheraton chains, has a chain of small, boutique hotels under the W brand. But Ian was the one who did it first. Now he plans to open a chain of lifestyle outlets called Shop.

Will it be a success? Who knows. Occasionally, even these trendmeisters miss. Branson's introduction of Virgin Cola into the United States was a flop. Lemelson lost his first lawsuit (against Kellogg's for paper cutout masks). Madonna's career has stalled once or twice since that day in 1978 when she gave up dancing and soft-core porn for rock and roll. (Wait a minute. . . .). But I wouldn't bet against any of them. These folks are to trend analysis what Michael Jordan and Phil Jackson are to basketball championships, and like these two, they have the rings to prove it.

That's enough on the professional trendmeisters. As I said, there's an even more interesting group over in the other wing: ordinary people who became trendmeisters.

It's lonely work building a business that is based on a trend whose potential only you can see. Think about it. Your coworkers tell you that you're nuts at least once a day. Every Sunday, your mom phones to ask when you're going to go out and get a real job to feed her young grandchildren. Your wife smiles bravely as you wax eloquent on where the *chronosynclastic infundibulum* market is headed.[2] Trendmeisters have only their vision to keep them company. These are the everyday heroes of the revolutions created by trends.

Trendmeister. Ed Kaplan
Location. Vernon Hills, Illinois
Trend. Digitalization
Pivotal moment. 1985

It was in late 1985 that Ed gathered the managers of Data Specialties, Inc. (DSI) together and announced that he'd just sold their main line of business and that the company only had enough cash to meet six more payrolls. In the coming half-year, they'd better find a way to build a new business, or everyone, including Ed, would have to find a new job.

They found a way. The new company, Zebra Technologies, was formed in 1986. The initial public offering (IPO) occurred in 1993, and the company grew like a rocket. It made *Fortune* magazine's list of the best small businesses 6 of the next 7 years. Today its products are sold in 90 countries and are purchased by 70 percent of Fortune 500 companies. While the old DSI has faded into obscurity, Zebra is now approaching $500 million in sales. And all of this came about because Ed understood what the trend to digital really meant.

The story starts at the end of the 1960s, in the very early days of mass computing. Back then, there were no such things as floppies and CD drives, and instructions to intelligent machines were transmitted via paper with holes in it. Paper tape was used to control devices like photocopiers and milling machines. It was in this environment in 1969 that two ambitious young engineers, named Ed Kaplan and Gary Cless, left General Telephone and Electronics (GTE) to form DSI, a company that made equipment to read long spools of paper tape. Data Specialties, Inc., quickly became a leader in its little niche. After a little more than a decade, the little company had 126 employees, a loyal customer base, and a sterling reputation.

Ed was worried, though, even in the early days. He fretted over computer trade magazines. He anxiously followed the development of disk drives and digital communication. He haunted trade shows and kibitzed with customers, finally reaching an uncomfortable conclusion: However successful DSI was, paper tape was a dying industry. Ed could see the day coming when those huge, narrow spools of tissue-thin paper would be replaced by a wire that ran from a computer in the office to the factory floor.

Ed did more than simply worry. He began searching for the product to replace paper-tape machines. Every week or so, an eager inventor would show up at DSI headquarters, carrying a box with what he or she thought could be the next big idea. Sometimes, it could get a bit silly. One of the would-be inventors brought a prototype built from an old lawn mower. Neither the lawn mower nor any of the boxes held the answer that Ed was looking for. He would kindly show the visitors out and go back to poring over trade industry magazines and technical journals.

By the late 1970s, Ed finally became convinced that he'd found the next big thing: bar codes. Universal product codes had been widely introduced in 1973. So far, they were being used mostly on the back of packages in supermarkets, but Ed could see a day when bar codes would be everywhere, from inventory control to the factory floor to the shipping department. Moreover, making bar-code printers seemed a lot like the paper-tape machine business—manufacture of a complex, high-speed mechanical device sold to industrial buyers.

Kaplan's management team was less convinced. After all, despite Ed's worries, DSI had its best years in 1981 and 1982. Ninety percent of the profits came from paper-tape machines, not from the tiny bar-code printer business that Ed was building. Indeed, no one knew if reliable bar-code printing in a harsh industrial setting was even possible. Running a factory is a bit different from a supermarket. In a factory, the bar code has to be perfect—solid black with crisp edges—so it can be read correctly the first time, every time. And in the early 1980s, no one had yet developed a reliable, deployable technology to produce pure black, the Holy Grail of bar codes. So DSI's management viewed bar-code printers as an interesting, but not very urgent, issue.

That brings us back to the day when Ed announced the sale of DSI and walked out of the conference room, leaving his disbelieving managers behind. He'd just sold a successful company in a still successful industry, and he invested everything in an industry that didn't even really exist. The fact that he sold the business underlines that others thought the future of paper tape was not as dim as he did. But he was dead right. His vision created one of the early technology success stories of the 1990s. For that, and for the style with which he did it, we hereby elect Ed Kaplan to the Trendmeister Hall of Fame.

Trendmeister.   Howard Schultz of Starbucks
Location.   Seattle, Washington
Trend.   Upscaling of coffee
Pivotal date.   1987

Every morning, I raise my latte to Howard Schultz. It's because of Howard that hundreds of thousands of Americans can start the day with a decent cup of coffee. Overpriced? Perhaps. But it's drinkable, and drinkable coffee was an endangered species until Howard came along.

There are two varieties of coffee beans, arabica and robusta. Arabica beans are dense and flavorful. Robusta beans are thin-tasting, harsh, and contain twice as much caffeine. Arabica grows slowly and only on cool mountainsides, making it costly to plant and harvest. Robusta, in contrast, grows quickly in moist lowlands, making it much cheaper to produce and thereby giving it its name. While many things determine the taste of the coffee we drink, the largest single factor is the ratio of arabica beans to robusta beans in the mixture. At Starbucks and Caribou, among others, the coffee is 100 percent arabica; however, cheap instant blends can contain no arabica at all.

From 1912 until 1956, most coffee in America was arabica. As a result, Americans drank some of the best coffee in the world. But in 1956, General Foods decided to stretch profits a bit by introducing a smidgen of cheap robusta into its market-leading Maxwell House brand. Other coffees soon followed suit, and by the 1960s, a smidgen had become a dollop; in the 1970s, when a huge frost hit the Brazilian arabica crop, widespread robusta substitution became commonplace.

In 1961, only a few years after General Foods' experiment, per capita coffee consumption in the United States peaked. Then, as more and more robusta made its way into American coffee cups, consumption declined for the next 2-plus decades. Americans turned to tea, carbonated soft drinks, beer—to anything to avoid drinking the thin cardboard soup that had come to pass for coffee.

Of course, not everyone gave up. Dutch immigrant Alfred Peet opened Peet's Coffee and Tea on Vine Street in Berkeley in 1966 and imported his own arabica beans, which he roasted in small batches in a roaster he'd brought in from Europe. In April 1971, three of Peet's loyal mail-order customers, Jerry Baldwin, Gordon Bowker, and Zev Siegl, opened another arabica coffee roaster in Seattle. And in an irony of ironies, General Foods bought the Scandinavian coffeemaker Gevalia in 1970 and began offering quality imported coffee by mail in the United States. However, these holdouts were like tiny fingers, unable to stem the flood of robusta that was pouring through the dike.

Howard Schultz did not start the trend to upscale coffee. In 1971, when Jerry, Gordon, and Zev were deciding on Starbucks as a name for their new business, Howard was graduating from Carnarsie High School in Brooklyn, more worried about finding a college football scholarship than good coffee. He didn't discover Starbucks until 10 years later, after he'd graduated from college, spent 4 years in the Xerox sales program, and moved on to become vice president of the U.S. division of the Swedish company Hammarplast. Hammarplast makes, among other things, high-end extruded plastic cones used to hold drip-coffee filters. Howard's role in the coffee saga began in 1981, when curious as to why a tiny Seattle store bought more of these cones than a giant like Macy's, he climbed on a plane and flew to Seattle to visit Starbucks.

Howard fell in love with the high-end coffee business instantly, but the business didn't exactly fall in love with him. The Starbucks team was pretty happy with things as they were, and were nervous that adding a high-voltage New Yorker like Howard would upset the laid-back West Coast karma of the small coffee store chain. It took master salesman Howard a year to finagle an offer to join them.

When the offer finally came, Howard left a promising career in New York for a job that didn't yet exist at a Seattle coffee company with five stores. It looked like insanity to his friends and parents, but Howard saw before anyone else—even the founders of Starbucks—the full potential of the nascent trend to upscale coffees. It was a bold move. Howard did not come from a wealthy family. He'd grown up in the Brooklyn projects and was the first member of his family to get a college degree. The salary he walked away from, $75,000, was good by any standards in 1981, but it was a princely sum to Howard. But he knew, he just knew, that the first company to provide Americans with good coffee would take the market by storm.

Of course, his recognition that Jerry and Gordon were onto something is impressive, but riding someone else's trend is not enough to get you into the Trendmeister Hall of Fame. (There's only so much space in the file cabinet. We have to be exclusive.) Had Howard stopped there, he might well now be a wealthy, but obscure, businessman in the Pacific Northwest. But he didn't. What comes next is what gets him his place in the Hall.

In the spring of 1983, while walking down a street in Milan, Howard idly started counting espresso bars. He was stunned by the number he found. Once he started looking, he began noticing them everywhere—on every corner, tucked in every hotel lobby, down every side street. Not just that, but everywhere there was a coffee bar there were happy people, laughing and drinking espresso. Howard had an epiphany: Coffee is more than a drink, it is a social experience, and just as there is fine coffee, there is a fine coffee experience. If Americans can fall in love with fine coffee, then the next trend must be fine coffee bars.

At the time, there was one espresso bar for every 2,000 adults in Milan. That translated into 100,000 coffee bars in the United States. Coffee roasting may be a good business Howard reasoned, but coffee bars could be an entirely new industry. Back in the States, he tested the first coffee bar in the back of a Starbucks store in 1984. A throng of customers made it an immediate success, and that should have been the start of the Starbucks we know.

The problem was the owners of Starbucks were unsettled by the success of the coffee bar experiment. They saw themselves as coffee roasters. Coffee bars seemed like a distraction, a different business, and not one in which they were particularly interested. By this time, they'd come to love Howard, accent and all. They even almost believed his argument that the way upscale coffee would make it to the American masses was through coffee bars. But they didn't buy into the trend the way he did.

So in early 1986, Howard left Starbucks to start a line of coffee bars. He left not only with their good wishes but $150,000 in seed money from the debt-laden company. His wife, who'd just had their first child, went back to work to support them, and Howard worked night and day designing and building the first Il Giornale coffee bar. What we know today as Starbucks is really the evolution of Il Giornale. Only a year later, Howard had the unexpected opportunity to buy the original Starbucks, which he combined with his three-bar Il Giornale business. The rest, as they say, is history.

Howard, for first recognizing the importance of the upscaling trend and the opportunity it provided to decommoditize coffee, for risking everything to act on that trend, for finding the perfect vehicle to make the trend happen, and for selling me a good cup of coffee, we elect you to the Trendmeister Hall of Fame.

We could go on and on and on with these everyday trendmeisters. There's an old saying that behind every great fortune is a great crime. The truth is a bit more encouraging: Behind every great fortune is a great example of trend analysis.

Let's look at Clay Mathile, as an example. In the 1980s, many young people made the decision to start families later than their parents and grandparents. To the giant pet food companies like General Foods, this was bad news. Fewer families meant fewer pets, their market researchers said. Clay Mathile of tiny Iams in Dayton, Ohio, correctly understood that the exact opposite was true. Childless couples would buy more pets, and with all of that disposable income, they'd be willing to spend on them as well. Guess who was right? General Foods is now out of the pet foods business, whereas Clay recently sold Iams to Procter & Gamble for more than $1 billion and has retired to his own island in Florida.

Trendmeisters like these are the ones who have built the world we live in today: Ray Kroc of McDonald's; Mike Egan of Alamo Rent a Car; William and Alfred Levitt, who invented the housing subdivision; adman Sir Martin Sorrell; Phil Berber of CyberCorp; Sam Walton of Wal-Mart; John Sperling of the University of Phoenix. In the next chapter, we will look in more detail at what we can learn from them.

CHAPTER 3

Fads, Fashion, and History

Now we've finished our brief tour of the Trendmeister Hall of Fame. In just a minute, we'll start our rocket sled ride through 60 trends in 60 minutes. But before we do, does anyone have any questions?

QUESTION: *What is there about these trendmeisters that really sets them apart?*

Trendmeisters are always curious. That's what drove Howard Schultz to jump on that plane to Seattle. They look in places where other people don't. That's what Jerry Lemelson and Ed Kaplan were doing when they pored over those dry technical journals. They're always looking for oddball connections. Branson sees a logical business link between record stores, airlines, cola, trains, and wedding services. Nobody else does, but he makes it work. Trendmeisters are very switched-on people. Being switched on is about awareness, not genius.

QUESTION: *What's the difference between trends and fads? Why do we care?*

Fads are very short-term trends that are caused by popular momentum. There's an old story about the California gold miner who decided to rid the mining camp of competition by starting a rumor of a strike in Canada. For a few days, he had the goldfield to himself, but the more he thought about his rumor, the more it sounded like there might be something in it. So he packed up and moved to

Canada himself.[1] Fads often have no more logic to them than that. Some fads work to a schedule. You can't necessarily predict what they'll be, but you can be pretty sure that one will happen—they're as regular as clockwork. Cyclical fads are called *fashions*. For example, according to my wife, purple comes in every 2 years or so. Each Christmas, there is a new red. Apparently, simple three-chord rock and roll is back.

Fads are to trends what lottery tickets are to a 401(k). All it takes is one winner and you're rich. (If only I'd known about purple!) The trick, of course, is finding that winner. Since there's no underlying logic to them, they're impossible to predict. It's a blind grope, like hunting a black cat in a dark room at night with a blindfold on.

If you're going to chase fads, remember this rule: Get in early and get out early. Because they peak so quickly, it's not possible to run fast enough to catch up, and because they come down so fast, it's easy to get stuck when they do. Ask all those small businesses with warehouses full of XFL uniforms.

Down the street from me lives our local dot-com millionaire success story. His secret? Sure, he was one of the first to found an Internet service provider (ISP). What made him rich, however, was being one of the first to sell. I have a dozen friends who jumped on the dot-com bandwagon just as it ground to a complete halt. Instead of big homes, they have drawers full of worthless stock options. They weren't any less talented or less committed than the millionaire. They just jumped on too late, and couldn't get off once it slowed down. That's the risk in chasing fads.

QUESTION: *If fads are really quick trends, what do you call really long ones?*

History.

QUESTION: *What causes trends?*

Trends happen for a reason. A ball lying on a flat, level surface never simply starts to roll across the floor of its own accord, unless you live inside a cheesy teen horror flick. In the real world, something has to change to make that ball roll. It could be a slap from a cat's paw, the vibration from a passing truck, or an earthquake, but there's always something; otherwise, the ball just sits there. Trends never start from nothing, and they never stop for no reason. They follow the same Newtonian laws that we learned in high school physics class: A body at rest will remain at rest unless it is acted upon by an outside force.

Alcoa, for example, has a division that makes shiny aluminum wheels for large 18-wheel trucks. Demand for those wheels has grown steadily, in part because they are a superb product that quickly repays the investment by improved fuel consumption. However, if you look carefully at the growth, you'll see that something else is responsible as well—a change in a law almost 30 years ago.

Here's what happened. When trucking was deregulated, the cost of shipping by road plummeted as driver-entrepreneurs cut prices to gain a piece of the new market. As a result, there was a huge demand for new drivers, so much so that a few unqualified drivers slipped through, causing accidents and forcing a national crackdown on licensing standards.

The new national licensing exam was so tough that it not only limited the number of new drivers coming into the industry, but some of the older drivers elected to retire. This exacerbated the driver shortage and created a very competitive market for drivers. Companies began competing for drivers, putting ads on radio, in truck stops, and on the rear doors of those huge rigs in front of you on the interstate. To attract drivers, trucking companies also started offering higher wages, perks, and flashy new trucks with shiny new wheels, which they buy from Alcoa. There's always a reason.

QUESTION: *People who make bar-code printers and pet food and who run coffee shops are in the Hall of Fame. Somehow I expected this trend stuff to be more glamorous. Was I wrong?*

Not always. Madonna, Branson, and Schrager are all pretty glamorous. But remember: Little trends can make you rich. Even little, boring trends can make a difference. In graduate school, I had an accounting professor who told the following story. In the 1970s, he stood in line in Fayetteville, Arkansas, to buy one of the first Hewlett-Packard (HP) calculators with a bond-pricing function. He took the new calculator and a newspaper with bond listings and drove to the office of a friend who was a bond trader. There he sat down and calculated the theoretical price of each bond and compared it with the price in the paper. Whenever he found an anomaly, he bought as many as he could afford. At first, he found lots of mispriced issues, and did very well. After a few weeks, everyone else caught on and there were no more bargains to be had. He then sold his remaining bonds, split the profits with his friend and used his half to pay his way through school.

QUESTION: *How important is timing?*

Timing is everything. Digital Equipment Corporation (DEC) figured out personal computers and American Telephone and Telegraph (AT&T) spotted the trend to cable TV. The only problem was that both companies spotted those trends 5 years after everyone else. There's no money in predicting the winner of yesterday's horse race.

Too early is better than too late, but not much. In 1993, John Scully bet the future of Apple on the world's first personal digital assistant (PDA), the Newton. The need was there, but the technology wasn't, and in 1998, Steve Jobs announced that Apple was pulling the plug on the Newton. Meanwhile, Palm Computing introduced its handheld 3 years after the Newton, in 1996, and it now sells almost $1 billion of the devices each year. The Palm folks didn't have any special secret advantage over the Newton folks; in fact, many of the Palm folks were former Newtonians who'd come over when it became obvious that Apple was losing interest in the device. They just timed it right. Computer Sciences Corporation pushed time-share computing in the 1970s, but hosting and Application Service Providers, which are the same things under a different name, only really took off with the development of the Internet and broadband communications in the 1990s. Every trend has its day.

QUESTION: *Sometimes it seems like trends point in two directions at the same time. What gives?*

For every trend, there is a countertrend. Hertz and Avis saw the increasing proportion and profitability of business travel and decided to build high-service rental car systems geared to corporations. At the same time, Mike Egan of Alamo saw the increase in the sheer numbers of leisure travelers and the fact that Hertz and Avis had little interest in serving them. He decided to create a low-service option for the nonbusiness market. Hertz, Avis, and Alamo have all three been very successful, while those who have tried to straddle trend and countertrend have struggled.

The trend/countertrend phenomenon even plays out at the most trivial of levels. For the 1970s and 1980s, the trend in cigarette marketing was toward macho imagery, as exemplified by the Marlboro cowboy. However, a significant portion of the population is deliberately moving away from macho symbols; therefore, it should come as no surprise that the most successful new cigarette is American Spirit, which has chosen the Indian to embody its non-Marlboro values. (Don't look at me—the purchase decision for cigarettes is a mystery to us all.) The opportunities created by countertrends can be every bit as exciting as those churned up by trends.

QUESTION: *Where do all the trends we're going to look at come from?*

For the most part, I came across these trends in the course of my client work. I am continually on the lookout for trends that might affect my clients' businesses. In the course of finding and analyzing those, I inevitably come across a great many that aren't very important to my clients, but are nonetheless pretty darn important. Relevant or not, I keep them all. In my office are bookshelves, notebooks, and file cabinets filled with files on hundreds of trends. And there are literally hundreds and hundreds of clippings from various sources along with stacks of analysis.

That brings us to another point. My guess is that some of these trends will be familiar to you and some won't. But the results of my trend analysis, the implications and opportunities, should all be new news.

As you read this book, you'll see a lot of statistics and anecdotes. A very few are for effect (e.g., if I say that something is a "gazillion"). Except for those few and obvious examples, however, any time you see a number or factoid, it has come from a reputable source.

The typical trend has a dozen or so factoids in it. To make this a faster read and to live up to the value proposition of 60 trends in 60 minutes, I have elected to neither footnote every number nor to list sources within the text. Instead, I have included an extensive bibliography at the end of the book. If you have a question or want to dig deeper, I encourage you to start with the source material.

QUESTION: *How much longer do we have to stand here doing Q & A? Can we go now?*

Okay, okay, but let me give you one more thought. In an ideal world, you'll buy two copies of this book. And no, that's not just shampoo marketing. (The best marketer in history was the person who thought to write "rinse, repeat" on the side of a shampoo bottle. He or she doubled the size of the category instantly.) I want you to buy two copies because I'd like you use them in different ways.

I'd like you to take that first copy and sit down and read it from cover to cover, taking note of the 10 or 15 trends that seem most important to you and your company. Then you should take those 10 trends and schedule a half-day for you and your team to dissect them, discuss them, and either prioritize or discard them. This exercise is called a *trendblasting workshop,* and we devote a chapter later in this book to describing in some detail how to do it. So far, every company we have put through a trendblasting workshop has come out energized and with a long list of potential new business ideas.

I'd also like you to buy a second copy of this book and a red pen. Put those two items in a place where you keep your snatch reading, that is, things you read in snatches (e.g., while you're waiting on the train). (To be blunt, in my house we keep ours in the bathroom. Some writers hope to earn a place of honor on the library shelf next to Shakespeare; I hope to earn a spot on the bathroom shelf beside the toilet paper.) Take this second copy out from time to time, read a few pages, close the book and let the ideas ferment a bit. Play with them, roll them around in your mind, get mad at me because you think I missed the point. Do whatever you do to process and internalize ideas. Turn *my* implications into *your* implications. Then share those new interpretations with your clients, colleagues, and friends.

The greatest joy I could get is if one day you walk up to me at a conference and pull out that second book and show me all those dog-eared pages, porcupined with little yellow stickies and the margins marked up with red ink. That is what this book is really for. (Of course, if you really do keep that second copy in the toilet, I'd rather autograph the one you keep in your office.)

All right folks, it's time to rock and roll. Let's go analyze some trends.

Economic and Geopolitical Trends

Economic and geopolitical trends are the monumental forces that make and remake our world—literally. They are the Amazons and Mississippis of the trend business—trends that brush civilizations aside and cut continents in half. A minor shift can create an economic or political flood, devastating and unstoppable. When the flood recedes, new nations and businesses grow in the fertile economic silt left behind.

We're going to look at nine such world-changing trends.

1. Interconnectedness
2. Little India is coming! Little India is coming!
3. My oh my, megalopoli
4. Barbarians at the gated community
5. Comrade Adam Smith
6. The incredible growing government
7. Balkanization
8. Company states
9. Babelization

A Quick Note on Process

Reading the preceding list, it might look like we've missed a few. What about megatrends like the information revolution, the death of geography, the population bomb, global warming, the disintegration of the Iron Curtain, the ascent of the scientific method, and the Age Wave?

Not to worry. We will explore every one of those trends, but with a twist that will make the output more useful. Let's go back to our river analogy. When the Mississippi approaches the Gulf of Mexico and reaches the delta, it breaks into a number of smaller waterways, like the Atchafalaya River and Red Pass. When megatrends approach the marketplace, they break up into smaller trends and trendlets.

We'll spend much of this book looking at those sorts of trends. For example, in the consumer section, we're not going to tackle the Age Wave, but we will dig into spin-offs such as Peter Pan–ism, prematurity, and bionicism. As we work through this book to draw out the implications of the 60 most important trends we face, you shouldn't be surprised to see the not-so-invisible effects of the economic and geopolitical megatrends again and again.

Yet, we have found that working with these smaller-scale, second-order trends simply produces more useful insights than does working at the megatrend level. Recently, I held a trendblasting workshop for a major consumer goods multinational in the Four Seasons Hotel in New York. Shelby O'Hara, the executive in charge, and I had carefully selected 10 of the smaller-type trends from the Helios database. We'd picked 10 that were important to their business and where the company could really use some fresh thinking. I explained the 10 briefly. Then Shelby spoke. She suggested we work from the list of 10, but said that if anyone had another trend in mind that they really wanted to work on, they were free to pick that one. We then asked each team to pick one, and we dispatched them to their breakouts to develop implications. You guessed it. Of seven teams, three picked one of the megatrends—the Age Wave—one that we had deliberately *not* put into the mix. That was fine. The problem, however, was that none of those teams said anything new. The non–Age Wave teams were brilliant, but the Age Wave teams didn't come up with a single big, new idea.

I don't think the problem is that you, I, and other business professionals are not insightful enough. I think it's just that there are entire organizations (like Yankelovitch and the Cato Institute) whose primary business is tracking and analyzing one or two megatrends. They do a pretty darn good job of it. There's not much left after they're finished grinding. Anyway, megatrends produce megainsights, the sort you base a presidential agenda on. We're looking for mini-insights, the specific kind you can build a billion-dollar business or a great career on, or on which you can base a winning brand strategy.

In each of the following 60 trends, our focus will be on implications and tangible ideas that you can use. To get to those, we'll follow a common structure. First, we'll define the trend. Then we will discuss why it's happening, and look at some of the implications that will result. After the implications, we'll run through a few opportunities at both the business and individual levels. To repeat myself, I hope that both the implications and opportunities serve more as thought starters than answers, and that you'll add implications of your own as we go. Got those yellow stickies and red pens ready?

Interconnectedness

The Trend

Increasingly, the world is becoming interconnected, and there is virtually no place you can't call, travel to, or send a FedEx package to quickly and cheaply. (At first glance, this may seem a bit obvious. We'll get to the not-so-obvious pretty quickly.)

Disconnectedness is the result of not being tied into networks that provide communication (movement of ideas,) transportation (movement of people), and distribution (movement of goods and services.) For example, the Lavani Valley in New Guinea isn't very distant. New Guinea sits smack-dab between two major nations, Australia and Indonesia, and is only 300 miles wide. But Europeans didn't reach the Lavani Valley until 1954, over 400 years after the coast was first sighted.

The reason? Getting to the Lavani Valley makes an expedition to the South Pole look like a weekender to Boca Raton. The Lavani Valley sits in the middle of the nastiest terrain the Earth has to offer. It is surrounded by dense jungle with virtually no edible native flora or fauna. Razorback ridges and roaring rivers isolate it from the outside world. Each valley is so disconnected that each village lives in its own world, sometimes ignorant that anyone and anything lives beyond the ring of mountains. New Guinea, an area slightly larger than California, has over 700 languages and dialects. However, even the Lavani Valley is interconnected now.

Factors and Factoids

Interconnectedness makes sense. Waycross, Georgia, the small town where I grew up, is 240 miles south of Atlanta and 1 hour by road north of Jacksonville. From my current home in Winnetka, just north of Chicago, it is 976 miles to Waycross. Twenty years ago, visiting my father meant a butt-numbing, droopy-eyed 19-hour drive. Today, I can make the same trip door-to-door in 7 hours on a flight that costs about $200.

Waycross is interconnected in more ways than just transportation, too. In terms of *communication,* families there can now get 82 television channels over cable and satellite, rather than 3. (And to get a clear picture for channel 7, you don't even have to talk your brother into climbing on the roof and turning the antenna.) A long-distance conversation with my father is no longer a once-a-week luxury, and I don't have to wait until after seven on Friday to call. In Waycross, as in most places in the United States, it is now possible for children to do their homework using the Internet.

There is a third dimension of interconnectedness, *distribution,* and along that, too, Waycross is now interconnected. Five choices of bread, all white and all sliced, have burgeoned into an entire aisle of wheat, French, and rye, along with croissants, bagels, and English muffins. Coors beer, once a rarity, is in the cooler of every 7-Eleven. People still read the *Waycross Journal Herald* and the *Atlanta Constitution,* of course, but they also read the *New York Times* and the *Wall Street Journal.* In total, Waycross is still remote compared with Times Square, but that remoteness is now measured in minutes rather than light-years. (See Table 4.1.)

Interconnectedness is rising and will continue to do so. In 1930, a coast-to-coast flight took 36 hours and cost the adjusted-wage equivalent of $4,780. Today, that same trip costs about $209 and

Table 4.1 **Way Down in Waycross**

Interconnectedness	1970	2001
Communications		
Number of TV channels	3	82
Cost of 3-minute long-distance call	$7.71	$0.21
Distribution		
Number of items in a grocery store	6,000	40,000
Transportation		
Trip to Chicago—time	19 hours	7 hours
Trip to Chicago—cost (est.)	$500	$200

Sources: Simon, Federal Reserve Bank of Dallas, Harvard, analysis by author.

takes 6 hours. Virtually every American now has access to a telephone and can afford to use it. The cost of a 3-minute coast-to-coast call has dropped from $341.45 in 1915 to $0.36 today on an apples-to-apples basis. There are now 69.8 million cell phones in the United States. That's one for every four people. Millions of Americans are connected to the Internet. We can even watch the war in Afghanistan live, thanks to tiny videophones carried by reporters.

Interconnectedness is not just an American phenomenon. Scandinavians are twice as likely to own a cell phone as Americans. By 2005, a billion people worldwide will be connected to the Internet. Worldwide, international air travel is growing at 5 percent per year. And you can buy Marlboros and Levis in Paris just as easily as you can buy Perrier and Moët & Chandon in Chicago.

Implications

Expect the world to get even smaller. Wider roads, faster planes, more broadband connections, and better logistics technology will continue to increase interconnection.

Expect interconnectedness to make the world a more interesting place. In an interconnected world, information, people, and goods flow back and forth across geographies very quickly. A dispute on the West Bank spills over to New York City. Scientists who mathematically model virulent diseases have found that because of air travel, any new plague will quickly spread to every corner of the earth relatively quickly, as AIDS has. Governments with introverted fiscal and monetary policies like Indonesia find themselves under siege as capital instantly flows away from them to more attractive markets. Isolationism is no longer an option. If we want to protect children in the United States from smallpox, we must inoculate children in India.

Interconnectedness extends and diffuses the short-term impacts of events. For example, natural catastrophes like famines, floods, fires, and earthquakes will be felt by more people, but each individual will be affected less. In 1998, Chicagoans chipped in to help victims of Hurricane Georges in the Dominican Republic, a catastrophe that would not have even been on their radar screens 100 years ago. As I write this, Cubans are receiving imports of corn from the United States to forestall famine due to crop failures. Firehouses in New York received gifts from Japanese schoolchildren following September 11. Interconnectedness transmits the shock away from the point of impact, like the roll cage of a race car.

Interconnectedness is the single most important trend in this book. (Many of the smaller trends that we'll see in the future sections will be caused by, or at least shaped by, interconnectedness.) But we said that we weren't going to focus on the megaimplications of megatrends. So let's bring it down a level. Interconnectedness has mini- and microimplications as well.

Consider business, for instance. Interconnectedness has already driven the shift of U.S. industry to just-in-time and make-to-order manufacturing systems. Have you tried to buy a new window, lamp, or bookcase recently? Chances are you didn't bring it home with you, but instead received it drop-shipped directly from the factory. And more change is coming.

For example, in an interconnected world, whenever you spot an opportunity, you better move fast. It will still be possible to walk down a street in Milan and find an idea that you can bring back to the States, like Howard Schultz did—but don't dawdle. In an interconnected world, ideas move at light speed, and someone else has baristas and espresso machines just one plane behind you.

Here are a few opportunities I've spotted that still have some legs to them.

The Opportunities

Business. Interconnectedness is now a necessity, not a nice-to-have, and people will pay for it. There are still many fortunes to be made plugging disconnected places into the network. Craig McCaw got rich building cellular networks in and fiber-optic pipes to smaller Midwestern markets.

Outside the United States, the opportunities to provide interconnectedness are virtually boundless. U-Paid Systems has started a business offering phone cards to poor people in remote villages in India, but with a wrinkle.[1] To make it true interconnectedness, they also offer these people voice-mail boxes, so they can more easily schedule calls with relatives in the United Kingdom and the United States.

Individuals. We'll also see jobs become more portable. You're working on a project in New York, but feel you'd be more creative in Zion, Utah, for a week? Bye. Now job portability isn't the same as telecommuting or working from home. Telecommuting is one of those experiments that will probably decline in a market with a glut of labor. For managers and those holding most regular jobs, telecommuting is just too much work and too expensive. However, interconnectedness does mean that the job can go with you, when you want it to, and unfortunately, as we'll discuss later, it can even go with you when you don't want it to. Blackberry's and laptop plug-ins in airports are just the tip of the iceberg of the job portability opportunity.

We could go on, but instead, let's pick up the pace a bit and just jump ahead to our next trend to see interconnectedness in action.

Little India Is Coming

Trend

Global cross-pollination of cultures is accelerating. Pozorrubio, a remote farming town in the Philippines, now grows mansions. Big houses are sprouting in the downtown, in the suburbs, and on the hillsides above the rice paddies. But you can't pay for or furnish a new mansion by cutting sugar cane, the traditional source of wages in Pozorrubio. The money fueling the new economic boom comes from remittances, money that is sent back from overseas by maids, nannies, and software engineers who work in the United States, Hong Kong, Japan, and Germany. In all, 1 of every 10 citizens of Pozorrubio now works abroad.

We're more interested in the flow of culture out of the Philippines, however, than the flow of dollars back in. When Filipinos come to Chicago to work, they can still eat traditional pork and plantain dishes at the Filipino restaurant on Devon. They've brought their cuisine with them. The influence of the Philippines is just one of many on the northwest side of Chicago. A few miles east on Devon is Little India, a crowded strip of restaurants, grocery stores, and electronics shops where you can buy everything from authentic Indian vegetables to satellite dishes that pick up the cricket match between Sri Lanka and Pakistan.

Factors and Factoids

Cultural cross-pollination comes from two sources. First is the movement of people across borders to live in new places, either permanently or, increasingly, temporarily. In 1975, 84 million people lived outside their home country. By 1999, that number had increased to 145 million. Some of that was forced dislocation (e.g., refugees), but much of it was people who have chosen to live outside their home countries for a time. And unlike most traditional immigrants to America, who for the most part actively worked toward cultural assimilation, these temporary visitors have no intention of leaving their culture behind.

Dense cities like Manhattan have long had their unassimilated ethnic pockets: Chinatown, Little Italy, Little Odessa. The new news is more pockets, and not just in big cities. Not too long ago a colleague from North Carolina surprised me by waxing eloquent about the new Indian restaurant in town. In Research Triangle Park, the number of Asian Indians has more than tripled since 1980. With this newly built critical mass, there's not only Indian food, but also classical Indian ballet instruction and concerts by touring Indian musicians. It's not Chicago's Little India yet, but it's not insignificant either.

Cross-border careers will continue. Places like the United States and Western Europe need workers, both skilled and unskilled. In 1970, 5 percent of the U.S. population was foreign born. In 1997, that number had climbed to 10 percent. The United States now allows about 100,000 foreign workers per year into the country on H-1B temporary visas, mostly to fill shortages in the high-tech industry. Not only that, but Western countries have found that foreign workers are a pretty effective form of off-the-books foreign aid. In 2000, emigrants sent $20 billion back to relatives in Latin America and the Caribbean. Experts think it will top $300 billion over the next decade. For countries like Haiti, Nicaragua, and the Dominican Republic, remittances constitute more than 10 percent of the gross domestic product (GDP). Employing workers is a less politically contentious and likely more effective way to help than government-to-government handouts.

It's not just immigration, however, that carries culture along with it. Tourism, the second source of cross-pollination, also contributes. Every time one of my neighbors vacations in Provence or Tuscany, they bring back new awareness and new tastes. And local stores like Pierre Deux pop up to serve those new preferences.

Implications

Milanese fashions in Dallas, Indian stadium concerts in New Jersey, edible food in London—all the result of cultural cross-pollination. Expect it to continue accelerating and to become more deeply infused as we move toward a global best-of-the-best cultural standard.

Opportunities

Look for ways to reshape your traditional business to better tap into these cross-border flows. International air travel will continue to grow. Travel agencies have struggled lately because airlines have slashed commissions and savvy travelers have learned to book on-line. Look for the segment of agencies that specialize in foreign travel to grow and do well. Many of us are comfortable booking our own travel to Kansas City, but we're going to be a little less bold choosing our own hotel in Tierra del Fuego. [Also look for safe alternatives to unsafe vacations (e.g., a Disney World safari).]

Think import/export. Western Union's traditional business of quick money transfer has faded as credit cards and automated teller machines (ATMs) have made it much easier to get cash remotely. But their business of secure money transfers across borders has boomed, so much so that dozens of competitors, including the U.S. Post Office's Dinero Seguro, have sprung up.

Consider new services that facilitate temporary people movement. For example, executives often have access to relocation services to arrange moving, to help look for schools, and to arrange driver's licenses and all the other paperwork that is attendant with cross-border relocation. Don't be surprised to see relocation services for the masses become popular. The typical new Indian immigrant now earns $45,000 a year and culture shock is not uncommon. Relocation services could help.

Most of all, however, widespread travel has created demand in Winnetka for high-end products made in London and Paris, and in London and Paris for products made in Traverse City and Dayton. At the same time, pockets of unassimilated immigrants create demand for everyday products not stocked at Safeway. Anywhere there's a micromarket—yes, even outside New York City and Chicago—there's an opportunity.

My Oh My, Megalopoli

The Trend

The trend is clearly toward big cities and more of them. For example, by 2015, London and its immediate suburbs will contain 7.6 million people. For almost 2 centuries, London was the prototypical megalopolis, one of the first cities to be given that designation by economists and writers. But by 2015, London won't even be on the list of the 20 largest cities in the world. (See Table 4.2). In fact, London won't even make the top 40.

In all, there will be 63 megalopoli, metropolitan areas with more than 5 million inhabitants. There will also be almost 200 more megalopoli-in-training (i.e., cities with populations of 2 million or more).

Factors and Factoids

One obvious factor driving the number of megalopoli is population growth. In 1960, there were 2.5 billion people on earth. That had grown to 4.4 billion by 1980 and to 6 billion by 2000. Demographers predict it will reach 8.0 billion in 2025 and 9.3 billion in 2050.

Table 4.2 **Twenty Largest Metro Areas in the World—2015***

1. Tokyo	28.9	11. Dehli	16.9
2. Bombay	26.2	12. Bejing	15.6
3. Lagos	24.6	13. Manilla	14.7
4. Sao Paulo	20.3	14. Cairo	14.4
5. Dhaka	19.5	15. Los Angeles	14.2
6. Karachi	19.4	16. Jakarta	13.9
7. Mexico City	19.2	17. Buenos Aires	13.9
8. Shanghai	18.0	18. Tianjin	13.5
9. New York	17.6	19. Seoul	13.0
10. Calcutta	17.3	20. Istanbul	12.3

Source: University of Vermont, Department of Economic and Social Affairs (filebox.vt.edu).
* Values are $\times 10^6$.

All of these people have to live somewhere. Why not in a megalopolis? And why not a third-world megalopolis? The big growth isn't happening in Europe, Japan, the United States, and Canada. Over the next few decades, most industrialized countries will actually shrink—Germany by 14 percent. (India adds as many people to its population every week as the European Union adds in a year—343,000. India's on track to surpass China by the middle of the century.)

Mexico City, São Paolo, Calcutta, Lagos, Karachi, Tianjin, and 12 other less-developed-country (LDC) cities are already on the bigger-than-London list. By 2015, 14 more cities will leapfrog the English capital. All but 1 of these 14 is in the developing world. The number of cities in the next tier down is also expanding rapidly. To our ears, their names may sound like something out of a Monty Python skit, but Taiyuan, Mashhad, Esfahan, Zhengzhou, Surat, Aleppo, Guayaquil, Surabaja, Datong, and Fushun already have more than 1 million people and will have more than 2 million by 2015.

What's not so obvious is that the trend toward larger cities is occurring even in places where there is no underlying population growth to speak of. From 1990 to 2000, North Dakota grew by 0.5 percent. Fargo, the North Dakota equivalent of a megalopolis, grew by 22.2 percent. (Fargo has a population of around 90,000.) Both rural areas and small towns in North Dakota are shrinking, but still the cities are growing.

What's behind this? Strangely enough, it's the same interconnectedness trend we just spoke about. Interconnectedness is accelerating the migration of young people to big cities. For them, big cities are opportunity pools, places where large corporations can offer technical and managerial jobs that will afford them a lifestyle they never could have dreamed of on the farm or in the small towns they grew up in. Fifty years ago, some hesitated to make the move because slow transportation and expensive communication meant cutting themselves off from friends and family. That's less and less a factor every day.

For example, mustered out after World War II, my father considered moving to New York, but instead settled in Sumter, South Carolina, where his parents lived. Faced with the same decision today, he'd probably make the move, and get a cell phone with unlimited long distance. Even during the time it has taken for you to read this page, my back-of-the-envelope calculation says that somewhere across the world, approximately 100 young people have jumped on buses and headed for the bright lights of the big city, be it New York City or Fargo.

Implications

Expect to continue to see the growth of megalopoli and metropolises and even regional hubs like Fargo. But while many want the opportunities that megalopoli provide, not everyone wants the lifestyle. So expect to also see the continued growth of *boomburgs,* defined in the United States as suburbs with a population of more than 100,000 people and more than 10 percent growth per decade. (Of course, demographers in India would consider 10 percent annual growth a successful example of family planning.) Boomburgs like Mesa, Arizona, and Naperville, Illinois, aren't true cities, because they have no center to speak of, but they are major population pockets.

The Opportunities

Business.   There's an opportunity to export trained professionals and technicians from the first world to help megalopoli build the hard and soft infrastructure they will need to support their huge growth. Today, many executives' careers include a stop in London or Paris. Going forward, these stops will far more likely be in the new megalopoli. For example, 47-year-old Rick Wagoner, now head of General Motors, spent a significant chunk of his career in São Paolo. Brian Dickie, now president of energy giant TXU, spent 5 years shuttling between Singapore and Jakarta for the consulting firm Booz-Allen & Hamilton.

Neither Mr. Wagoner nor most Europeans and Americans actually want to live in a megalopolis in an LDC for their entire careers. And therein lies a great opportunity for first-world-based businesses that offer affordable, exportable expertise and that have a business model to bring people back home again.

Individuals. Watch for *salmoning*. Never heard of salmoning? Me neither, but I needed a word to describe the circular migration many of us will go through in our lifetimes. Salmoning seemed to fit.

Look for people to be born and grow up in rural areas, small towns, or even small cities like Fargo or St. Louis, leave those cities to find good jobs in larger cities, retire to Phoenix, and then move back to where they started or where their children live toward the end of their lives. They will live their lives like salmon, in a vast circle encompassing thousands of miles, but ending up very near where they started. Said simply, if you build nursing homes, build them in New Jersey, too, not just in Boca Raton.

Barbarians at the Gated Community

The Trend

Uh oh. I just can't figure out how to say this one in a nice way. One of my friends is a venture capitalist, a Stanford graduate who lives in a lovely $5 million home in Portola Valley (part of the area better known as Silicon Valley to those of us who live east of Oakland.) He has a beautiful wife, two BMWs, a Porsche, and nine Glock pistols—one for each car, his boat, his ski condo, and another for every major room of his house. This fellow, we'll call him Steve (because that's what his parents named him), isn't alone. Increasingly, the trend is toward self-protection and fortressing.

Most Americans are shocked by a common sight in the Third World: middle-class homes surrounded by a high concrete wall topped with broken glass. Now insecurity is coming to us. Welcome to Paranoia-ville, folks.

Factors and Factoids

What's fueling this trend? First, there are simply a lot more rich people around. We're not talking about millionaires—a million bucks is no longer considered wealthy or even unusual. One of every 12 American households is now a millionaire. No, we're talking multi-millionaires, or even ten-millionaires, a group that includes 1 of every 100 U.S. households.

Thought of another way, we could empty out New Mexico and replace its entire population with ten-millionaires (which old-timers in Taos and Santa Fe might argue is already occurring.) We're witnessing a new phenomenon: For the first time in history, there now exists what some socioeconomists are calling a *mass upper class*. And it is growing. The United States now has four times as many ten-millionaires as a decade ago.

Those on the rich side of the fence know they can't count on the police to protect them. Seven out of 10 robberies are never solved. So increasingly, they are looking to protect themselves and their possessions. They see it as a case of barbarians at the gates, or the gated community, as it turns out.

The Opportunities

Big business. Who's going to win from this trend? Anyone in the security and protection business for a start. One of the best businesses in America is the prison business. The number of Americans in prison grew from around 300,000 in 1980 to well over 1.3 million today. Sure, one-third of that growth was drugs only, but then again, two-thirds wasn't. But that's not all. Not only is there money in locking the bad guys in, there's money in locking them out as well. In the early 1970s, there were around 2,000 gated communities in America. Now there are over 20,000. Four million people now live beyond a guardhouse.

There are additional protection industries we Americans haven't even thought of yet. In high-crime countries like Brazil, the latest craze is armored vehicles. There are 10,000 on the street, and 25 factories are turning out another 1,000 a year. Indeed, it costs around $25,000 per vehicle, and the extra 300 pounds of steel and Kevlar doesn't help gas mileage, but it's become a status symbol in crime-infested Rio. By the time this book comes out, U.S. carmakers will be offering optional *personal protection packages:* smashproof glass, emergency signals, and tires that can be driven when flat. In South Africa, increasingly cars come with transponders keyed to satellites, so within 15 minutes of a car theft or carjacking, police can be notified and begin tracking the vehicle. It's taking hold in the United States as well.

There will also be opportunities to help provide the tools to those who provide the security. For example, ChoicePoint has built a multimillion-dollar business integrating the FBI's many databases with public ones to make data easily accessible to those in law enforcement.

Small business.   Private security is already a $104 billion business. There's no reason to believe it's going to stop here. Security systems are standard equipment on 30 percent of new homes. That means there are 70 percent where they're not standard—yet. Also, look for high-tech to play a role (e.g., web services that provide cameras in day care centers that parents at work can call up at any time). Locks, self-protection classes, security systems, and anything to do with protecting home and property is going to be big business over the next century or so.

Willie Sutton, when asked why he robbed banks, answered scornfully, "Because that's where the money is." To find new business opportunities from this trend, simply look at where the money is, then where it isn't, and draw a line between the two. There's the opportunity.

Countertrend?

It's not quite a countertrend, but one interesting statistic is that crime has actually dropped over the last decade. Still, sociologists say not to relax, that this may just be an artifact of a temporary shortage of teenage males, and that echo booms will soon restock the system with potential felons.

Comrade Adam Smith

The Trend

The Berlin Wall is down, the Soviet Union has been dismantled, and Cal State offers an MBA in Moscow. Karl Marx must be spinning in his grave, eh? Maybe, but it's more likely that he's grinning from ear to ear. Herr Professor Marx envisaged a state with protections for workers, medical benefits, and lifetime income security. To accomplish all of that, he thought the key was for labor to own the capital. Check. Check. Check. And check. Through a variety of vehicles, American laborers now directly and indirectly own many American corporations.

Factors and Factoids

Labor now owns the capital, or at least a big chunk of it. Only 1 percent of Americans owned any stock in 1900, only 13 percent as late as 1980. But in 1998, 52 percent of Americans owned stock either directly or indirectly. And the numbers are significant. According to the New York Stock Exchange, approximately 25 percent of the stock market is now owned directly by pension funds. There's $8 trillion in all in pension funds. Another $6 trillion is invested in mutual funds, much of which is invested in the stock market. Seventy percent of those mutual fund holders have annual household incomes of less than $75,000.

Marx was right in a more direct and interesting way as well. Sure, many employees now own stock in the companies in which they work. Company plans make stock purchase cheap and convenient. Increasingly, however, employees have actually banded together to buy the company itself.

What has made this possible are employee stock ownership plans (ESOPs), vehicles that allow employees to borrow against their retirement plans to buy all or part of the businesses that employ them. The ESOPs were established in 1974 with the enactment of the Employee Retirement Income Security Act (ERISA). Since the new law, there has been an explosion of employee-owned corporations:

- In 1987, the employees of Avis borrowed $1.7 billion to buy their company.

- In 1992, Union Carbide sold 55 percent of a $50 million bottled-gas business to its employees.
- In 1994, United Airlines swapped 55 percent of its stock for $4.9 billion worth of wage and productivity concessions.

In all, 15 million Americans, or 12 percent of the workforce, share ownership of 11,000 companies that employ them. Employees own a majority of 2,500 of these, ranging from giants like Publix Super Markets, United Airlines, and SAIC to medium-sized companies like BNA, National Spinning Company, and Charles Machine Works to smaller companies like Crane Technologies Group.

Okay, it's probably not exactly what Marx had in mind. (For example, he probably didn't envisage United Airlines employees going on strike against themselves. My suggestion for a slogan: "We're not going to take our crap any longer.") But it can't be that far off. All in all, over the last 2 decades, we've seen Karl Marx and Adam Smith become comrades, their revolution plotted in the most unlikely of places, across the kitchen tables of America.

Implications

Okay, listen closely, because I'm only going to say this three times in this whole book: The dot-coms had the right idea.[2] In this case, they understood the powerful allure of ownership.

I know. I offered a young MBA, "Michael," a job for $150,000 a year plus bonus. He turned me down to go to Boston to sleep on a couch and help a friend work on a business plan for a portal concept. The friend promised him $25,000 a year and 25,000 options. I tried to convince Michael, who graduated from Northwestern, that $150,000 was worth a good bit more than $25,000 plus 25,000 unpriced options of an unlaunched company with a potentially infinite number of shares. But I lost the argument. Maybe it was about greed, but I don't think so.

Ownership was a powerful motivator 100 years ago, and it is a powerful motivator today. Ownership is also about pride and emotional satisfaction. People want to own the house they live in and the company for which they work. It goes beyond investing. Owning the company is insurance, protection against an unexpected plant closure or lay-offs.

The Opportunities

If you're a growing company, offer generous job titles and employee ownership as currency to attract talent. Employee ownership is also a good way to cash out of difficult-to-sell personal service businesses. Once your company gets large enough, for example, more than 100 employees, think about spreading the ownership around a bit.

Related Trend

Now that Americans have become comfortable with the idea of owning stocks, maybe they've gotten too comfortable. Many Americans now have accounts with on-line brokerages. Some worry that many people who are investing do insufficient research and, as a result, are assuming risks they don't need to take. With the losses created by the dot-com meltdown and the collapse of company ESOPs like that of Enron, in which many employees lost their life savings, look for new and more restrictive rules around individual investing.

More rules means more government, which makes sense, of course, given the trend to. . . .

The Incredible Growing Government

The Trend

Quick, name three things you'll never see in this lifetime. Time's up. How about (1) snow in Key West, (2) a Cubs/Red Sox World Series, and (3) a shrinking government?

There has been so much talk about the budget surplus that it would be easy to conclude that the government is shrinking. That would be wrong.

Factors and Factoids

True, in the 1990s, government expenditures as a percentage of the GDP dipped, but that was because the GDP grew, not because the government shrank. The trend is for government spending to continue growing. At the beginning of the century, U.S. government spending as a percentage of the GDP hovered in the midteens. At the end of the century, it was around 34 percent. Given the long-term trend upward and the fact that the European countries are already all above 40 percent, it's a safe bet that government spending will continue to grow as a proportion of the U.S. economy.

In the unlikely event it does stabilize in percentage terms, that still doesn't mean that the government is going to shrink. The last time there was actually a reduction in the absolute size of the government was in 1965, 1 of only 6 such years since 1936. Even during the Reagan years, with all the rhetoric about the need to rein in government, government outlays almost doubled—from $590 billion to $1.1 trillion.

What's driving this? Simple, the ratcheting effect. Every January, congresspeople and senators head to Washington, case files stuffed with requests by constituents. Over the next 300 days, the legislators will pass somewhere between 500 and 1,000 new laws. And though the scale is different, a similar scenario is replicated in 50 statehouses and in thousands of municipalities each year as well. The net result is hundreds of new laws each year, many of which require new programs, new departments, new buildings, and new parks and roads, all of which add up to new spending.

Every year the budgeting process may trim back a few expenditures, but every spending cut is met with vociferous opposition from whoever is currently gaining from that program today. So the number of ways to spend money still grows faster than decisions to stop spending. It's a ratchet. Governments tend to get bigger and bigger. If left unchecked long enough, as in the former Soviet Union, they can even get so big that they simply collapse under their own weight. (Not that we're close to that level.)

Implications

Big business. The government is a boom market—rain or shine, recession or expansion. This year, the government will spend $1.6 trillion. That's $1,600,000,000,000, over 1 million millions, enough money to cover every square inch of New York City in $20 bills. Of course, not all of that trillion-dollar pot of money is an opportunity; much of it goes to things like paying postal workers and sailors. But around $200 billion goes to purchases. True, big business already knows about the government business. And many companies better known for their nongovernment business still find the government a huge and profitable market. General Motors, Tenneco, and West-inghouse, for example, each sell more than $3 billion a year to the government. Still, there's room for more.

Small business.   Not all small businesses realize that getting the government as a customer is a great way for small businesses to become big businesses. Take Globalquest Solutions, a small woman-owned start-up in Buffalo that provides tech support. They've gone from a 650-square-foot office to one that is four times that size be-cause of government contracts. Who knows where it might end up for them. Mighty EDS also started out doing tech support for the government, and today it has more than $19 billion in revenues. And the opportunity is not only in selling to the government, there's also money to be made in becoming the government. If the priva-tization trend continues, look for small businesses to replace gov-ernment functions. For example, some have proposed privatizing or parceling out the printing that is now done by the Government Printing Office. Indeed, the paperwork is tedious, and the delays can be maddening—but still, $3 billion is $3 billion.

Not only are governments growing in size, but they're also grow-ing in number, as the next trend shows.

Balkanization

The Trend

In July 1999, Sir Sean Connery proudly donned his kilt, the green tartan of the highland MacLeods, to attend the inaugural ceremony for the Scottish Parliament. It was the first such gathering since 1707. Their parliaments are part of a much larger trend toward more, not fewer, independent nations. Even as we speak of trends that are pushing the world closer together (e.g., interconnectedness), there are countertrends (e.g., balkanization) that seem to be pulling it apart again.

Factors and Factoids

In 1945, the United Nations (UN) charter was signed by 51 nations. By 1961, the number of countries in the UN had almost doubled. And by September 2000, it had almost doubled again, to 189.

Pop quiz. Where are Kyrgyzstan, Kiribati, Myanmar, Zebrano, Azerbaijan, Eritrea, and Tuvalu?

Extra-credit question. Which one of these is not a country, but a trademark owned by General Motors?

(For the answers, see note 3 for this chapter in the endnotes.)[3]

While the world may be becoming a better-functioning and more efficient machine, it is clearly a machine with more political parts. How far could this subdividing go? Well, if we use the number of languages as an outside estimate of the number of potential individual self-governing units, that implies a UN with 6,528 members. To seat delegates and interpreters, that incarnation of the UN would clearly need a bigger building.

Of course, the idea of a 6,000-seat UN is a little silly, but a 400- or 500-seat UN within the next century isn't. There are already any number of real new states waiting to be established, like Kurdistan (from Iraq, Iran, and Turkey,) East Timor (from Indonesia,) Euzkadi (from Spain,) Tibet (from China,) Quebec (from Canada,) Jammu and Kashmir (from India,) and Palestine (from Israel.) Also look for the emergence of more city states (e.g., Singapore), small ethnic enclaves (e.g., Serbia), and reconstituted versions of older nations erased by wars (e.g., Estonia).

Is this proliferation of states a good idea? Probably not. One would be hard-pressed to argue that the citizens of most of the countries created in the last 40 years in Africa and Asia are better off than they were before. More often, both their economic and human rights situations have deteriorated with secession. Nor is the world overall necessarily better for having the Soviet Union's weapons arsenal divvied up between the Russian Federation and all the new -stan states in central Asia.[4]

Still, look for balkanization to continue. Large, central governments are an easy target for ambitious politicians stirring the self-rule pot, promising gains that may or may not be realized, and playing on tribal, religious, or ethnic prejudices to drive home the point. Of course, central governments could prevent balkanization. But in the main they won't. The former Soviet Union was an amalgam of at least 15 republics. As long as there was a strong army to hold it together, it was a single country. But when that force was removed in

1991, it quickly fragmented. The United States was able to prevent a similar breakup in 1861, but half a million soldiers died in the conflict. Few nations are now willing to pay those sorts of prices for togetherness.

The exceptions will be largely limited to totalitarian backwaters. Many of the islands of Indonesia remain a part of that nation only because of what are, in effect, occupation armies. China will continue to keep an iron grip on Tibet, Mongolia, and Hong Kong. Iraq isn't going to permit the creation of Kurdistan. But over time, fewer and fewer countries will put forth the effort required to hold nations together. We'll see more and more new countries formed and kingdoms disunited.

Implications

Business. Trade, not just in goods, but in the free flow of ideas and people, is the lubricant fueling the new world economy. More borders make free trade harder. The solution? Trade groups. Look for more and more trade agreements, such as the European Union (EU), Mercosur, the Association of Southeast Asian Nations (ASEAN), and the North American Free Trade Agreement (NAFTA). By creating common standards, lower tariffs, single currencies (maybe), and reduced paperwork, trade groups can dismantle many of the barriers that statehood creates.

Of course, not all trade groups will be created equal. Just like English soccer or American baseball, there will be major and minor leagues. Mexico, Canada, and Belgium get to be in the major leagues by the happy accident of geography. Australia, New Zealand, Japan, and Chile aren't quite so lucky. So expect the geographically disadvantaged to either finagle their way into the major leagues or find themselves falling further and further behind.

Here's one possibility: Remember mercantilism? In mercantilism, every large populous country had colonies. The rough idea was that colonies supplied the raw materials and the central country provided manufacturing. Mercantilism became very unpopular in the 1960s. Third-world countries rushed to throw off their colonial ties and establish their own base of automotive, steel, and electronics industries. In turn, advanced countries no longer automatically bought produce and raw materials from former colonies.

Don't be surprised if we see the revival of mercantilism, although it won't look quite so stark as old-style colonialistic mercantilism. In the new mercantilism, the central country would provide the technology, arms, and education, and the colonies would contribute labor-intensive manufacturing, personal service workers, and beach-front vacation space. This may not be politically correct, but it would be politically practicable. Indeed, we could argue that we're already on the road. Look no further than the retirement communities that are springing up on the Mayan Riviera and the maquiladoras (manufacturing plants) that are clustered along the Mexican border, assembling parts for U.S. automakers.

Net, net, we're going to have more political entities, but fewer economic ones. At a minimum, look for more and stronger trade groups. At the extreme, we could recut traditional trade flows and reestablish a long discarded economic model.

Individuals. In this new multistate world, travel is going to be a much more dangerous and less certain thing. Every year, *The Economist* newspaper devotes an issue to wars. There are usually around two dozen or so going on at any given time somewhere around the world. Well, twice as many countries could well mean twice as many tiny wars, and twice as many opportunities to find your tour bus late for lunch because it's pinned down in the crossfire between the South Yemenis and the Zebrano Liberation Front.

Instead, we will tend to travel to stable megastates, like France, or safe mercantile partners, like Australia and the cleaned-up portions of Mexico. Those that do travel the smaller or less stable states will do so from the safety of tourist fortresses, like Club Meds or cruise ships. (Even though both are faring poorly at the moment, long-term prospects for the category are very good.)

The Opportunities

Maybe that international relations degree my daughter is getting isn't such a bad idea after all. The business of managing crossing borders, in all its manifestations, will continue to provide opportunities for individuals, big businesses, and even small guys, like all those flower importers clustered around the Miami airport.

But let's go forward a step—balkanization has another mind-boggling implication, and therein lie more opportunities. Is it possible that we're headed for a day when governments will no longer be the largest social organizations on the planet? On to the next trend. . . .

Company States

The Trend

Are company states really all that new? After all, the first was the East India Company, founded 400 years ago. The British government gave it trade franchises that effectively allowed it to rule the Indian subcontinent. And what about United Fruit, notorious for orchestrating the overthrow of the Guatemalan government in 1954 because its president proposed land appropriation?

The large multinational corporation has been around, growing in importance, and bumping up against states for centuries. But here's what's new: It used to be company towns, like Pullman, Illinois, or Ludlow, Colorado. Now, it's company states. These new corporations are bigger and more sophisticated than the average nation. They are not just taking on a few functions normally provided by government like Pullman or dabbling in foreign policy like United Fruit. This is for real, a bona fide quasi statedom, with all that it implies. Here are some stats.

Factors and Factoids

There are now 40,000 corporations in the world whose activities span national boundaries. For example, Altria, nee Philip Morris, operates in 170 countries. It is one of the 200 multinationals that now control well over one-quarter of the world's economic activity. That share is increasing.

To put it in more graspable terms, in a comparison of GDP and revenues, General Motors is bigger than Norway; Ford is larger than Saudi Arabia; Japanese giant Mitsui is bigger than Ireland and New Zealand combined. Fifty-one of the 100 largest economies in the world are now corporations, the rest countries. One-third of the world trade now comprises intercompany transactions. Even as countries are fragmenting and getting smaller, corporations are consolidating and getting bigger. Cy Freidheim, CEO of Chiquita

Brands, has predicted the "trillion-dollar enterprise." That's half again as large as Canada.

This huge growth in megacorporations has come about because evolution rewards efficiency. The New York Stock Exchange and Nasdaq send the same message to corporations that saber-toothed tigers sent to prehistoric antelopes: Get fast or get big or your DNA stops right here. Public corporations have undergone 401 years of relentless evolution. Even private companies are forced to improve as they compete with the hyperefficient public ones.

Corporations can become so efficient, in part, because they don't face the same constraints as do countries. If GM has 10,000 workers who are unproductive or who lack the skills it needs today, it can just send them home. Nigeria can't outplace 10 million illiterate subsistence farmers.[5] General Electric can locate itself close to its major markets. Iceland is stuck in the middle of the North Atlantic. Corporations can evolve as fast as viruses, continually morphing into ever more efficient forms.

Evolution is inexorable, be it in biological organisms or social ones. So we can expect to see the trillion-dollar company state, and if the world were rational, it should probably get Samoa's seat at the UN. Don't expect everyone to be as calm about this as I am, though. The bigger the entity, the bigger the target. Expect a new and more vicious wave of anticorporatism. Eventually, don't be surprised if the World Trade Organization protests evolve into something far more sinister and serious.

Implications

It's no longer enough to think in terms of selling in the United States and Canada, now you need to think about selling in the United States and IBM. Both have their own ponderous regulations and requirements, their own language, and their own customers.

Think of each of these giants not as a single customer, but as a market. For example, Focus 5 used its relationship with Ford in the United States to expand to Brazil. And a single company market is not necessarily small, either. Microsoft grew to behemoth size itself because of its relationship with IBM. Weiden and Kennedy became a major ad agency because of Nike. J. R. Simplot grew to over $1 billion supplying potatoes to McDonald's.

The Opportunities

How can you tap into these markets? First, commit. Look at the big consulting firms and accountancies. They have reorganized around customer groups, and de-emphasized geographies. For example, consultants report to the head of the worldwide auto practice, not the managing partner of the Cleveland office. Look at ad agencies with huge offices in Seattle, Atlanta, and Detroit, built just to serve single clients.

Second, take time to learn the language. You wouldn't relocate an executive to Tokyo without investing in a few Berlitz classes. So don't go to General Electric if you don't speak the lingo. If you're going to call on Boeing, bring an interpreter with you to Chicago, a former employee who knows how to navigate the labyrinthine vendor approval process. (Personal experience says it takes around 18 months from the first contact to the first sale in a global multinational corporation, and 17 of those months are spent learning whom to talk to and how to say it.)

Third, be ready to pick sides. If you work for Coke, you don't work for Pepsi. Sure, maybe you'll be small enough or work in an industry friendly enough that you won't be forced to make a choice. But don't count on it—sooner or later, the question may come up, and when it does, you'll need to have thought through the answer.

Sprechen Sie DaimlerChrysler?

Babelization

The Follow-On Trend

When the Pope gives speeches in the Middle East, he uses English even though it's not the first language of the Pope or the people to whom he's talking. That's the same language his pilot used to communicate with the control tower as he landed the papal plane, the same language that has become the de facto official second language of the world, spoken to varying degrees by 1.5 billion people. No other language comes close to English for ubiquity. Mandarin has far more primary speakers, but fewer total. Nor is any other language gaining speakers at the same rate as English.

English is already the language of commerce (including advertising), movies, and science. At the Switzerland-based European
Laboratory for Particle Physics, CERN, the scientists from 82 countries communicate in English. English is even making inroads into
diplomacy—the EU now uses English along with French at its informal meetings.

Does that point to a world where we will all sing in perfect har-
mony, or at least in a single perfect language? Nope. We may well
see a day in which most people in the world have some level of pro-
ficiency with English, but we are very unlikely to see a day where
English is the preferred communication method of a majority of the
world's population. It is far more likely that we will actually see an
increase in the number of active languages—*babelization*.

Factors and Factoids

Again, just as in balkanization, countries *could* prevent babelization—
but they won't. The current trend is to support more language tolerance, not less. In 1987, Hawaii wiped out a century-old law
forbidding the teaching of Hawaiian except as a foreign language. In
1990, the federal government reversed its 100-plus-year-old policy of
discouraging Native American languages. Governments just aren't
willing to make the political investment required.

Babelization is being driven by language activists and scholars.
They worry that half of the world's 6,500 languages may be extinct
by the end of this century. They point out that of the 300 languages
spoken in the United States in 1492, only 175 are still spoken, and
many of those by a handful of old people. Without intervention,
they worry that English, and particularly bad English, will simply
displace other languages.

Activists are using both the carrot (education and awareness)
and the stick (laws.) In Hawaii there is a network of schools, Punano
Leo, that educates children in the native Hawaiian language, to the
exclusion of English. Organized groups like the Académie Française
in Paris, the Association of German Language in Berlin, and the
Office de la Langue Française in Montreal are actively fighting the
English invasion. France, Brazil, Canada, and Germany all have
considered or passed bills that restrict the use of English and man-
date the use of other, longer-established languages.

Implications

Business. The big takeaway is that as the official discrimination against other languages in the United States becomes less intense, expect Spanish to continue to grow in acceptance and importance. Historically, immigrant languages fade away by the third generation. Don't expect that this time. With a continual influx of immigrants and less stigma attached to not speaking English, Spanish will likely continue to grow, and there's a reasonable chance that the United States may become a bilingual nation in a few generations.

In other parts of the world, expect second languages like Russian to lose share to English, now that ethnic minorities are no longer forced to learn them. Instead, expect small, remote nations to speak a local dialect and English.

Individuals. Bad news for us folks. We Americans will finally be forced to join the rest of the world and learn a second language—even while, worldwide, English continues to take off like an *a'ala'au* (that's *rocket* in Hawaiian).

The Opportunities

Language schools, translation services, multilingual marketing—all of these will continue to grow and expand. Nestlé of Switzerland already publishes every significant memo in four languages.

Possible Countertrend

As English spreads, some linguists predict that it will morph into a family of similar but mutually unrecognizable dialects, just as Latin turned into French, Italian, Spanish, Portuguese, Romanian, Provençal, and Catalan. A few years ago, a subtitled movie, *My Name Is Joe,* played in the United States. The language of the actors was English, but it was the working-class English of Northern England. And it's not just accents, but different words and grammar, as well. For example, recently we visited South Oakland. Although my teenage son carefully studies rap videos and considers himself hip to the point of self-parody, he was nonetheless unable to communicate easily with the teens in the household we were visiting. When they spoke Ebonics, the street English of California, he was completely unable to follow the conversation.

CHAPTER 5

Technology Trends

In 1997, the Dallas Fed put out a list of the top 10 inventions and discoveries in history:

1. Electricity
2. Microprocessor
3. Computer
4. DNA
5. Telephone
6. Automobile
7. Internet
8. TV
9. Refrigeration
10. Airplane

At the same time, the Fed also nominated candidates for another iteration of the list of 25 developing technological areas that could change the world. That list included materials science, organic computers, recognition technology, lasers, virtual reality, optics, genomics, photonics, artificial intelligence (AI), and nanotechnology. (What's striking is what was *not* on that list: polymerization, cloning, biometrics, machine vision, encryption, and oceanography, among others.) *Technology Review* magazine has its own list with yet more technologies, including flexible transistors and brain-machine inter-faces, to mention but a couple.

What's the point here? It would have been just as easy (perhaps easier) for the Fed or *Technology Review* to make a list of 50 or 100 transformational technologies. How then can I pick just 10?

I selected these 10 by first asking a simple question: What makes a technology most interesting? The answer, I decided, was that tech-nologies are like billiard balls: They're most interesting when they're crashing into stuff, be it other technologies or new markets. Think of each technology as a ball and each market as a pocket. It's the action and interaction that are exciting. Until those two things hap-pen, every tech trend is just a second-place project at the county sci-ence fair. Most of the time, we look at tech trends from the lab outward, a pure technology starting its journey to the marketplace. We don't look at them from the market perspective, and we don't look at them in combination. But not here.

In this section are 10 such collisions of technologies, and my take on how these will hit the market:

1. *Instant obsolescence.* There's a new patent issued in Amer-ica every 3 minutes. One hundred twenty-five new products arrive in supermarkets every weekday. Colliding technologies: cellular, ergonomics, satellites, medicine, cloning, micropro-cessors.

2. *Infinite reach.* Technology has always put us within reach, anywhere, any time, and in multiple ways. Colliding tech-nologies: voice recognition, cellular, AI, fiber optics.

3. *Swarm to warm.* The first great U.S. migration was east to west, the second north to south, and it's all due to technology. Colliding technologies: epidemiology, refrigeration, materials science.

4. *Pills "R" Us.* In 2000, we spent $121 billion on prescription drugs, plus billions more on over-the-counter (OTC) remedies. Colliding technologies: pharmacology, nutrition, nanotech.

5. *Itsy, bitsy, teeny, weeny, little microscopic machines.* The next big thing in technology is small. Colliding technologies: microtech, nanotech, AI, biochemistry, chaos theory, robotics.

6. *Bionicism.* There are now dozens of replacement parts for the human body, and we've only just begun. Colliding technologies: materials science, metallurgy, telemetry, medicine, pharmacology.

7. *It ain't heavy, it's my product, brother.* There's been a lot of attention paid to miniaturization, but even more striking is the increased weightlessness of many of the products we use every day. Colliding technologies: microprocessors, materials science, ergonomics.

8. *Down in the data mine.* Information is gold, and we now have the technology to dig down into the data and get it. Colliding technologies: wireless, microprocessors, data compression, number theory, data storage.

9. *One extra lifetime per person, please.* Technology has added 15 years of life on the average over the last century. Now the trick is to make those 15 years worth living. Colliding technologies: epidemiology, hormone therapy, nutrition, pharmacology, biomedical engineering.

10. *Helpless in Seattle.* We love technology but do not understand it. How will we cope in a world where everything is a black box? Colliding technologies: telecommunications, ergonomics, digitalization, AI.

That's it, our 10 technology trends. Ready? I'll rack, you break.

Instant Obsolescence

The Trend

We are seeing both an increase in the amount of technology in the world today and, even more important, an increase in the rate at which it is being introduced—and retired. Iridium spent 12 years creating a worldwide phone system. It was an extraordinary technical and logistical feat. Their software developers wrote 20 million lines of computer code. The companies' engineers launched 88 low-orbit satellites. Together they created a communications network that literally covered every inch of the planet, with enough capacity to handle the 27 million users they expected by 2007. Instead, the company had 55,000 customers when it declared bankruptcy in 1999. Bad forecasting? Nope. Iridium's technology was effectively obsolete before it could be deployed.

The system was originally envisaged as *the* standard business tool for anyone who needed to travel and work worldwide. By relying on satellites, coverage was literally global. And since it was a single network, there was no problem using the same phone and the same number in any country. Investors pictured a busy mining executive chatting away as she boarded a plane in France and resuming her conversation when she reached her destination at a copper pit in remotest Chile. They poured in $5 billion of capital.

But even as investors were handing over their checks, cellular technology was developing—fast—and almost before those checks could be cashed, iridium was left with no market. Digital standards made it possible to develop handsets that would work internationally. Handsets became smaller and cheaper than the $3,000 bricklike iridium phone. Cellular networks quickly spread worldwide, even in poor countries. By the time iridium was operational, the only markets that weren't served well by cellular were tiny and limited to a few people who worked in impossibly remote locations (e.g., bush pilots in Alaskan canyons, military personnel on secret missions, and field explorationists for oil companies). And that niche was too small to be commercial. Iridium's 88 satellites are twinkling memorials to instant obsolescence.

Factors and Factoids

In 1995, slightly over 100,000 patents were issued in the United States. By 2000, that number was over 150,000, a growth rate of more than 10 percent per year. In 1996, the United States was the second most patent-intensive nation on earth, with around 175 patents per million persons. Japan edged us out with around 180. Japanese output grew from just over 50 per million in 1975. To understand just how much technology is being created in the United States, consider this: Only nine countries produce more than 50 patents per million. The others in the club are Switzerland, Sweden, Finland, Germany, Canada, the Netherlands, and France.

Most of these patents weren't for blockbuster breakthroughs, like cloning or cold fusion, but for tiny incremental improvements to common items. This continuous stream of innovation means that from a technology perspective, everything gets a little better every day.

Let's take a look at turn signals. My 80-year-old father thinks that turn signals are one of the great achievements in automotive, perhaps human, history. He remembers a time when signaling a turn meant rolling down the window and sticking your arm outside, which meant that in cold or rainy weather, people didn't always bother. They just turned. As a young man, my father only drove at one speed, pedal-to-the-floor, so these drivers caused him more than a few near catastrophes, and thus his infatuation with the technology of turn signals. He couldn't get over how this simple device had made his world so much safer.

But wait, Dad, it gets even better. Turn signals are brighter now. They're positioned where they're easier to see. They turn themselves off when the turn is complete. With the flasher button, turn signals can now be used as emergency beacons. And on trucks with long trailers, there's now an additional turn signal located halfway down the trailer so that we drivers who are stuck in the blind spot get warning of an impending lane change. Even the lowly turn signal has continued to improve. It was just such a series of small improvements that left iridium without a market.

What's more, as the creation rate of new technology has increased, so also has the rate at which we are absorbing it. As the chart in Figure 5.1 indicates, the time it takes for technology to become available to the mass market is getting shorter and shorter.[1] Roughly speaking, it took around 50 years for new innovations to become widely available in the nineteenth century, half that long in the early part of the twentieth century, and half that in the second half.

There are several factors driving this technology boom. Economically, we now have a market that can afford new products, making companies willing to invest in research and development (R&D). Total R&D expenditures in the United States in 2000 were almost a quarter of a trillion dollars. Three-fourths of that was spent by the private sector. Industry R&D spending continues to grow at a steady rate of around 10 percent. Also, companies know they have no choice. Their competitors will reverse-engineer their products the second they hit the shelves. If they want to stay ahead, they must

Figure 5.1 **Time to mass market of major innovations.**

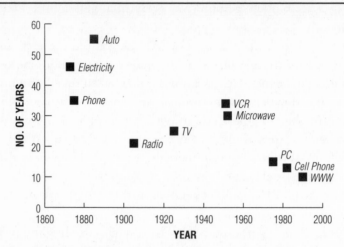

Sources: Dallas Federal Reserve Bank, Industry Standard, *author's analysis.*

invest to find newer, better technology. As we invest more in looking for new technology, not surprisingly we find it.

There's another thing going on here as well, though, that might be less obvious. Technology, especially today, is a team sport. Despite the fiercely competitive nature of academic and industrial research, most technological problems are simply too large and too complex to be tackled by one person. Specialization is the order of the day. The interconnectedness trend, by linking all these specialists together, has greatly increased the efficiency of technological development.

For example, if Thomas Edison needed a piece of lab equipment, rarely could he just order it from a catalog. Much of the time he was forced to make it himself. But now, companies like Agilent Technologies have entire buildings of scientists devoted to making scientific instruments, creating technology to help make more technology. And equipment is not the only way the work of one scientist can enable the work of another. By mapping the human genome, Johns Hopkins researchers made it possible for a host of pharmaceutical researchers to attack problems in new ways.

Isaac Newton wrote to Robert Hooke, "If I have seen further, it is by standing on the shoulders of giants." Today in medicine, clinical researchers stand on the shoulders of bench pharmacologists, who stand on the shoulders of basic chemists, who stand on the shoulders of molecular physicists. There are literally thousands of scientific and medical journals that report new results each month. (And to no one's surprise, rarely do scientists wait for exciting new journals to arrive in the mail. Instead, they view new papers on-line before they are published.)

Implications

Expect products to be out of date before they are taken out of the box. In the months between when this book was written and when it hits the stands, 44 million computers will have become obsolete. Expect new products to go from must-have to paperweight overnight. Palm, the maker of handheld scheduling devices, has seen its stock take a beating not because of a lack of new products, but because of too many. They have produced new and improved wireless devices so fast that they're stuck with warehouses full of old ones.

Interestingly enough, instant obsolescence doesn't really mean many products will go away, just that the market for them will shrink dramatically. There's still a market for slide rules, typewriters, and even buggy whips. It's just no longer very big.

Expect companies to put themselves out of business with improved products. Take tires. Over the last 20 years, the price of tires has fallen by one-third, and their life has risen by 50 percent. That means the cost per mile to the consumer has been cut in half, or looked at another way, the tire makers' potential sales per vehicle have been halved. A pair of the newest Michael Jordan sneakers now costs more than the average set of four tires, and probably won't hold up for a trip or two around the world, like the tires will. Good luck, Michelin.

Expect technologists to become rock stars, à la Steve Wozniak. In January, PPL Therapeutics announced the birth of cloned pigs, two days before an American team was set to announce a similar discovery in the journal *Science*. The American researchers howled, not only because the Scots stole their spotlight, but also because PPL has a record of making announcements of breakthroughs that send their stock price soaring but don't always hold up. (Last year, they claimed that they'd found a way to deage cow cells, but have since admitted that they may have been premature in their announcement.) More interesting, however, was how PPL announced their discovery—not in a refereed journal, but in a PR release.

The Opportunity

There are many opportunities here. Since this trend is getting a bit long, let's tackle just one—coping with the so-called wreckage that technological innovation leaves behind. Take the products we mentioned earlier. Small companies that sell slide rules and make buggy whips are thriving. Later, in Chapter 7, "Consumer Trends," we'll talk about how some consumers crave *authenticity,* and to some that means *old technology.* That's not the only way to profit from instant obsolescence.

Consider Technology Recycling LLC in Denver, which now operates in more than 100 U.S. cities. Not only do the people of Technology Recycling fix, upgrade, and resell used equipment, they also break useless stuff down so it can be safely recycled. Cadmium, used in a laptop's central processing unit, is 200 times more lethal than lead, and dumped in a landfill, can easily leach into groundwater. Technology Recycling has processed more than 100 tons of digi-junk since it was founded in 1998.

Warning! Once a product hits the mass market, it attracts competitors the way roadkill attracts flies. If you invest in developing new technologies, don't plan to have decades to recoup your investment. Think years—maybe months.

Infinite Reach

The Trend

MIT has a sophisticated media lab to predict the future convergence of electronics, telecoms, and computing. I have Brian. Brian is a full-on geek. Not only does he go to the annual digital summit, COMDEX, but he takes his family as well. Brian subscribes to every computer magazine and e-zine known to man, woman, or machine. He has more gadgets than an electronics superstore, adds more every month, and is currently shopping for a wearable computer. (Pity his poor wife Carol. How many times has Brian come home from a business trip with a new device trailing behind, its little cord wagging hopefully? *Him:* "It just followed me home, honey. Can we keep it, huh, can we keep it? I'll take care of it, I promise." *Her:* "That's what you said about the copier/fax, but I'm the one who always has to take out the toner.")

You don't want to be behind Brian at an airport security checkpoint when they make everyone take all their electronics out of their bags. He carries two cell phones, a personal digital assistant (PDA), a Blackberry, two laptops, a global positioning system (GPS) receiver, a pager, and a miscellany of plug-ins, connectors, and wires. Once in Minneapolis, a consulting team complained about not being connected to a printer. Brian pulled a local area network (LAN) kit out of his bag and rewired the room for a LAN, crawling around on his hands and knees in his suit.

I bring this up because Brian has almost achieved the geek equivalent of true enlightenment: infinite reach. He has created a system through which he can be reached anywhere, from the client's office in London to the ski lift in Park City, anytime, with one phone call. Maybe we're not to Brian's level yet, but we're all headed to being in touch all of the time.

Factors and Factoids

Here's how it works. I call the number of Portola Valley Consulting, Brian's company, and a computer program called Wildfire answers the phone. Wildfire asks me for my name and, if I'm on the list, not only gives me the option of leaving a message or a page, but being routed to Brian. The computer then works a list of phone numbers, trying to find him. Most of the time, Wildfire does find him, although it is not at all unusual to have Brian answer the phone with, "Talk fast. I'm in the Manchester Airport and this will cost a fortune."

Brian dreams of a day when Wildfire will shoot him an e-mail, telling him that I called and when, that he can pick up on either of his laptops or on his Blackberry. A competitive offering, Webley, already does that. But for complex geek reasons, Brian hasn't switched over from Wildfire to Webley—yet.

There's more to him being in touch as well. He can pick up all of his e-mails in Manchester, answer them on the flight, and download them in JFK airport in New York. He can also grab the electronic version of the *New York Times, Wall Street Journal,* or the *San Jose Mercury,* and read those as well. If he has to, he can even tell Wildfire to route his calls to the phone in the seat armrest, and stay in touch during the flight.

There are obviously a whole slew of technologies at work here. The backbone of infinite reach is cellular and, in particular, cellular networks that will relay calls across borders (this is much harder than it sounds because the United States uses a different portion of the electromagnetic spectrum than the rest of the world). But there's also voice recognition software (Wildfire,) the Internet, fat pipes (fiber-optic cables,) a contact database, and AI. Most of us, to be sure, haven't reached Brian's level. However, most of us do carry at least one portable communications device, which keeps us in more-or-less constant touch with the rest of the world. And with call forwarding and pagers, we're continuing to approach true infinite reach.

More is coming. There are wireless connections to the Internet in some Starbucks. Smart phones carry loads of phone numbers and the like (not much point in having a phone if you don't know anyone's phone number). Their number is expected to grow from 2 million to 21 million over the next 3 years. Sales of companion personal computers (i.e., ultralight PCs that are even smaller than notebooks) are expected to double, as are PDAs. High-speed Internet connections, satellite TV, you name it, we're moving toward constantly being plugged in.

Implications

Expect the number of devices required to achieve infinite reach to shrink. Ten years ago, I listened to British telecommunications guru Hugh Collins predict that the replacement of the analog cellular standards with digital would lead to the creation of the universal personal communicator (UPC). The UPC would always be on, fully encrypted, follow us anywhere we went around the world, and allow video-to-video calls. Over time, Mr. Collins said, it would make land lines unnecessary. Brian says he's right, and that we will eventually go to fewer, more powerful devices.

Brian also says we can expect the number of contact numbers to shrink. Yes, he says *shrink.* Today, my clients and colleagues have six phone numbers for me in their PDAs: office toll-free main, office direct, office fax, cell, home, and home office. That's unwieldy and unnecessary. In the future, each of us could have one number, which we would have for life and take it with us from place to place, job to job, and device to device.

For example, we wouldn't have an office number and a home number, just our number. When we arrive at our first day of work at our new employer, we'll just feed in our UPC number. When we resign, they'll simply delete the number from the phone system. Numbers will no longer be linked to a physical location, but to a person. At the very least, we will have cheap Wildfire-like equivalents that provide one touch point for those who wish to reach us.

Another implication? Expect this infinite reach to rewrite the rules of etiquette. If a client says, "I'm on vacation, but you can call me," does that mean you should? We'll talk more about the implications of this trend on society and consumer behavior a bit later in the book.

The Opportunity

Think portable office. Dockers is now advertising Mobile Pants, a pair of pants with special pockets that hold all that electronic gear. Companies are making desks for cars. Look for workstations in recreational boats before it's all said and done.

Think also about the confluence of infinite reach and barbarians at the gated community. Dr. Peter Zhou has invented a chip that could be worn or inserted under the skin that would transmit the location of an animal at all time. It sounds a little ghoulish, but such a chip would allow parents to find lost children, for example. (Although, I'm sure the last thing my teenager wants is a device that lets me track him from one place he's not supposed to be to another.)

Think *countertrend opportunity,* as well. The more plugged in people are, the more they need to occasionally unplug, and the greater the need for products and services that can help them do that—from rafting trips down the Grand Canyon (no phone service inside the canyon, unless of course you have an iridium phone) to day spas.

Swarm to Warm

The Trend

Three hundred years ago, living in the Southern United States was punishment for being broke. Now it's a reward for being rich—all because of technology.

In England, between 1700 and 1750, the industrial revolution displaced hundreds of thousands of untrained laborers from the agricultural and home-based manufacturing (e.g., weaving) sectors. Many ended up in London's streets, drunk on cheap gin (the crack of its day), and dependent on crime for their livings.

To cope with the first modern crime wave, the English built new prisons and instituted capital punishment for hundreds of crimes (from murder to burning a hayrick to poaching a rabbit.) Still, the crime boom continued and the prison population swelled. So in 1717, Parliament passed 4 George I, c. II, the Transportation Act.

Georgian-era ideas on punishment were draconian, and the threat of transportation was intended to be a strong deterrent to those considering a career in crime or even those thinking of borrowing money for frivolous purchases (like food, presumably). They sent these prisoners to the most heinous places they could find: the southern colonies of America.

What was so bad about Savannah? For Englishmen of the eighteenth century, heat was both disliked and feared. There was the risk of heat stroke. Remember: Most Englishmen of the time wore wool, not cotton. Also doctors of the period believed that heat bred "poisonous vapors" that caused malaria and yellow fever. Only people who had no choice would live in warm climates.

Today, it's the exact opposite. States like Florida, Georgia, Texas, and Arizona are highly desirable places to live. If you drew a line across the United States passing through the bottom edge of Virginia, you'd find about one-half of the U.S. population today lives above that line and one-half below it. But 100 years ago, three-fourths of the population lived above that line. The first great American migration was from east to west; the second one is from north to south.[2]

It's not that we've built up immunity to the vapors, though. Of all the inventions that have fundamentally changed the United States, not many have had a greater impact than air conditioning. We now live comfortably in places once thought to be uninhabitable.

Factors and Factoids

Twenty-two U.S. metro areas (greater than 600,000 inhabitants) grew more than 20 percent in the 1990s. Eighteen were in the South or the Southwest. (The other four were Denver, Portland, Sacramento, and Salt Lake City. Seattle was almost a fifth—it grew at 19.7 percent.)

Second on the list is Phoenix, where July temperatures normally reach 106°F and have reached 113°F. That's why its population was 5,544 in 1900 B.A.C. (before air conditioning) and still only a little more than 100,000 a half-century later. As a benchmark, during that same time the population of Chicago grew by almost 2 million. After 1950, when air conditioning became common, the population of Phoenix grew by more than 1 million while Chicago's fell by a similar amount.

And consider these stats: By 1960, 7 percent of all new cars came equipped with factory-installed air conditiuoning. In 1990, 94 percent of all new cars and trucks came with air conditioning. Between 1973 and 1993, the percentage of U.S. homes with central air grew from 17 to 44 percent, and the proportion is still rising. Eighty-three percent of all new homes (and 99 percent of those built in the South) now come with central air.

Is air conditioning the only factor driving the swarm to warm? Not really. There's also improved pest control. Malaria (spread by mosquitoes, not vapors) was a major killer in the southern states until the 1930s. And there's sunscreen. Light-skinned children in sunny states used to wear long-sleeved shirts and hats whenever they went outside. There's even improved paint that will stand up better to the constant beating of a warm climate. And of course, refrigerators, a first cousin of air conditioning, play a role by improving both the quality and safety of food. But it is air conditioning that has changed our world the most.

Implications

Expect a continued migration to warm in the short to medium term. Longer-term trends might send some people back north. But it probably won't be back to the gray states. (We'll discuss some exceptions in Chapter 6, "Societal Trends.") Instead, look for sunny places like Colorado and Idaho to boom.

You know, there could be something even bigger going on here. We are approaching a time when our technologies will allow us to live absolutely anywhere we please in relative comfort, from Anchorage to El Paso. We cannot control whether it boils, rains, or snows, but we can make it essentially irrelevant through technology. In both World War II and the Korean War, cold accounted for 10 percent of all casualties. That says that the day could come when people choose to live in places that today are still considered too harsh, like the Alaskan and Maine coastlines. Could we be headed for a day when the wealthy keep their primary residences in Kennebunk and a summer cottage in New York City?

The Opportunity

The obvious opportunity is in Boise real estate, and similar ones based on building businesses in potential grants areas. But there are more subtle ones as well. Sure, the house is air conditioned and so is the car, but it gets awful hot out there on the fourteenth green. That's why an entrepreneur has just introduced a golf cart with air. Anything that reduces climate dependency, be it protection from hot or cold, wet or wind—from cool packs to wear around your neck to battery-operated jackets (North Face) to lightweight clothing made of breathable waterproof fabrics (Gateway Technologies)—will find a market.

Pills "R" Us

The Trend

On TV, I recently saw an advertisement for a machine that automatically dispenses pills at the appropriate times. That seems like a godsend to me. I can't even remember to take a vitamin, and would never be able to keep it straight if I had to take 25 pills of assorted sizes, shapes, and colors a day like my mother-in-law does. A computer-controlled pill organizer is very timely technology.

But we're going to need a row of them on the kitchen counter, one for everyone in the family, regardless of their health, because we have become a nation of pill poppers. Just like the old song from the

1960s, there are pills to make us larger and pills to make us smaller. Specifically, we take pills to increase our muscle mass and pills to decrease our fat. We take pills to kill pain and pills to kill microbes. We take pills to increase our social confidence, improve our love-making, grow back hair, unclog our arteries, and stop us from sneez-ing. We take pills to wake us up and pills to help us sleep. We take pills to prevent kids, and we give our kids pills to make them health-ier and to help them study. We take pills to counteract the side effects of other pills. We even give our pets pills (and expensive ones, at that) to treat everything from arthritis to cholesterol.

Each year, U.S. pharmacists fill more than 1 billion prescriptions. Twenty-five percent of Americans take at least five medications per week. Pills "r" us.

Factors and Factoids

Prescription drug expenditures in 2000 were $121 billion. The 40 million Americans who are on Medicaid average 28 prescriptions a year, some of those one-offs and some refillable. Over-the-counter drugs aren't as big in dollar terms, but they're bigger in the number of pills. Sixty percent of all dosages are nonprescription, and 110 mil-lion Americans will take an OTC drug within the next 48 hours. Extrapolating from industry shipment data, we're spending twice as much as a decade ago and, by implication, taking twice as many pills.

There are four reasons for our passion for pills:

1. Pills work, and we believe they work. Since 1998, 17 million Americans have tried Viagra. That's one in every six males.

2. Pills are wonderfully convenient—portable, easy to use, and inconspicuous.

3. Pills are cheap—relatively. Pharmaceuticals comprise only 15 percent or so of the total cost of our health care. Since they work, our doctors encourage us to use them. Since they're cost-effective, our HMOs and insurance companies prefer them to options like surgery, and they encourage doctors to prescribe them.

4. Technology is the real engine behind this trend. There is a continuous flow of new drugs able to tackle almost any

problem. For example, drug researchers now say they're closing in on a treatment for Alzheimer's. Not only that, but doctors are developing sophisticated drug regimes, programs that combine different drugs into treatment programs that can tackle even the most complex set of ailments, like AIDS.

Let's focus on that final factor, the new drug pipeline. According to Steve Hebel, CEO of the company that publishes the bible of the pharmaceutical industry (*Drug Facts and Comparisons*), in 1992 Medi-Span, a database used by hospital pharmacies, contained info on 117,000 drugs. It now contains information on 206,000 drugs. The number of new drug approvals is increasing. The FDA has cut the approval time for a new drug by two-thirds and is approving double the number of new medicines of only a decade ago. (See Figure 5.2.)

What's fueling all these breakthroughs? Investment in R&D. Investment in health-related R&D has doubled in the last 15 years. The legal drug business is now the most R&D-intensive industry in

Figure 5.2 **New drug approvals and the average time for approval process. *Note: Approval time* is the time from marketing application submission to final approval for marketing, including both FDA review time and the time companies take to answer questions that arise during the review**.

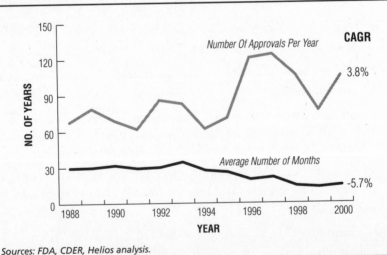

Sources: FDA, CDER, Helios analysis.

the United States. Pharmaceutical companies spend more than $18 billion a year on research, 11.8 percent of sales, and almost twice as much per dollar of sales as any other industry, including electronics. All of that investment pays out in a continual stream of improvements to existing drugs and new drugs to treat or cure heretofore unaddressable problems.

Implications

Expect a constant stream of new miracle drugs. New technologies like the human genome database promise to exponentially increase scientists' abilities to identify possible causes of disease states and to design new chemical compounds to attack them. There are now plans to create supersmall pills with islets of insulin-producing cells on the inside, protected by a porous shell that will let the tiny insulin molecules out but not let big white blood cells in.

Expect the public's propensity to take pills to grow, despite occasional drug recalls and exposés on *Sixty Minutes*. Fueling this appetite, as if it needed fuel, will be drugmakers themselves, who increasingly are turning to consumer advertising to encourage people to ask their doctors for drugs by name. Zoloft spent $46 million on advertising in the first 10 months of 2001. Prozac spent $32 million. In total, ad spending on prescription drugs jumped from less than $1 billion in 1997 to $2.5 billion in 2001.

Expect politicization of the pharmaceutical industry. Pills have become such an integral part of our lives that there is now discussion of pharmaceuticals as a public good, like electricity or water. For example, public outcry forced pharmaceutical companies to donate AIDS drugs to Africa. Holman Jenkins of the *Wall Street Journal* argues that dual-dosage drugs, like Zantac, that come in both over-the-counter and prescription strengths, are more a result of politics than logic. They exist because having a prescription-strength option allows consumers to get their insurance companies to pick up the tab.

The Opportunity

There are at least two opportunities here. First, of course, once an industry gets large enough, it creates a set of satellite industries to serve it. Pharmaceutical companies will continue to become larger and more complex, creating a whole envelope of what Chris Mellor, former

CEO of Adis, calls *pharma-space,* an industry devoted to serving the needs of the pharmaceutical industry.[3] For example, ads for pharmaceuticals must be written by specialists, who understand the strict FDA rules on what can and can't be said. Z-S, a consulting firm in Evanston, Illinois, helps pharmaceutical companies restructure their salesforces to cope with all the growth they've undergone. Adis supplies a database that tracks new drug introductions around the world.

The second opportunity lies in competing with the giants. Most of us don't have the $10 billion or so that it takes to set up a new drug company, but consumers are also becoming interested in natural pharmaceuticals, which are, at this stage, far less regulated than FDA-approved drugs. Herbal supplements have grown at almost the same rate as branded pharmaceuticals over the last 5 years. So far, only 30 percent of U.S. households use herbals versus 75 percent for vitamins. Sounds like an opportunity to me.

There is also a set of indirect effects, which I haven't quite figured out yet. An obvious one we'll talk about when we get to Chapter 7, "Consumer Trends," is products to make that second lifetime more livable ("Booms or Bust"). Another, for example, will the confidence that "pills can cure anything" turn us into a nation of risk takers? Some suggest that the development of drug regimes to treat HIV has made high-risk segments less careful.

Itsy, Bitsy, Teenie, Weenie, Little Microscopic Machines

The Trend

Uh oh. I can see some of you are getting restless. You picked up this book to read about hot new trends. Maybe you wanted to get a few ideas for work. Perhaps you thought you'd pick up a tidbit or two for conversation. And I've been giving you technology breakthroughs like air conditioning and cell phones. Yeah, like that's going to keep the discussion going at lunch. "Hey, anybody want to hear about the latest advances in climate control?"

Well, since you put it like that, maybe I should push the boundaries a bit. Maybe it's time for some real techno-pyrotechnics, a look at what's got all the kids at Cal Tech buzzing, something that is eyebrow-raising and jaw-dropping. Something that's BIG! Or rather small.

The biggest trend out on the edge right now is the science of the small—things like nanotech, molecular engineering, and micromachines. Here's the basic idea. What if we could build little—tiny—machines. Suppose that we could dump a truckload of sand, and hundreds of thousands of little antlike machines would each grab a grain and assemble it into a new patio. Or what if we could make the machines even smaller, for instance, small enough so they could crawl through your arteries and repair a tiny tear on the wall of a major vessel? Or what if we could create even smaller devices, ones that could manipulate individual atoms? These nanomachines could lay out very precise (and small) microprocessors, or even transform a pile of grass into a steak or a steak into a pile of charcoal brickets.

Theoretically, at least, we can. We're just still working out the details.

Factors and Factoids

In 1959, Richard Feynman, the great physicist, gave a speech entitled "There's Plenty of Room at the Bottom," in which he challenged scientists to realize the potential of microtechnology. Feynman offered $1,000 to anyone who could build the first electric motor that could fit in a cube smaller than $\frac{1}{64}$ inch per side.

The world of small science is an odd place, with its own strange language, and it is played at out a level that few of us can readily conceptualize. That is, most of us think pretty comfortably in units down to a millimeter, the size of a grain of sand. But the science of the small starts from 10 to 100 times smaller than that, at the level of bacteria, the smallest living things. Microtechnology works from that point down to the level of large molecules, which can have billions of atoms. Nanotechnology then takes over, and continues all the way down to the level of individual atoms.

These technologies are at least partially realized. The first ever Biological Microelectromechanical Systems (BioMEMS) and Biomedical Nanotechnology World Conference was held in 2000. At it, scientists talked about machines that can splice genes and create gene chips, or oligonucleotide arrays. (They're already available.) Scientists from Harvard presented papers on microfabricating a skin equivalent using lasers.

At Massachusetts Institute of Technology (MIT), micro- and nanoscientists are working on projects like printing entire computers on a small piece of plastic, and precisely placing little plastic spheres (0.5 micron across) on a substrate. Those same labs are now creating a single-electron transistor by using an atomic force microscope to write 10-nanometer-sized titanium oxide lines and dashes. (No, there is no easier way to say that.) The Center for Bits and Atoms at MIT is building quantum dots, nano-sized boxes for holding electrons.

And more is on the horizon. Nanotech, or molecular engineering, could lead to superconductors, flawless diamonds, ultrathin films, and perfect bearings and rotors. It could even allow us to glue pieces of molecules together.

All that is pretty interesting, I think, at least what I can understand of it. But for most of us, the easiest thing to get our heads around is the logic of micromachines.

Feynman's basic proposition was that machines can get smaller and smaller, almost to molecular size. In the early 1980s, scientists began to realize that these micromachines don't have to be completely mechanical, but can be partially inorganic and partially organic or biological. Nor is it necessary that we set up little microfactories where humans build all these micromachines; instead, we can just have the micromachines themselves build them. Once we get them built, it would be too cumbersome to try to control them centrally (picture 100,000 invisibly thin wires running from a control panel to our pile of sand.) So it's important that these tiny machines can be individually programmed to do individual tasks. In sum, micromachines will likely have three key characteristics: (1) organic/inorganic composition, (2) the capacity for self-replication, and (3) individual programming. None of those technological planks is anywhere near reality today.

Building small machines sure seems like a large task, but if we do create such devices, we will be able to perform tasks with a precision and efficiency not possible today. With micromachines, or mikes, we could build smaller, faster microchips, dig out cancer cells and repair the damage left behind, scrub cholesterol from artery walls, and erase DNA errors. If we had nanomachines, we could put them to work on polluted land, collecting the toxic chemicals and heavy metals, or send them into the atmosphere to reweave the ozone layer.

Implications

Small tech could replace every factory on earth. Picture this. What if, instead of ordering a new car, you just piled up some scrap metal in the backyard behind the rose bushes, had GM send you a box of preprogrammed mikes and nanites, dumped the box on the pile, and went away for a few hours. You wouldn't worry that you hadn't piled up exactly the right amounts of steel, rubber, and glass for the mikes to work with, the nanites would just have to rearrange a few atomic structures to make a bit more nickel and a tad less iron. It sounds preposterous, but lots of technology sounds preposterous the first time around.

Now there is one teensy problem with nanites. To get enough to really do any significant work, like build our car in the backyard, we'd need millions. Rather than having GM ship us all those, it would be a lot more practical to have the company send us a pre-programmed hundred, then have those build some more, and so on, until they have enough to get started on the car. This is called *self-replication,* and of course you see the problem. What if the nanites lost interest in building the car, and instead decided just to keep turning out more nanites? Theoretically, *theoretically,* mind you, they could disassemble the world, and it would only take about 5 hours. Scientists call this the *gray-goo problem.*[4] Hmmmm. That's troubling. Let's make a note to work on that some more before we actually launch the product.

The Opportunity

Around 80 companies are now active with micromachines, or MEMS, and 60 of those are small businesses of under $10 million per year. Projections say the market should go from under $200 million in 1997 to $30 billion in the early part of this century. Still, as cool as they are, the near-term opportunities lie not in micromachines, but in more mainstream applications of micro- and nano-technology. In the very short term, small tech should lead to much smaller and faster microchips, enable a new generation of laboratory equipment, and create new medical sensors. If you're looking for a hot, way-out-there technology, this is a real contender.

Bionicism

The Trend

The term *cyborg* was first introduced by the National Aeronautics and Space Administration (NASA) in the 1960s to describe the ideal astronaut, a human with mechanical additions that would allow him or her to better survive in space. In 1972, Martin Caldin wrote a dark, edgy science fiction thriller called *Cyborg*. The following year, ABC made the book into a tongue-in-cheek television show called the *Six-Million-Dollar Man*.

In the TV show, Colonel Steve Austin is an astronaut who loses both legs, an arm, and an eye in a plane crash. A shadowy government department called the Office of Scientific Intelligence spends $6 million to rebuild him, giving him legs that allow him to run 60 miles an hour, an arm that can rip through steel doors, and an eye that is a combination microscope/telescope and range finder.

We are now entering a time when many body parts can simply be replaced with synthetic equivalents. And the day is coming when, like Colonel Austin, it won't just be an issue of replacing parts, but upgrading them.

Factors and Factoids

In all, there are already dozens of replacement body parts available, a list that includes joints, tendons, prosthetic feet, legs, hands and arms, silicone noses, heart valves, cochlear implants, tooth implants, pacemakers, artificial hearts, and breast implants. (Okay, breast implants are not replacements, strictly speaking; they're more like additions.) Millions of people worldwide already live with replacement parts. In 1999, 191,583 women had breast implants. (Through the 1990s, the average bra size in America went from a 34B to a 36C.) In 2000, there were 160,000 hip replacements and in 1997, 196,000 pacemaker and defibrillator implants. And it's not just parts replacements—we're also getting bionic procedures as well. There are almost 1 million laser eye surgeries a year.

More and better are on the way. The FDA recently approved testing of a pacemaker that will send data on the heart's performance back to a doctor's office. Illinois researchers have surgically installed microchips in the eyes of three blind men, hoping to cure blindness. An artificial titanium-and-plastic heart has been used in six people so far. (Putting medicine aside for a moment, researchers have experimented with identity chips, small devices implanted just below the surface of the skin, that allow access to restricted buildings. I'm not sure what to call that. At any rate, I don't want to get off track here, so. . . .)

Bionics is the merging of biological, electronic, and mechanical systems to restore or improve basic human physical performance. It is the apex of technology convergence, requiring integration of technologies rooted in physical, chemical, and biological sciences. Take a simple hip replacement: There's the hip itself, a steel or titanium marvel of materials science; the surgery, an intricate and complex process of gluing bones and tendons to the new hip; and the follow-up, which includes a sophisticated drug regime to prevent the body from rejecting the new part. With more complex devices like self-contained artificial hearts, the number of technologies and the amount of interplay between them increase exponentially.

Implications

Expect continued growth of bionics. We're boomers, we're going to need those new parts. Also expect considerable debate over who pays. Breast implants cost $6,000. Laser surgery costs $1,000 per eye. An artificial heart operation costs $75,000, and up. And expect debate over who gets what procedures when there is no one to pick up the tab, like an uninsured patient with a worn-out heart.

Expect bionics to take it to the next level, and expect there to ensue a whole new level of ethical debates. We've pretty much accepted the need for devices and procedures that restore performance to the level it was at earlier in an individual's life, like artificial joints, fillings in teeth, and dialysis machines. We've also bought into the idea of devices and procedures that restore performance to an idealized human standard, like breast implants, eyeglasses and laser eye surgery, and orthodontics. But how do we feel about bionic devices that enable human performance well beyond what are standard levels today?

It hasn't been much of a problem so far, because most bionic devices haven't been as good as the original, much less better. Still, there are some examples. Here's one that most of would not think of as a bionic device: power steering on a large sport-utility vehicle (SUV). True, it's not body specific. Still, it meets the test of being more than just a device to save labor. Power steering allows millions of Americans to do something that they would otherwise find almost impossible to do: turn the wheel of a parked, long-bed pickup truck. If it weren't for power steering, SUVs would be about as popular at the mall as tractors. The only people driving them would wrestle steers for a living. Nobody cares that power steering gives an unequal advantage to small, weak people because the technology is available to everyone, and because no one else is really disadvantaged in the process.

But what happens when we start seeing devices that create large advantages to normal people (i.e., turning normal bodies into superbodies)? At what point does that become unfair, for instance, in sports? NFL running backs break knees and ankles with painful regularity. Why not just give each a set of titanium and elastic legs like Colonel Austin's that will run 60 miles an hour? Seem silly? A few years ago, Tiger Woods had laser eye surgery. Sixty percent of recipients of laser eye surgery end up with better than 20/20 vision. Scientists say microscopic and telescopic vision is around the corner. What if Tiger decides to have surgery to install a telescope and a range finder in his left eye? Is that fair? Who decides? Expect it to get sticky.

Finally, I hate to say this, but we've had the six-million-dollar man and the six-million-dollar woman. Next, expect us to start working on the six-million-dollar dog. Hip replacements and chemotherapy for pets are already common. People are also starting to invest in doggie orthodontics and pet dialysis. Veterinary pet insurance had revenues of $50 million last year, and that could double in 2 years.

The Opportunity

Because there are so many technologies involved and because they're so complex, there are almost endless opportunities here. The human body is wonderfully complex, with more than 200 bones, dozens of

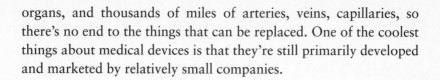

organs, and thousands of miles of arteries, veins, capillaries, so there's no end to the things that can be replaced. One of the coolest things about medical devices is that they're still primarily developed and marketed by relatively small companies.

It Ain't Heavy, It's My Product, Brother

The Trend

Motorola's first cell phone weighed 2.5 pounds. Ten years later, in 1973, Compaq introduced the first portable computer, a suitcase-sized marvel at 28 pounds. Today, cell phones typically weigh between 3 and 6 ounces, and laptops range from 2 to 9 lbs.

If we don't have to carry it, we want it big and substantial, like an SUV or a home theater. But if we *do* have to carry it, we want it as light as possible, like the laptop this book is being typed on. We want weightless in everything from clothes to bicycles to beer cans, and technology is giving it to us.

Factors and Factoids

Getting lightweight involves several different technologies. Advances in microtechnology have allowed engineers to build smaller and smaller chips, to the point where an entire computer can fit on a ring. Technology is now beginning to shrink mechanical systems the same way. Better computer programs, for example, allow more precise calculations of tolerances and load factors, meaning engineers don't have to throw extra mass into structural pieces to provide a safety factor. Translation into English: thinner, stronger car bumpers; smaller gears; slimmer walls on cell phone casings; bicycle frames that weigh less than 3 pounds.

Another technology, robotics, allows tiny components to be built and assembled into smaller and smaller devices. For example, the newest manufacturing machines can precisely place gears as small as a period, and can do so far faster than any human.

Our old friend, interconnectedness, plays a role as well. One reason that computers, cameras, and music players can get so tiny is that they don't have to carry around bulky things like data storage. The iPod holds 1,000 songs, but it doesn't need to carry with it 100 CDs. It can leave the originals on a server somewhere, and tap in as needed. Similarly, small laptops can leave data and even applications on bulkier machines located elsewhere, and just plug in from time to time for uploads and downloads.

I should probably clarify here that *small* is not exactly the same as *light*. For example, industrial designers painstakingly work to create products in the tightest package available, to save space, not weight. (Modern car engines are so compact that partial disassembly is required to perform the most basic maintenance.)

As small as things get, they still have to be made of something, and what that something is also determines the weight. Increasingly, as the chart in Figure 5.3 shows, we are substituting lighter materials like plastic for heavier ones like steel.

In fact, materials science is getting even more esoteric than just simple plastics. Sony and Panasonic use titanium and magnesium alloys in laptop exteriors to provide great strength with very low weight. In Europe, Volkswagen sells cars that get 99 miles per gallon, in part because the hood is made of titanium and magnesium. Ping uses carbon fibers to make the shaft of golf clubs, providing more strength and whip, and less weight. The latest Kevlar canoes weigh less than 40 pounds and can easily be portaged by a single person. There's a new synthetic fiber called Meryl Nexten, made of

Figure 5.3 **The use of steel, aluminum, and plastics over time.**

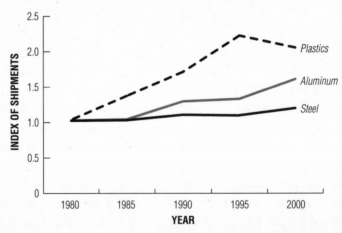

Sources: Association of German Plastics Manufacturers, World Almanac, International Iron and Steel Institute.

hollow-fiber yarn. It insulates 25 percent better than polyester, wicks moisture away from the body 33 percent better than cotton, is almost impossible to tear, and weighs a little more than half of what a conventional fabric does. I could go on, but I'll stop.

No, I won't. Let's pack a briefcase, with as much gadgetry as possible, and try to stay under a 30-pound weight limit. Following is my first cut at a packing list:

Cassiopeia Fiva notebook computer	2 lb
Nokia 8890 cell phone	0.2 lb
Palm Pilot m500 (to keep addresses and calendars)	0.25 lb
Blackberry (to receive pages and e-mails)	0.3 lb

Whoops, I've got far more technology than I had with my old gear, and I'm still only at 3 pounds, less than one-tenth of what that original Motorola brick and Compaq portable weighed. Maybe I'll throw in some more stuff so I can work in the hotel room, and maybe a few fun things as well.

HP personal printer	4 lb
HP CapShare 920 (handheld copier)	0.75 lb
Plus V-807 digital video projector	2 lb
Belkin universal surge protector	1 lb
Sony digital-relay CD-RW drive (if I want to burn a CD)	1 lb
Audiovox 1680 personal DVD player	6 lb
iPod	0.4 lb
Konica KE-300Z digital camera	0.4 lb

Now, not only can I call people and work on my laptop, I can also create and print reports complete with photos and present those to a roomful of clients. I can put that report on paper, or on a CD, and while I do all that I can also listen to music or watch a movie. How much are we up to? Eighteen pounds. Let's throw in a pound of AA batteries (around 12 dozen) to run all this stuff. Now we're up to 19 pounds.

I'm running out of gear here. Wait, I've got it. How about a videophone with an Inmarsat satellite uplink like the ones the CNN folks use. That way I can videoconference into the office from anywhere in the world. That whole kit is only another 8 lbs. That's 27 pounds total. Toss in a few cables and we're probably approaching our 30-pound limit. Thirteen devices, with almost the full capabilities of the most modern office, and we're still under what a computer and a cell phone were only 2 decades ago. Brian would be so proud. Now if only I can find a bag to hold all this stuff.

Implications

Expect the weightlessness trend to continue in some sectors (e.g., sports equipment, outdoor gear, clothing). Eventually, expect paper to be replaced by ultralight electronic crystal e-books. If something can't get any lighter, expect it to have wheels, like modern luggage. If it's heavy enough that it's hard to pull, it will have a motor attached, à la the latest baby strollers.

This trend does have a limit, though. Some semiportable devices (e.g., vacuum cleaners and speakers) are now getting heavier to improve performance. And don't expect all electronics to continue to shrink. If cell phones get much smaller, even the daintiest of us won't be able to punch the keys.

The Opportunity

Take weight out of everything you make. Sony, Nike, Callaway, and Patagonia do. And if you make anything that has to be bulky or heavy, either find a way to make it easy to move, or carry it for your customers.

Down in the Data Mine

The Trend

Data mining is all about digging into data and finding patterns—and it's all the rage. Here are a few examples: scientists are using the data from space probes to hunt for extinct volcanoes on Mars; casinos are leveraging information from slot machines to identify which customers should receive free dinners to entice them back; tobacco companies are installing CRM systems to track customers by name; security agencies are poring over travel itineraries to spot potential terrorists; insurance companies are analyzing claims data to lower the premiums on your new Porsche; and cruise line operators are modeling bookings to set prices for less desirable cabins.

Factors and Factoids

There are two types of data mines—numerical and textual. In a typical company, about 90 percent of the actual data are text, but most of the effort so far has been over on the numbers side. Until relatively recently, however, there just weren't that many large, clean data sets of either numbers or text. There was the Census, the Library of Congress, and a few large commercial data sets like A. C. Nielsen. Still, for the most part, data sets were scattered, incomplete, and small.

In the last decade, however, we have been generating data at a truly extraordinary rate. For example, the effort to map the human genome has been going on for decades. By the mid-1990s, scientists had completed 5 percent of the map. In the last 5 years, they've knocked out the remaining 95 percent, and a high-tech start-up named Celera is already commercializing it, selling access to eight pharmaceutical companies at $2 million each. Teradata is a billion-dollar company whose business is managing companies' data mines. For Kmart, they keep 92 terabytes of data, 10 times the entire printed collection of the Library of Congress. Teradata manages 76 terabytes for Federal Express, 53 for Office Depot, and 48 for American Telephone and Telegraph (AT&T). The average Fortune 500 company manipulates a terabyte of data a day, and that's growing at 57 percent a year.

Why the sudden boom in data mines, or huge data sets? First, we've seen a tremendous increase in data capture since digitalization. Now every phone call is logged, every transaction at a convenience store is recorded, and every time a car passes through the EZ pass lane on an expressway, that event is documented in a computer somewhere. New data capture technologies such as bar coding and wireless (that little Mobil Speedpass that hangs on a key chain) have made it relatively painless for convenience stores to capture what was sold and who bought it.

Simultaneously, the cost of organizing and storing that data has dropped precipitously. Since 1977, the cost per instruction (industry lingo) to process data has dropped by a factor of 1,000, and the speed with which it can be processed has increased by a factor of

100,000. Data storage costs have dropped at a rate that is almost as impressive. So we're now building *huge* collections of data about just about everything.

And now that we have data mines, we're developing the tools to extract insights from them. Tools are the most exciting part of data mining. There is the development of new search tools for text data [e.g., Standard Generalized Markup Language (SGML) for libraries and Google on the Internet]. (Just for fun, I just asked Google to search the Internet to find the word *the*. It took 0.31 seconds to complete the search and find 2,420,000,000 hits.) Also, there is the creation of new algorithms to plumb numerical data sets.

There's a famous story in mathematics told about Gauss, among others. It goes like this. One day, young Carl Freidrich and a friend were caught talking in class. The teacher called them to the front of the room, scolded them, and as punishment told them to return to their seats and add up every number between 1 and 100. Gauss paused and said, "5,050," smiled, and sat down.

How did he do it? Well, of course, it is possible to add up every number in the series: 1 + 2 = 3; 3 + 4 = 7; 7 + 5 = 12; and so on. But it is time consuming and very easy to make a mistake. There is an easier way. What if instead of adding each number to the next in line, you added them like this: 0 + 100 = 100; 1 + 99 = 100; 2 + 98 = 100; 3 + 97 = 100; and so forth. There's clearly a pattern here, one that says that there will be 50 pairs of 100, or 5,000, plus 1 number left over, 50.[5] It takes about a minute for each of us to do that calculation, and we can do it in our heads.

Now apply a variation of that to sorting a deck of cards. It's much faster to go through and divide the deck up by suit first, then order them. These are the sort of algorithm improvements that make data mining a practicality. The trick with data mining is not just to find new insights, but to find them very quickly and without a lot of work.

Implications

Expect data capture to continue to improve. Ford bought 5,000 PDAs to give to factory floor supervisors to input data. Other companies are developing key chain credit cards, which also capture and send back data.

Expect more resources devoted to data mining. Some corporations already spend more than one-third of their budget on information technology (IT). Data mining software investments have doubled over the last 3 years.

Expect the debate over privacy to rage. The ore within most commercial data mines is composed of large files on individuals and their buying behaviors. And *Wired* magazine says, "Privacy is history—get over it." But most of us haven't bought into that, and don't want to.

Taken to its logical extreme, lost privacy and individual marketing actually get pretty creepy. The day I run out of soap in the shower and the radio announcer in the background suddenly interrupts the song to say, "Hey, Sam, have you tried new Bud's Suds for Studs?" is the day the radio goes flying out the window and I move to a remote cabin in Montana. See you there.

The Opportunity

There are opportunities everywhere here. ChoicePoint mixes and matches databases to accumulate information ranging from tax records to speeding fines, all of which it organizes by social security number and resells to Fortune 1000 companies and government organizations like the FBI. Sound boring? Their revenues were almost $600 million in 2000, having doubled in just 5 years. Axciom is building a database that includes every household in America. Their revenues in 2000 were almost $1 billion, having doubled in just 2 years.

But it's not just big companies that are doing this. Apigent, Alloha, and Vital Link Technologies help retailers use their real-time sales data. (That's why the guy at RadioShack gets your phone number when you buy a few dollars worth of batteries for cash.) Knowledge Discovery One and Marketing Analytics help retailers like Walgreens develop algorithms to predict the success of promotions. digiMine works with customer databases. SRD uses data mining to spot deadbeats for casinos. (Interesting side note: most of these companies are in states like Oklahoma, Arkansas, Minnesota, Texas, and Illinois.) Even if you're not game to jump into the data mining business, there's still value in data mining. Dig into that shoebox of receipts and know the numbers. Know who are the good customers and who aren't—and most important, why.

One Extra Lifetime per Person, Please

The Trend

Thomas Hobbes famously summed up life in the middle ages: "Nasty, brutish, and short." And life stayed short until the middle of the twentieth century. In 1900, average life expectancy was only 47.3 years. But by 2000, it was 76.9, a difference of almost 30 years.

In other words, we now have an entire extra lifetime with which to work. No wonder we have second homes, second degrees, second careers, and second families—we now have a second life. We can thank medical technology (both preventative and curative) for 15 of those gifted years, and technologies like food processing and hygiene (e.g., antibacterial soaps) for the other fifteen.[6]

Life expectancy rose pretty steadily during the twentieth century, often in concert with advances in medical technology improvements. Here's a rough estimate of the increase in lifespan by decade, and a sampling of some of the medical breakthroughs of each period.

Decade	Increase in Years	Selected Technology Achievements
1900–1910	2.7	Chemotherapy, syphilis testing, typhus vaccine, ECG
1911–1920	4.1	Insulin, vitamins A and B, x-ray spectroscope
1921–1930	5.6	Penicillin, vitamins D and C, diphtheria, whooping cough vaccine
1931–1940	3.2	Sulfanilamide, sulfapyridin, sulfathiazole, antihistamines, PAP test
1941–1950	5.3	Neomycin, bacitracin, tetracycline, streptomycin, dialysis machine
1951–1960	1.5	Erythromycin, polio vaccine, oral contraceptives, mammograms, pacemaker, defillibrator, Acyclovir
1961–1970	0.9	Human heart transplant, measles vaccine, CAT scan, artificial heart
1971–1980	1.1	Laser surgery, MRIs, ultrasound imaging, balloon angioplasty
1981–1990	1.7	Meningitis vaccine, AZT (for AIDS), laparoscopes, synthetic HGH, cyclosporin
1991–2000	1.5	Human genome project, DNase, cloning, protease inhibitors

---

Factors and Factoids

Three broad thrusts have led to this extraordinary increase in life-span. The first is a decline in infant mortality. In 1915, 1 in 10 babies died at birth. When my younger brother (the same one to whom this book is dedicated) was born prematurely in a rural hospital in 1955, he weighed slightly more than 3 pounds. The doctor carefully wrapped him in a towel, placed him in a shoebox, and told my parents to take him home, but not to expect him to make it. Today, 84 percent of babies delivered at 28 weeks live. You might have seen this story in the news—in 1999, Nkem Chukwu gave birth to octuplets at 20 weeks, 4 months before her due date. The *largest* was less than 2 pounds. Seven survived.

Now the infant mortality rate in the United States is one-tenth of where it was a century ago, down to 1 in 100. (Sadly, African-American babies are still twice as likely to die at birth as white babies, and outside of the United States and Europe, the infant mortality rate is still 1 in 10.)

If you did survive childbirth in the first half of the twentieth century, that was still no guarantee of reaching old age. Just to get to adulthood meant running a gauntlet of microbes and viruses. Periodic waves of smallpox, diphtheria, polio, cholera, malaria, tuberculosis, typhoid fever, whooping cough, and measles raged across the country, leaving dead, maimed, and blind in their wake. According to Moore and Simon, "Just three infectious diseases—tuberculosis, pneumonia, and diarrhea—accounted for half of all deaths in 1900."[7] Diseases that we no longer even think about, like diphtheria, malaria, tuberculosis, and whooping cough, each affected 1 person per 1,000 each year before 1950. Virtually every family had at least one brush with these deadly illnesses during their lives.

And there were times when every house on every street was affected. Consider, for example, the Great Influenza Epidemic that started in Fort Riley, Kansas, in March of 1918. Before it was done, it had killed 548,000 Americans and another 21 million people worldwide. We still can't cure viral diseases like the flu, but we do have vaccinations to prevent them, and the technology to help people survive them. For example, there's no cure for AIDS, but there are treatment options. The AIDS death rate (in the United States) fell by 50 percent between 1997 and 2000.

Infectious diseases are not the only things that we now survive, thanks to medical technology. Cancer survival rates have almost doubled since 1960. The death rate from heart attacks has fallen by almost two-thirds since 1950. We now survive car crashes, fires, even drownings. Put it all together, add in 15 years that are a result of lifestyle changes (e.g., more protein, fewer cigarettes, and more baths), and we have 30 more years of life, a whole new lifetime to play with.[8]

Implications

Do expect us to die from different stuff. For example, the fourteenth leading cause of death is now pneumonitis, where food or drink is breathed into the lungs and causes pneumonia. Pneumonitis is a disease of the elderly, as are rising causes of death like Alzheimer's and septicemia.

But don't expect this trend to continue at the same rate. That is, the maximum lifespan isn't going to get too much longer. Life expectancy increased at about 4 years per decade in the first half of the last century and about 1 year per decade in the second half. University of Chicago researchers say that's about it. According to Jonathan Thatcher, head of the Kronos Clinic in Phoenix, there comes a point where everything simply wears out at once, and things just can't be replaced fast enough. (I am paraphrasing here. Jonathan's exact language is considerably more scientific.)

The Opportunity

There are three basic types of opportunity here. First, there's the opportunity to make aging less visible [e.g., cosmetic surgery (see "Bionicism," earlier in this chapter)]. Second, there's the opportunity to make products for the newly aged (see "Boomers or Bust"). But the biggest opportunity here is for medical technology to shift its focus from helping us live longer to making that second lifetime better. The latter stages of life today can be unpleasant, due to poor health or problems like dementia, which cause a loss of independence and self-reliance. Thatcher calls the alternative *dying healthy,* defined as being as active and independent as possible for as long as possible. *Antiaging* clinics are popping up everywhere. Reputable physicians and scientists, like those at Kronos, hate that term.

However, move the hype out of the way and there's a real need underneath, and right beside it, a real opportunity.

Helpless in Seattle

The Trend

Time for another pop quiz, but with no trick questions this time. Answer each of these sentences with Yes or No.

1. I know how to transfer calls at the office and conference people in without losing the call. (Yes/No)

2. My thermostat is programmed to lower the temperature and regulate the furnace when we are away from home. (Yes/No)

3. When the auto mechanic explains the problem with my car, I usually understand the explanation. (Yes/No)

4. If there's a TV show I want to see but it's on at an inconvenient time, I just program my VCR to record it. (Yes/No)

5. My digital watch is set for the right month, day, and time zone. (Yes/No)

6. All the other digital clocks in my other devices (e.g., my coffeemaker) are set for the right time as well. (Yes/No)

7. I use more than just the timer on my microwave, and use the microwave for more than just reheating food. (Yes/No)

8. I hooked up my new digital camera to my PC and figured out how to download pictures without asking my teenager to help. (Yes/No)

9. My cell phone is programmed with the numbers I call most frequently. (Yes/No)

10. When stymied about a problem with a new computer, I simply call the help line, confident that I can sort out the problem with their help. (Yes/No)

To score, give yourself 10 points for each Yes, 0 points for each No, and something in between if that seems more appropriate.

How'd you do? Ninety percent of those who have taken the quiz get below 50. We have absolutely no idea how to get even a fraction of the value out of all these wonderful gizmos and gadgets around us.

Most of us are comfortable with technology. We use technology almost every waking moment of every day. We even use it to do things, that when you stop to think about it, would have sounded downright nuts to our great-grandmothers. For example, we strap ourselves inside thin aluminum tubes fueled by exploding gas to be shot 30,000 feet into the sky, confident that aviation technology will get us back down again. We take powerful poisons as part of chemotherapy, counting on the words of pharmacists that the chemicals will do what they're supposed to and not do what they're not supposed to. We rely on a switch on the wall to heat our homes when the temperature drops to −27°F. Our very survival these days depends on technology.

As my pop quiz score proved, however, don't expect me to understand it. Because I, like most of us, am helpless in Seattle. And Chicago. And Miami.

Factors and Factoids

Here's why we don't know how it works. Nobody knows except the people who designed it.

Take the family car. Fifty years ago, every mechanic understood every single element of how cars operated. The mechanic at the local garage, faced with an engine that wouldn't start, would first see if the plugs were sparking. If so, he'd check the carburetor. If it wasn't the plugs or the carburetor, he'd work the problem backward until, sooner or later, he managed to get the engine running again. There were only so many cars, they were simple, and they didn't change much. Mechanics diagnosed problems, often visually, and prescribed fixes.

Today's cars, however, are heavily reliant on electronics and sealed componentry. There's no way for a mechanic to hold a plug against the block and see if an electronic circuit is working. Instead, he or she must rely on sophisticated factory diagnostic machines that spit out error codes that tell him or her what needs to be replaced. Just to keep up and understand how to use the diagnostic machines requires almost continuous reading and formal training. Even then, a mechanic's real understanding of what's going on inside that engine control computer is almost nonexistent. At best, he or she understands how to use the technology that understands the technology.

Modern technologies are simply too complex to be understood at any but the most superficial level. According to James Gleick, your electric toothbrush has 3,000 lines of computer code in it. Even worse, many modern technologies are not designed to be understood and worked on. Kitchen appliances are glued together, not screwed. Switches are sealed shut. The people who designed them never intended you to take them apart, figure out how they work, and set them right. Instead, they deliberately make them so that the price of a complete replacement is only a fraction more, say 50 percent, than a partial repair.

Implications

Expect technology to become even harder for laypeople to understand. Technologies will become more complex, change faster, and become more specialized, making it almost impossible for most of us to keep up, knowledge-wise.

At the same time, expect technology to become easier to use. Designers have learned that none of us can pass the techno-quiz, and they've started working around us. My cell phone knows, for example, I won't set the time properly. So it doesn't even ask me, it just sets itself. My computer keeps track of daylight saving time. My new digital camera has controls my dog could figure out. Expect industrial design to increasingly come up with ingenious products like the Apple iPod, which is so intuitive that its full capabilities can be used by the most technologically challenged.

But beware. ("Danger, Will Robinson, danger.") The more technology does for us, the less we need to do. Forty years ago Isaac Asimov predicted that the day would come when we would become so reliant on calculators, that we'd totally lose our ability to do simple mathematical functions. I'm there—I can't even add two numbers together anymore. Expect our grandchildren to have no idea how to work a manual can opener or start a fire without a gas jet.

The Opportunity

RadioShack's strategy since 1993 has been to help people deal with the confusion of technology, so it has retrained its 32,000 employees away from helping people build radios one transistor at a time and toward counseling people on how to turn on their new cell phones.

J&S Computer in Winnetka makes much of its income going to people's homes and helping them get on the Internet.

Where's the gold here? Help people to navigate the maze. Wrenchhead.com and RepairClinic.com provide pictures to show you how to do simple home appliances and auto repairs.

Advertisers have already picked up on this need to explain technology to nontechies. Take IBM's new commercials, in which they explain how computer systems work together by showing a team of basketball players wearing jerseys with names like Infrastructure and Linux. It's simple, and we get it.

Societal Trends

Now let's take it down a layer. Economic/geopolitical and technol- ogy trends shape our world. But we are also shaped by how we react to those broadest of trends, the changes that our societies make to cope with those huge external pressures, which are trends in their own right. In this section, we're going to look at 10 such societal trends.

1. *Polytheism.* Our increasing tendency to supplement our traditional religious belief system with other faiths and activities. (It's more interesting than it sounds, trust me. But then again, you probably won't trust me because you and I don't trust anybody. See item 4, the "Trust Deficit" trend.)

2. *Postnuclear families.* The death of the myth of the dad-plus-mom-plus-2.2-kids family model.

3. *Retribing.* Our tendency to join large social groups with common interests, irrespective of geography or family connections.

4. *The trust deficit.* The legendary City News Bureau of Chicago had its slogan on the wall, "If your mother says she loves you, check it out." The Bureau is defunct, but their skepticism lives on in all of us.

5. *Contradictory consumption.* Why do we see Greenpeace stickers on gas guzzlers? Because we now live in a world

where there's no such thing as the right thing, only the right-est, and that's not as clear as it seems.

6. *The neverending traffic jam.*   It's a crowded old world out there, and getting more crowded far faster than can be explained simply by population growth.

7. *You talking to me?*   Well, somebody is—an ad every 20 seconds, an e-mail every 6 minutes, and at least one phone call per hour on average (which suggests that somewhere out there are a lot of nonchatty people that bring the average down).

8. *Instant polling.*   What do you think of the book so far? Never mind that, what about this section? This chapter? How about this sentence? Like the structure? Word choice? Punctuation? It's my punctuation that you have an issue with, isn't it? You'd rather I'd used a semicolon. Log on right now and tell me.

9. *Lawyers, guns, and money.*   Or have your lawyer log on, especially if you're suffering emotional distress over the whole thing. That's what we're doing as a society, increasingly looking to the courts to solve more of our problems more of the time.

10. *Screw you very much.*   Finally, most think we're becoming a very rude society and that we are poorer for it.

Ten trends. Buckle up and let's take a flyover of the world we live in.

Polytheism

The Trend

There are some fads and trends that people would just as soon forget, like perms for men and leisure suits. And those of us with 17 cases of canned peaches and a dusty generator cluttering up the basement want to forget Y2K.

But while both Y2K and its predecessor, Y1K, have been busts as apocalyptic events, they are still useful as trendpoints. Taken together, they explain why my son's high school swim team now practices yoga and why Shirley MacLaine hasn't been tied to a stake and burned. (It's going to take a few minutes to explain that last sentence. If you're sensitive about either religion or technology, you may want to move on to the next trend now.)

Let's start with Y1K. What was the biggest concern for the man on the street in December 999? If you guessed Ye Olde Superbowle, nice try. The right answer is Judgment Day. Across London, roving wild-eyed ministers promised that at midnight, on December 31, Christ would return to sort souls into those destined for paradise and those condemned to eternal damnation. Thousands listened, abandoned homes and belongings, built huge wooden crosses, and headed to hilltops to pray. Needless to say, nothing happened, except for a spate of burglaries of empty houses.

For Y2K, though, very few went to church, much less mountaintops. Instead, we installed cots in data centers. Our greatest fear in December 1999 wasn't God, but technology. What caused the striking shift between 1000 A.D. and 2000 A.D.? Why was the panic caused by God in Y1K and technology in Y2K? Why did people build crosses in 999 and buy generator sets this time around? And what does all of this have to do with Miss MacLaine?

Simple. Polytheism.

Factors and Factoids

Here in the States, we're more afraid of our computer crashing than we are of being struck with a lightning bolt from heaven, are more likely to fall in love at the gym than in Sunday School, and are more likely to watch SportsCenter five times a day than go to morning and evening mass. At first blush, it may look as if we're just no longer as religious as we once were. (I'm using *we* to mean Americans and Western Europeans whose religious background is Judeo-Christian.)

But people are still spiritual. Religious portals are among some of the most frequently hit on the web. Ninety-five percent of us still believe in a higher power. And we're still respectful of those higher powers. Even those of us who scoffed at the Y2K hysteria still took an extra $200 out of the automated teller machine (ATM) on the December 31. (Or you at least bought another bottle of water. Come on, admit it.)

The big change is not that we're less religious, but that increasingly we also believe in, or are at least willing to entertain the idea of, multiple higher powers, be it Buddha or science or the healing value of crystals. The reality is that we've supplemented a singular, all-encompassing religion with a smorgasbord of smaller religions and quasi-religious activities.

Why are we becoming polytheist? Perhaps it's because there are simply more religions about. There are almost 6 million Muslims and over 1 million Hindus in the United States. There are Buddhists, Druids, Navahos, Scientologists, Wiccans, Atlanteans (and 2,000 more, according to the *Encyclopedia of American Religions*). Inevitably, as different belief systems exist side by side in society, they come to exist side by side in individuals as well.

My Catholic wife also practices Yoga, a set of rituals derived from Hinduism. Her friend, Lenny, considers himself a Zen Buddhist and a Jew. In my briefcase I carry a nomole, a small stone rice god I picked up in Africa 2 decades ago, even though I am a Baptist. Millions of self-identified Christians bought the *Celestine Prophecy*, a new-age self-help novel espousing a belief system that is more akin to reincarnation than standard Christianity. Who knows what Harry Potter–addicted children will grow up to believe in?

Whatever it is, we're okay with it. Only 44 percent of us believe that only one set of values is right, and 70 percent think that it is up to each individual to decide what is right and wrong. Boomers are seekers by nature, introspective, inquisitive people. Naturally, our explorations have taken us away from where we started, and up to 20 percent of Americans say they no longer practice the religion of their parents. But roughly one-third of those who say they have embraced New Age religions say they have not broken from the church. The big news here is that most of us have not replaced our original religion, we've simply added more on top of it. We have become de facto polytheists.

Implications

Wrong or right, expect it to continue. Don't expect people to become less spiritual; instead, expect individuals to increasingly cruise the religion buffet line, creating their own designer belief systems.

Expect church attendance to stay low or even fall further.

(Although polls say that 40 percent of Americans attend church regularly, quantitative analysis suggests it is half that at best.) The young are less likely to go to church regularly, suggesting continued erosion.

Expect people to continue to replace church-related activities with quasi-religious ones, like sports and exercise. Pundits like Jim Rome already call sports "America's secular religion."

The Opportunities

Many of the more obvious ones have already been capitalized on. For example, self-help gurus and programs like EST have already offered up alternative belief systems. Oprah has built a media empire focused on finding and packaging spiritual hors d'oeuvres. Psychiatrists and counselors have replaced the clergy as counselors, and the television networks have slowly but surely begun to encroach on times once reserved for worship. Increasingly, books that synthesize religious tenets from various sources are making the best-seller lists. There's also an emerging market for vaguely spiritually connected stuff, like aromatherapy and spa vacations.

Still, it would be risky to say there's not more room here for growth. It's hard to predict where this might go next, but let's take a flyer. What about creating and producing mainstream products with a claim to new religious authenticity? You've heard of natural products? How about supernatural? How about Wiccan wear? The Goth package on a Chevy Silverado? Buddha insect repellent? Crystal Lite with real crystals in it? The combination of polytheistic tolerance and boomer curiosity might combine to create some wild and wonderful new offerings.

And where society goes, advertising soon follows. Look for mainstream brands to insert *spirituality* into commercials.

Postnuclear Families

The Trend

There was a time, from 1969 to 1974, when the *Brady Bunch* was the window into our societal soul. It was this inane and vapid TV show that explored a new type of family, one that would soon become the norm in America, if not on TV.

In America, sitcoms are the white mice of the media—they're cheap, they breed fast, and they're expendable. As a result, from *All in the Family* to *M*A*S*H* to *Sex in the City*, sitcoms are how we experiment with our thorniest societal issues. The Nielsen Ratings and *TV Guide* track the results of those experiments. For example, when *Will and Grace* won an Emmy, that was not just about acting (obviously). It was also an acknowledgment from mainstream America that we have accepted homosexuality.

But let's get back to Marsha, Greg, and the gang. The 1950s and 1960s airwaves were chock-full of family sitcoms. There were the *Ozzie and Harriet Show* (1952 to 1966), *Father Knows Best* (1954 to 1960), and *Leave It to Beaver* (1957 to 1963). All portrayed a classic model of family life—monogamous, heterosexual, white parents; beautiful, unblemished kids; a dad who went to work each day and a mom who stayed home, cleaned, cooked, and even had time to put on makeup and pearls for dinner.

Even today, that's *still* the model typical of most shows. The families in *Married with Children* (1987 to 1997), *Roseanne* (1988 to 1995), and the *Simpsons* (1990 to today) may be dysfunctional, but they're still nuclear: Al and Homer go to work; Bud, Bart, and Lisa go to school; Peg and Marge wear pearls and stay home; Roseanne and Dan still sit around the kitchen table dispensing parental wisdom to Darlene, just as Ozzie did to Ricky.

It was shows like the *Brady Bunch, Different Strokes,* and *Murphy Brown* that first showed America a completely new type of family unit, a hodgepodge of people banded together not by birth but by choice—the postnuclear family.

Factors and Factoids

Although over half of all Americans believe in the traditional family model, it's not necessarily from personal experience. Less than 24 percent of households are now composed of a wife, husband, and children under age 18. Only just over half of adults are even married, down from three-quarters 30 years ago. There are now more than 5 million households where people live together unmarried. (See Figure 6.1.)

The proportion of kids who live in a household with two parents has dropped from three-fourths to one-half, and the number who

Figure 6.1 **Proportion of U.S. households defined as *traditional* family.**

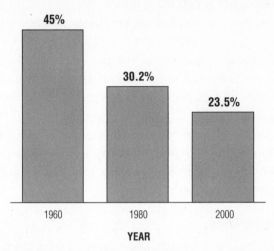

45%

30.2%

23.5%

1960   1980   2000

YEAR

Sources: U.S. Census, Wall Street Journal, *author's analysis.*

live in a home with just one parent has tripled. Fifty percent of those who marry this year will find themselves in divorce court. Thirty percent of U.S. kids are now illegitimate, and illegitimacy is no longer associated with just the poor and uneducated. Even traditional families are often not so traditional. One of every six traditional families is now reversed, where the dad stays home and the mom goes to work.

Americans are still not completely comfortable with all this moving about. Half of us still *say* the traditional model is best, double the ratio of our counterparts in Germany, Spain, India, Taiwan, and Thailand. And a resounding majority of us believe people should stay married for the sake of the children, if at all possible. Still, every study, from the U.S. Census to the University of Chicago, says exactly the same thing: Traditional families are far more common on cable channels than around the dinner table.

Implications

Expect us to continue to see more and more postnuclear families. In many European countries, as in the United States, the proportion of illegitimate births now hovers around 30 percent. The Swedes, who seem to live on the social frontier, have now okayed homosexual adoptions; New Hampshire has quietly removed its ban; Florida's ban is under siege through the courts.

Recent statistics that have shown minor upticks in traditional family pillars, such as women leaving the workforce to stay home with their children, have proved illusory. More people are *talking* about it—almost one-quarter of all parents regularly discuss having one or the other quit and stay home to raise the kids, but so far, not many have done it. In fact, as the labor market tightens, expect employers to become more demanding and less tolerant of working at home—forcing more women back into the 9-to-5 grind.

All together now, "Here's a story of a lovely lady, who was bringing up three very lovely girls. . . ."[1]

The Opportunities

Our infrastructure still hasn't quite caught up with the new postnuclear reality. That's an opportunity. Sure, we now have day care and parental leave programs. Most school forms now have two spaces for parent contact data. But it's still logistically more difficult to live in a postnuclear family than in a traditional one.

The key to finding opportunities is simple: Think Ozzie and Harriet. Single moms and lesbian couples often need or would prefer to outsource the services that Ozzie could provide—handyman help, babysitting, sports instruction. That's one reason businesses like the Strike Zone in Wilmette, Illinois, which teaches kids baseball, have sprung up. Single dads and gay couples often need or want the inverse, services that Harriet provided. In TV land, most postnuclear families have a butler or a set of extra dads (*Full House*) around to take up the slack. In the real world, things are a little more difficult, and the opportunities to help are larger.

Retribing

The Trend

We are born to a tribe, usually defined by geography, religion, and kinship. Increasingly, however, many of us instead gravitate to tribes of our own choosing.

- On August 1, unless I can figure a reasonable way to weasel out of it, I will attend what is arguably America's largest retribing event. My brother and I will ride Harley-Davidson motorcycles from Houston, Texas, to Sturgis, South Dakota. There we'll meet up with a half-million other bike riders, all members of the Harley tribe. This tribe cuts across not only geography and kinship, but it also runs against the grains of demographics and social class. CEOs from Chicago will sit down on the curbside and share a beer with unemployed auto mechanics from Fresno.

- At the end of that same month, 25,000 people will come to the Black Rock Desert, 120 miles north of Reno, Nevada, for the annual festival known as Burning Man. Teachers from Sarasota will join nuclear physicists from Berkeley to camp for a week in the desert, set off fireworks, listen to loud music, and attend New Age seminars.

- In August, instead of riding to Sturgis, South Dakota, with me or camping in the desert, you can pick from Celtic festivals in Monterey, Kalamazoo, and New York City. Across the world this year there will be 350 Celtic festivals, most of them not in the United Kingdom. (One that caught my eye is to be held in Tokyo. Clan Maclanahan-san does have some poetry to it. Another will be held on the cruise ship Norway, aka the "Celtic Love Boat." I swear I'm not making this up.)

Factors and Factoids

We are not only born *to a tribe,* we are born *to tribe.* That is, we like to be part of well-defined social groups. Our ancestors formed packs and swung around African treetops. Some of us join country clubs. Our children join fraternities and sororities. For the most part, tribes are associated with place (e.g., churches, civic organizations, even bowling leagues are all geographically driven). Historically, most people have had limited chances to join nonlocal social groups.

Belonging to nongeographic tribes used to be not only rare, but risky. Don grew up in Chicago, in a Southside neighborhood located behind what used to be the stockyards. One night he told us about his days as a Golden Gloves champion in the late 1950s. "I really had no choice," he said. " 'Back-of-the-Yards' was an Italian neighborhood. Every day I'd go to school and some kid would say, 'Why don't I ever see you at mass over at St. Anthony's?' Then I'd tell them I went to St. Aloysius, they'd figure out I was Polish, and somebody would smack me. Then I'd go to the parish and some kid would ask me where I went to school. I'd tell him and he'd say, 'But that's an Italian school.' Then he'd smack me. By the time I was seventeen I'd fought every kid in Chicago."

But now, thanks to interconnectedness, we are no longer limited to geographic tribing and retribing options. People can now use the Internet to help form new communities, and chat on the telephone to a fellow tribe member across the country for $1. Cheap travel makes it possible for the new tribes to assemble relatively easily. Retribing is now a global activity.

The Implications

Expect the continued growth of large tribes that span geographies. Expect geography-based tribes, like the Rotary, Lions, and Kiwanis Clubs, to struggle. All of us can only belong to so many groups, and as we join new ones, the ones that came before must by necessity wither away. It will mean more tribe time, but less face-to-face time.

Expect retribing to have a light and a dark side. The light side is my 17-year-old son, who is passionate about water polo, now is linked in with similar fanatics around the world. He knows about next month's tournament in Australia, who's competing, and who's not. The dark side is in tribes like the Davidians, the Aryan Nation, and al-Qaeda, which attracted recruits from dozens of nations and cities, including the suburbs of San Francisco.

Expect tribal affiliations to eventually supplant traditional ones, exactly as Marshall McLuhan predicted 30 years ago.

The Opportunities

Business. A word of caution is warranted when talking about the business opportunities created by retribing. All those for-profit on-line communities found that out the hard way, when their business models that were based on advertising, subscriber fees, and e-commerce collapsed. It takes patience to build a business around a tribe, just as it does to build one around a community. But it can be done. The Oprah Book Club is a business built around tribe, as is Liquid Blue, official tee-shirt suppliers to Deadheads around the world. The key is to pick a tribe for which you have a natural affinity and to invest time in really understanding it.

What sorts of opportunities lie in retribing? Obviously, there's a business in promoting communication and assemblies: The merchants in Sturgis get about $175 per day from every biker who attends the rally; Burning Man sells tickets; a cruise on the Celtic Love Boat costs more than a typical run-of-the-mill cruise. There's also money in providing emblems and badges. Tribes have insignia, be it official Harley leathers or Celtic-design shirts. And finally, there will also be money in safety. Due to the dark side of retribing, there's going to be a need for safety services (e.g., vetting of applications and transaction processing).

Individual. Aside from business opportunities, the potential of retribing to create groups of passionate people to enjoy each other is an exciting one. This is America. Reinvention of self is a god-given right, like freedom of speech and speeding. And retribes are the great self-reinvention vehicle. A poor kid from Kansas who earns a Harvard Business School ring has used retribing to become something else entirely than defined by birth. And more power to him or her.

The Trust Deficit

The Trend

As a generation, we're suffering from a trust deficit.

Factors and Factoids

In 1989, 55 percent of Americans trusted the evening news. By 1994, that number had dropped to 12 percent, exactly the same percentage of people who say they trust corporate advertising. In general, consumers think there's about a 50-50 chance that companies "would do the right thing if faced with a serious problem with one of their products."[2]

We think the news media is biased; we think corporations have their fingers crossed; and we suspect the government could be up to anything, from covering up those really responsible for the Kennedy assassination to concealing autopsies of aliens to hypnotizing Mark Chapman so he'd kill John Lennon.

As the old joke goes, just because we're paranoid, doesn't mean they're not out to get us.

- You never won at McDonald's Monopoly game because the company that packed the game pieces kept the winners for friends and family.
- Turns out Ford and Firestone have known about those tire problems for years.
- Does anyone believe those executives of tobacco companies testifying before Congress that they don't know smoking causes lung cancer?
- It could be worse. Does anyone also believe a certain former U.S. president is the only adult on the planet who doesn't know what sex is?
- And those glowing reviews of Sony Pictures movies by David Manning of the Ridgefield Press? There's a Ridgefield Press, but no David Manning. The blurbs were concocted by someone in Sony's PR department.

Our mistrust is well placed and trust would be, well, misplaced. The motto of the 1960s was "Don't trust anyone over thirty." The slogan of the new millenium is "Don't trust anyone. Period." Gosh, that sounds harsh, but it's true. We've become a generation of Mulders. Santa's not getting down that chimney without a government-issued ID with a recent photograph on it.

Implications

Trust and credulity are like tonsils. Once they're gone, they're gone. We will remain a cynical lot, a generation who takes everything we read or hear with not just a grain of salt, but with a whole teaspoon. There are many implications of this, and almost all of them are a little depressing. But one immediate result for those of us in business is it's going to become harder and harder for us to get our messages across.

Expect us to move to a new code of behavior for everyone in any sort of public role, be it business or politics. This new code of behavior will comprise the following three rules:

1. Tell the truth, always. It sounds corny, but to summarize Mark Twain, the truth is easier to remember anyway.

2. Don't joke about serious stuff. To our mistrustful ears, it won't sound funny. Okay, here's when people trot out the "We've-lost-our-sense-of-humor-due-to-political-correctness" complaint. Well, so be it. In this newly cynical world, people aren't going to trust that some of your best friends are minorities and that you meant no harm with that joke. If you wouldn't want to read it in the newspaper, just don't say it.

3. If you do blow it, admit it and face the music.

Expect any sentence to be tripled for covering up. Bob Davie was caught misappropriating funds as a young assistant coach. He confessed, repaid the school, and was later named coach at the prestigious University of Notre Dame. George O'Leary, before even having time to move into his new office, was fired as Davie's replacement after it was discovered that he had fudged his resume to get his first job and never owned up.

The key to succeeding in this distrustful world will be to never forget that we're talking to a group of customers and employees who are just as cynical and distrustful as we are.

The Opportunities

Business. Companies that use evidence-based advertising will do better than those who make vague emotional claims. Show skeptical consumers the data that say your product really works better and you'll move product while they puzzle over flat sales.

In fact, don't just rely on advertising to talk to your customers. Supplement any message to consumers with word of mouth and/or good press. Even if your advertising is convincing, we consumers are going to want corroboration and not from David Manning.

Finally, be as protective of your good name as a father interviewing his daughter's first prom date. What's the one media outlet that everyone, black and white, male and female, trusts? Everybody trusts *Consumer Reports* because they have never, ever allowed their brand to become tarnished. *Consumer Reports* refuses to even accept advertising. They've been wrong, but never on the take, and people remember that. If your brand does get tarnished badly, think about shelving it. Draconian? Yes, but remember—once that trust is lost. . . .

Contradictory Consumption

The Trend

One of my old pals from the Peace Corps, Christine, gets apoplectic if you just say the word *SUV*. To her, sport-utility vehicle (SUV) owners are the absolute embodiment of selfishness. How can anyone with an ecological conscience drive a Lincoln Navigator? she wonders. She's not alone. There are some truly scary chat rooms devoted to the anti-SUV crowd. But why have socially conscious people replaced their VW Beetles with Cadillac Escalades and turned the thermostat back up to 72 degrees? It is because we live in a society where it is no longer possible to simply do the right thing—we can only optimize for the *rightest* thing, and what the rightest thing is can be very far from clear. Sure, that suburban mom cares for the environment, but she also cares for the safety of her kids, and the two aren't necessarily the same thing.

Factors and Factoids

People want to do the right thing. In terms of the environment, at least, we all agree increasingly on what that right thing is: recycling, nonnuclear power sources, and fuel-efficient vehicles. In 1968, espousing those causes would have gotten you teargassed in Chicago. And speaking of people who got teargassed in Chicago in 1968, today 98 percent of the people in Madison, Wisconsin, participate in the city's recycling program. Okay, maybe Madison is not a typical community. Still, between 1991 and 1994, curbside recycling programs in the United States increased eightfold.

But we also drive SUVs, put up strand after strand of Christmas lights, and do all the other things that people like Christine would argue are still excessive in a resource-constrained world. Even in Madison, the streets are full of Chevy Suburbans. If anything, despite our good intentions, the trend is toward more energy usage, not less.

At the end of the 1970s, carmakers sold over 3 million subcompacts and almost no SUVs. Today, they sell over 2 million SUVs, more than subcompacts. The average weight of cars fell from 3,349 pounds in 1978 to 2,805 pounds in 1988 as carmakers increased their use of plastics and lightweight materials. Since 1988, the average weight is now back up to more than 3,000 pounds per car. Subcompacts and compacts get more than 30 miles per gallon, and sales are dropping. Large pickups and SUVs get under 20 miles per gallon, and their sales have been growing.

Christine would argue that this increasing gap between intentions and actions means we're all just plain dumb or seriously confused. She's wrong. The problem is it's not that clear what the right thing is. Why not? Because our elected government has pushed the decisions down to us and, at the same time, made them more difficult to make.

One unit of the government runs ads on the need for energy conservation, pushing us toward subcompacts. But at the same time, world oil prices, adjusted for inflation, fell by 60 percent between 1978 and 1998. Adjusted for inflation, gasoline prices at the pump have dropped by about 20 percent over the same period. So even though the six o'clock news says we're running out of energy, the prices on the pump say just the opposite.

We each must optimize these conflicting signals to the best of our ability. The result ends up being a nation of SUVs and Volvos with Greenpeace stickers on the back bumpers, dropping off the recycling on our way to work.

Implications

We will continue to see this need to optimize what are an inherently conflicting and irrational set of messages with regard to the environment. Over the next 20 years, energy usage in the industrialized nations should rise by around 30 percent, far higher than population growth over the same period. Energy consumption in the developing world should grow four times as fast as population. This increased usage will add a tremendous loading of carbon emissions to the environment, and the government will continue to urge us to use less energy.

At the same time, all governments will endeavor to keep energy prices low and stable to promote economic growth. Allowing an instantaneous return to true market pricing can have very extreme social results. In Venezuela in 1989, gasoline sold for about a dime a gallon. When the government removed the subsidies, the resulting riots caused at least 256 deaths and looting in seven major cities.

And in 2001, California decided to allow electricity to move toward true market pricing, only to have Governor Davis screaming for price controls as soon as summer air-conditioning bills showed up. So it's very unlikely that we'll see another oil shock, at least if politicians have anything to do about it.

We will simultaneously continue to see low energy prices push us toward bigger vehicles and an increased awareness of carbon emissions and their effect on global warming push us toward Vespa scooters. Each of us will have to balance conscience and economics. It's up to us to sort it out.

The Opportunity

The opportunity is not in developing products and services that help people do the right thing, because it's never going to be clear what that is. Instead, help people do the *rightest* thing. Design products and messages that address the social issues with which we're all trying to deal within the context of how we live today.

Who's doing this today? In the area of energy, companies like Honda are producing hybrid cars that run on gasoline and electricity. Allied Systems is testing microturbines and Canadian start-up Ballard is pioneering new hyperefficient fuel cells that run on hydrogen.

Energy, however, is not the only place we're seeing opportunities created by balancing conflicting signals. There are lots of places where there's not a right answer, but only a rightest one. As I write this, President Bush is making a speech for us to get back to normal, but to continue to support the war and pay attention to Attorney General Ashcroft's warnings of impending terrorist attacks. We're told to trust Social Security, but to save anyway. Spend to help the economy, but don't run up debt. And anywhere there's an impossible conflict between social issues and the exigencies of daily life, there's an opportunity.

- United Way corporatized giving, making it convenient for people to support charities.
- The jury's out on whether organic food is really better, but it has now become a $7.7 billion industry. The U.K. market for organic food grew from $160 million in 1993 to $640 million in 1999. The number of organic farms in Europe has grown

from around 10,000 in 1990 to well over 120,000 today. People are buying even though organic, natural, and ethically congruent food costs more—free-range turkeys cost a dollar a pound more than the old cooped-up kind. Farmers and food manufacturers have found a way to help people do the rightest thing.

- In the United States, Green Mountain Power has shown that some consumers will pay more for electricity that comes from hydro or wind, rather than oil and nuclear. They offer people a package of green and brown energy, for example, 50/50, for a modest upcharge versus purely green. And people are buying.

- And in the United Kingdom, there are 36 ethical investing funds with around $4 billion in them. Although definitions vary, in general, these funds won't invest in liquor, tobacco, oil, cosmetics (concerns over animal testing), or nuclear energy. Instead, they put their money into wind turbines, software, health care, and telecoms.

So don't even try to change fundamental consumer behavior (e.g., car pooling) or convince them to ignore economics. They won't. Instead, try to help people balance their social caring with the economic and logistical realities with which we all must deal every day.

The Neverending Traffic Jam

The Trend

Mount Tamalpias, north of San Francisco, is where many car commercials are filmed. You know the ones—beautiful sunshine, waves of lush golden grass, blue ocean in the background, and happy drivers whipping shiny red cars around empty S curves. Well, maybe it is like that, if you're filming a commercial and can get the Park Service to close the road for you. But if you're a normal schmuck on vacation, the view is more likely to be the red brake lights of the minivan in front of you. Because the road up Mount Tamalpias, like almost everywhere else in America, is often congested.

Ever feel like you spend a major portion of your life stuck in traffic? You do, in the neverending traffic jam that we now all live in.

Factors and Factoids

In 1999, the typical driver in LA spent 56 hours per year in traffic delays. That was the worst in the nation, but not by much: Atlanta and Seattle, 53; Houston, 50; Dallas and Washington, 46. In Chicago, where I live, we spent an average of 34 hours per year backed up, three times as many hours as we spent when I first moved here in 1983. Last time we Chicagoans counted, 24 minutes of every hour were spent in traffic tie-ups.

What's causing this? Sprawl, the tendency of megalopolises to grow like middle-aged former athletes—out not up. In 1940, the largest cities in the United States packed more than 10,000 people per square mile. Today, only three large cities have a density of more than 7,500 people per square mile. Instead, the growth of U.S. megalopolises has been through the boomtown phenomenon. Mesa, Arizona, was founded in 1950 and now has almost 400,000 people. Nearby Gilbert had 5,700 people in 1980, and it now has more than 100,000. It grew 276 percent in the 1990s. Around the edge of every metropolis, be it Boston or Bombay, there now exists an endless spread of strip malls, subdivisions, and traffic lights.

Sprawl creates traffic jams in three ways. First of all, things are just farther apart, making it necessary to drive for everything. In the city, a carton of milk is an elevator ride away. Out in the sprawl, it may be miles from your home in a gated subdivision to the nearest shopping area. For most of us, that means a car trip. Not only are things farther apart out in the 'burbs, but they're harder to get to. Because cities have a well-defined center, it is easy to construct fast and cheap public transportation that goes to a single central point. And the volume of traffic in and out allows convenient schedules with frequent arrivals and departures. As anyone who has tried to use suburban bus lines will attest, it doesn't work that way out in the 'burbs where businesses and public building are scattered across miles and miles of what used to be woods or prairie.

In the city, whether to own a car or not is an option. Not so in the 'burbs. You need one. Period. So you get one, and then, because you have one, you use it. Even when public transportation is a viable alternative, it still becomes more convenient to simply hop in the car and drive. The net effect is more people, more cars, more miles, and more traffic jams. Between 1960 and 1996, the number of passenger miles driven grew four times as fast as population growth. Most of that growth was in local traffic, not on long cross-country family vacations like we took 30 years ago. (Now we just fly for those.)

Look at how this works. Until the early 1990s, Sears's corporate headquarters was located in the Sears Tower, in downtown Chicago. But Sears's headquarters is now located in Hoffman Estates, located about 30 miles northwest of downtown. Many Sears executives live in Chicago's North Shore communities, 30 or so miles due north of the city and 30 miles or so due east of the new headquarters. But even though the mileages are similar, whereas the trip to the old headquarters was a 30-minute train ride, no train serves the new headquarters. Nor is there any expressway that cuts across. Instead, unless you drive in at 5 A.M. as the CEO does, it's a slow, hour-long, stoplight-to-stoplight crawl each way.

Why not just build more roads you ask? That's what many experts propose. But roads are costly and take a long time from drawing board to ribbon cutting. Those lead times are increasing due to environmental regulations and right-of-way acquisition, especially if they're built in built-up areas. More important, many experts are skeptical that new roads are the answer, since the better the roads, the more people decide to drive, which increases traffic. (In Virginia, a road built to connect rural Loudon County has turned its small towns into miniboomtowns, drawing people from Washington, D.C., Maryland, Virginia, and West Virginia.)

Others have proposed limiting sprawl through new laws. Surveys say that this is the solution favored by three-fourths of Americans. One of the major plans in Al Gore's campaign was the Livable Communities Initiative, which proposed tax breaks for communities that relieved traffic congestion. The problem is that it's not that easy to do. We don't have a system that tells suburbs that lots have to be smaller and houses closer together. Nor is there any way to tell large corporations that they can't put the new headquarters out in a distant suburb.

Implications

Where's it all going to end? William Gibson, in his brilliant book *Neuromancer,* talked about a world where there was one vast traffic-choked suburb that stretched from Atlanta to Baltimore. Let's hope that we're not headed there, but it still looks like sprawl will continue, and with it congestion. As a result, it's hard to see where we won't continue to spend more time in our cars, much of it not moving. Expect the neverending traffic jam.

The Opportunities

Business.   There are big bucks in figuring out how to make traffic move faster and more smoothly. Take EZ passes that speed getting through tollbooths. The next iteration of this could be smart roads (i.e., roads with lanes that only drivers who pay a surcharge can use). So far, public opposition to Lexus Lanes has been pretty fierce, but that may fade. For example, there has been little outcry over American Airlines offering first-class passengers their own security checkpoints with shorter lines. Are first-class roads far behind? It's a cliché, but it's still true—after a certain point, people no longer want money as much as they do time. Look for big companies to make major investments in trying to sell commuters back their lost travel time.

Of course, most won't be able to afford special helicopter limos. For the rest of us who are stuck in traffic breathing fumes, the trick will be to help us make that time less unpleasant and more productive. Richard Branson followed this logic when he designed Virgin Airlines. He figured no one enjoyed air travel and spent a great deal of his time thinking of ways to make travelers hate it less. His innovations included a meal choice in coach and massages in first class. Where are the equivalents for commuting? Obviously, cell phones and one-handed food (most McDonald's milk shakes are sold at breakfast time), but what else? How about talking books loaded up with today's newspaper? (Note: When I showed this chapter to a friend of mine who's a marketer, she said, "Oh, what a great opportunity to reach consumers. They're trapped." Well, not really. Someone has already thought of that. See the next trend.)

You Talking to Me?

The Trend

We now live in a world of constant communication, where every waking second of every day is spent taking information in and reacting back to it.

Factors and Factoids

A few years ago I prepared a simple analysis for a speech in São Paolo. The analysis looked at the amount of time each day that I spend communicating compared with the amount of time spent communicating by a mythical ancestor of a millennium ago.

Here's how I built the analysis. According to the *Domesday Book* of 1086, 75 percent of people were agricultural laborers, so that's what I assumed my ancestor would have been. (There's certainly no reason to believe any of *my* ancestors were kings or priests. Not only does my family not have a coat of arms, it was probably the late 1700s before we could afford a coat with arms. Da-da-da boom.) Serfs and villiens (free serfs) typically worked a 6-day work-week, taking off Sundays, feasts and festivals, and weather days. They rose just before light, and went to bed soon after dark, both because they were exhausted from the backbreaking labor in the fields, and because firewood and torches were scarce commodities. The ancestor would have been completely illiterate, so any communication he received would have been limited to the spoken word, either conversation, sermons, or perhaps the performances of wandering minstrels. Because of the physical intensity of agricultural labor, conversations would have consisted mostly of exchanges before and after work and during breaks.

For my ancestor, communication would have been limited to about 4 hours per workday and perhaps 14 hours of communication on the other day. Suppose, on average, 7 hours per day was spent in communication, and the other 17 spent in silence.

To test my conclusion, I thought back to my days in a small rural village in West Africa in the mid-1970s. The subsistence farmers in Manjoru had kerosene lamps, which lengthened their day a bit, and a few even had cassette players. But they probably communicated no more than 9 hours of their day. So 7 hours a day for my ancestor seems pretty reasonable.

In contrast, I communicate probably 16 hours a day. But even that doesn't really capture the difference, because I communicate on two or three levels at the same time. I talk on the phone while I answer e-mails. I read the scrolling stock prices off the screen in the elevator as I ride up to visit my largest client. I talk to my son while I watch football, while he talks to his girlfriend or his best friend on the cordless phone. (Or even both, using the magic of conference calling.) Like everyone else walking down the street in New York, I have one eye on the street, the other on the Times Square Jumbotron, and a cell phone permanently attached to my ear. I listen to the radio and read billboards as I drive, and my four-times-a-week stroll through O'Hare is a communications gauntlet, with ads ambushing me from every direction. My day is a communications soup, a minestrone of passive and active communications. If it were possible to convert all my communications (visual and aural) into words, I probably communicate 10 or even 20 times more than my ancient counterpart.

I'm not alone here. The typical person makes eight phone calls a day, twice as many as 10 years ago. Ninety-seven percent of school-aged people in the United States can read, and one of every five buys a daily newspaper.[3] We watch TV an average of 4 hours per day. And while, traditionally, TV was a relatively passive form of communication where we sat while the Big Three networks blasted it in, increasingly, it is an interactive communication medium as we surf between hundreds of channels or jump back and forth between the TV and the Internet during a sports broadcast.

Possibly the ultimate indicator of how pervasive communication has become in our life is the emergence of professions that my ancestor could not have imagined, jobs that are purely communications, like newspaper editors and call center workers. Almost 2 million Americans now work in call centers. That's over 3 percent of the workforce.

Implications

Expect communications intensity to increase. A few years ago, there was an article on a real estate broker from LA lamenting the loss of quiet time. According to her, her daily commute used to be her quiet time. But now she couldn't get a minute's peace because if one of her two cell phones wasn't going off, something was coming in on the fax. It's an image dripping with irony, but we all have the same problem.

Expect us to continue loading up on communications devices—landlines and cell phones, pagers, wired and wireless e-mail, TVs, radios, CD and DVD players, while at the same time keeping traditional communications methods like newspapers and mail in the mix. Don't be surprised to see new houses have walls of TVs, all turned to a different channel, perhaps with automatic cycling.

Expect to see businesses capitalize on our apparently endless appetite/tolerance for communications by inserting them everywhere, from ads sculpted in sand on the beach to ads plastered on the walls above urinals to ads embedded in informational communications like directory assistance. Expect an increase from passive to more active forms of communications, especially for advertisers.

Expect a noisy world where you will be communicating, or communicated to, every waking minute of every day. Expect simultaneous personal, business, and commercial messages conveyed through multiple devices in multiple modalities (e.g., graphical, text, aural). You talking to me? Yep. And so is everybody else.

The Opportunities

There are two big buckets of opportunities from this trend. The first is easy. Communications is good business. AT&T couldn't provide broadband to the home and make a buck at it, but then again, they gave up the world's greatest monopoly so they could get into the PC and credit card markets, so what do they know? Someone will make money providing communications services not only to big businesses but to small ones and to homes.

The second is a little trickier. Obviously, there comes some point where the level of communication is just too much. As writer Gunter Grass says, where "the sheer volume of information dissolves the information. We are unable to take it all in." So there's an opportunity to help people sort it out, to shield them from the cacophony. Regina Fazio Maruca, the business writer, suggests building a business around quiet time and quiet zones.

But be careful. People as a species have proven pretty capable of sorting through enormous piles of information. As we'll talk about later in the consumer section, Chapter 7, "Consumer Trends," we have already raised looking right past advertising to an art form. Further, people are nervous about having someone else sort through communications for them. Witness the demise of all the My portals that promised to organize the web for us.

Even though I absolutely hate all the spam e-mails I get and have never answered an on-line come-on for anything, from mortgages to Viagra to Brittney's phone number, I still haven't installed a filter to stop them. Human nature is to increase communication, not decrease. The winners will be those like Amazon and magazines that winnow down and concentrate the information we see, but without being obvious about it.

Instant Polling

The Trend

In 1948, three major polls predicted that Thomas Dewey would win over Harry Truman in a landslide. At the most recent election, eight polls weighed in with an opinion. (If you're curious, *Newsweek,* CBS/*New York Times,* and the *Wall Street Journal* all predicted a 3-percentage-point margin for Gore. Three others called it for Bush, and two showed it a dead heat. So if you'd been astute enough to add all eight together, you would have exactly predicted the real outcome.)

We love polls. We love them even when they contradict each other and even when we don't know who was asked or exactly what the question was. We don't care that people may be expressing opinions about issues where they cannot possibly have any clue what they're talking about. We just want to know what we as a group think, and increasingly, we want to know what we think right now.

Factors and Factoids

Why do we love polls so much? Part of it is we just like scores. We want to know who's winning and who's losing. That's why we have sports polls for everything from professional football and basketball to collegiate baseball, football, basketball, field hockey, and water polo. We have polls by sportswriters, coaches, computers, and fans. Be it elections or sports or topical issues, we care who's ahead and who's winning.

But our natural competitiveness is not the only reason we like polls. Decision theorists have long argued that decisions reached by teams are more often right than decisions reached by individuals, even really smart and knowledgeable individuals. Most of us, consciously or subconsciously, believe that. For example, on *Who Wants to Be a Millionaire?* it's the audience poll that always seems to pay off. When dining in a strange city, we turn to *Zagat's*, a restaurant guide based on readers' contributions. So we also value polls as the best possible estimate of what the real answer might be. Most marketers refuse to make a major decision without poll data to justify it. Aggregated opinion has a persuasive power that individual opinion does not.

Finally, there's another reason polling is on the uptake—technology. Technology is making polling faster and easier. Wireless keypads can allow an audience to choose their favorite video clip, or allow votes on sensitive topics at a national sales meeting. Large outbound call centers can do a nationwide poll overnight and get a quick answer on where the voters think they stand before the 9 A.M. press briefing. Technology sorts through thousands of zip codes and telephone numbers in seconds to provide a call list that is statistically random, or nonrandom, for example, depending on whether you want to know what all Americans think of the proposed tax bill or whether you are just interested in the views of elderly people.

Even telephone surveys are slow, though, compared with Internet polling. Simple polls are everywhere on the Internet. On professional football games, thousands of viewers log on during the game and express their opinions on everything from the player of the game to the most recent referee's decision. My Netscape homepage wants to know whether I keep my New Year's resolutions. At CNN.com, you can express your views on the looming political issues of the day. At the end of a recent A&E program on a notorious murder trial in Oklahoma, there was an opportunity to log in and vote on whether you agree with the jury's decision. The Internet has taken polling to a whole new level.

The Implications

There are some obvious implications to this, such as the likelihood that marketers will eventually come to test every single communication with consumers at every single stage of the process. For example, some companies already test advertising at several points—positioning statement, creative concept, and first cut. Right now, that process takes months. For almost a decade, Ken Lambert, formerly an executive at ad giants BCOM3 and Y&R, has been predicting the emergence of an instant feedback model, where all this happens in a 3-day, collapsed time frame using multiple prese-lected consumer panels wired into a central test facility.

There's no reason to believe that Ken's vision isn't spot on, that the process won't be broken down into more and more steps and tested at more and more points more and more times. The thing is this, that new efficiency is not necessarily all good. Several studies have shown quick-and-dirty polls are not particularly accurate. And the emergence of by-the-numbers creative development in Holly-wood has led to movies and sitcoms of unrivaled averageness and predictability. Of course, therein lies an opportunity: A whole indus-try of independent filmmakers has sprung up to create truly break-through work. But I'm getting ahead of myself.

Instant polling will continue to spread. Internet marketers have found that instant polls are the quickest way to create interaction with their website, and to build a high-quality list of web addresses. Marketers and politicians have found it's now possible to get data to help make real-time decisions. So expect polling, and particularly instant polling, to grow.

Expect the broader instant feedback concept to grow as well. For example, with supermarket scanners, we could see a day when mar-keters at headquarters monitor sales of toothpaste and, if sales are slow, adjust prices in real time.

The Opportunities

Any time you can talk with your customers, it's an opportunity. Every business, large or small, should have a standing panel of cus-tomers and employees with whom it can quickly test new strategic and tactical moves. Now this doesn't mean you'll always want to do what the research tells you to do, but at least you'll know.

Lawyers, Guns, and Money

The Trend

The title comes from a great song by Warren Zevon about a young man in trouble who begs his dad to "send lawyers, guns, and money, the shit has hit the fan."[4] It's a neat encapsulation of one of the great trends of our time, litigiousness. America is already the most liti-gious country on earth, and it's getting more litigious every day.

Factors and Factoids

In 1999, there were more than 90 million cases filed in the state courts of the United States. Most of those were traffic cases, but 15,122,009 were civil cases, citizen against citizen, company against company, and citizen against company. The number of civil cases is up by one-third from 1984, when there were 11 million.

Why the boom in legal actions? There are three reasons: First, lawsuits are very effective remedies for a whole range of problems. They really are. Second, we have a serious infestation of lawyers, the highest on the planet. Third, lawyers are allowed to work on contingency.

Let's start by looking at the effectiveness of lawsuits. Lawsuits pay. Ninety-five percent are settled ahead of time, often because the defendant wants to avoid the cost and bother of the legal process. And if they do go to jury trial, plaintiffs win 49 percent of the time. That means that in 97.5 percent of the time the aggrieved party gets a payout. The size of the payout? It varies. Winning a judgment for slander and libel only yields $25,000. (That's for all the lawyers who didn't like my infestation joke in the last paragraph.) But a win in a product liability or medical malpractice case typically pays out around $250,000. Then there's always the chance of a jackpot win. Twenty-five percent of medical malpractice jury awards top $1 million. So for individuals seeking financial compensation for having been wronged, lawsuits are both reliable and profitable.

However, lawsuits have also become the preferred tool of social activists on both ends of the spectrum. That's because lawsuits also pay off in a currency that some value more than cold cash—time. The legal process is lengthy and time consuming, and a case can take years to wind its way through the legal process. Some have found that using the courts to delay outcomes achieves the same end as actually winning the suit. Those pushing what opponents call a *no-growth agenda* have been particularly adroit at using the legal system.

For example, environmental activists have employed a two-step legal strategy. First, they have used the courts to force the Department of the Interior to list over 1,200 species as threatened. Then whenever specific development projects are proposed near the habitats of threatened species, the activists sue in state courts to halt the project or delay it while the impact is evaluated.

In 2001, the Bush administration asked Congress to declare a moratorium on adding new species to the list. Good luck. Historically, moves to limit lawsuits haven't worked very well. For example, the Private Securities Litigation Reform Act, passed in 1995 under the Clinton administration, was intended to reduce the number of securities class-action suits. But they're still being filed in record numbers.

That's the demand-side explanation for the blossoming of lawsuits. There's a simple, and equally valid, supply-side argument as well. That is, we have a lot of lawsuits because we have a lot of lawyers. The United States has an *extraordinary* number of attorneys, even compared with countries with very similar legal systems like Canada, England, Australia, and New Zealand. For every 300 Americans, there is a lawyer. That is at least half again as many per population as countries like Canada and the United Kingdom, which have very similar legal systems.[5] The number of attorneys in America has quadrupled in the last half-century. (See Figure 6.2)

And because the United States allows lawyers to take cases on a contingency basis, we have seen the emergence of speculative class-action suits instituted by legal *factories*. In 2000, the Cendant Corporation, owner of Avis and Ramada, settled a suit with its

Figure 6.2 **Growth in the number of lawyers in the United States.**

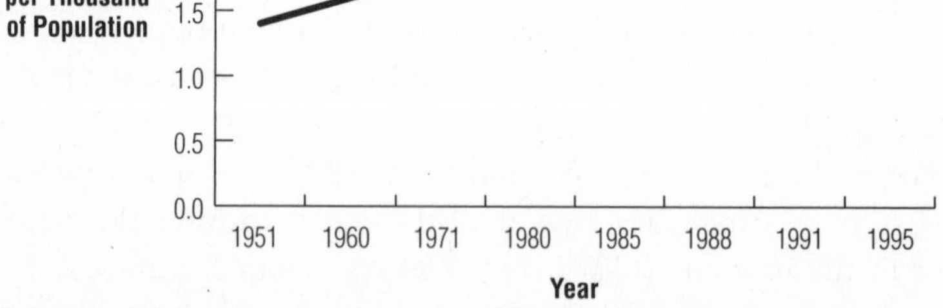

Sources: BLS, Helios Analysis.

stockholders for $2.8 billion. An estimated 20 to 30 percent of the proceeds of such suits go to the attorneys. Abusive? It depends on which side of the table you sit. But whatever it is, with $700 million in fees up for grabs, it's not going away any time soon.

Implications

Expect more lawsuits, targeted especially against big institutions. Does *big institutions* mean corporations? Not necessarily, one of the biggest problems facing churches today is defending themselves from legal action. Thousands of churches have been sued for everything from slip-and-falls to sexual misconduct to clergy malpractice. That latter category has led to wrongful death suits by the families of people who committed suicide and even charges of brainwashing. Any institution is a target, profit or not-for-profit, large or small, public or private.

Expect the chief counsels to continue to grow in importance within corporations, perhaps even becoming co-CEOs in some cases. Not too long ago, the CEO of a high-tech start-up told me of his plans to sue a major computer manufacturer because their equipment had grossly underperformed promises. I asked if he expected to win. "Not really," he answered. "Those guys get sued by clients all the time. Sometimes I think they're just a big law firm who sell computers on the side." More and more corporations will find Legal as a part of the strategic inner circle of top management. (And a corollary, expect to see more and more lawyers in management positions.)

Also, expect the law profession to move from profession to industry. That means bigger and bigger law firms, more competitive bidding for projects, and more professional marketing. There's already a fair bit of marketing by legal firms. On Chicago cable TV, Peter Francis Geraci earnestly implores viewers to call and listen to a free tape to find out how bankruptcy can sort out their finances. Even this is professional and restrained compared with Wallin & Klarich in LA, who specialize in criminal law and advertise for clients to call 1-877-4NO-JAIL. Expect it to move up a notch though, both in visibility and in class.

Also don't be surprised if law firms branch out. A committee of the American Bar Association has already proposed that legal firms move into areas like mergers and acquisitions advisory. Right now, there are laws that limit lawyers who are not in a law firm from practicing law directly (e.g., those who work for corporations) and limit what businesses law firms can engage in. This could change within a generation.

The Opportunities

Here's the biggest opportunity—lawsuit prevention. For example, Ergodyne has built a successful business providing back supporters to workers whose job involves lifting. Back injuries are hard to prove or disprove, and they're costly in court. It would be far better to simply prevent them—and the suits that result. Big Five consultancies help their clients set up sexual harassment prevention programs. They are part of what the *Los Angeles Times* has called the *antiharassment training industry.*

Prevention won't be enough, so lawsuit resolution will also become bigger business, be it private eyes who shadow workers' compensation cheats or insurance companies. For example, employment practices liability (EPL) insurance, which covers sexual harassment, discrimination, wrongful termination, and other employment-related legal areas, has grown from a seldom-seen product offered by only a few companies to a must-have coverage.

Finally, for both small businesses and individuals, look to the legal industry to become a market in and of itself. As firms get bigger, we'll see other firms spring up around them to serve them. For example, right now, Harvard guru David Maister has built a very successful consulting practice built around law firms. New York firm Bliss and Gouverneur provides PR services to those in the legal industry (and other service industries). If you're a small business, you can think of law firms just like those smaller machine shops in Detroit think of the auto industry, as a potential market.

Screw You Very Much

The Trend

Not too long ago, someone called me "rude." I confess to being a little sensitive on the topic, especially since this is not the first time it has come up. See, I don't think I'm rude. I seldom intend to offend anyone, except my brother-in-law (and that doesn't really count). It just happens. My excuse is that I'm socially tone-deaf. I can no more pick up social rhythms in a conversation than I can follow musical rhythms on a dance floor. (To help you calibrate, the last time I tried to samba, an off-duty paramedic tackled me and held my jaw so I wouldn't swallow my tongue. My social skills are no better than my dancing.)

The good news, I guess, is that at least I'm not alone. Almost everyone agrees that we live in a time of bad manners and ever increasing rudeness. And it's not just in the big cities, like where I live. It's everywhere, it seems.

Factors and Factoids

Eighty-nine percent of Americans think rudeness is a serious problem, and 8 out of 10 think it has gotten worse over the last decade or so. Fully, 9 out of 10 think that rudeness leads directly to violence, although from the survey data it's not clear if the violence is done by rude people escalating from word to deed, or done by the victims of rudeness. The latter is certainly plausible—four out of five Americans report getting enraged in response to rudeness. Think of road rage as the twentieth-century version of dueling with pistols at dawn, a violent objection to a breach of manners.

Nor is this just an American problem. In a 1998 survey by The Yomiuri Shimbun, 87.7 percent of respondents said they felt manners had deteriorated in Japan. A few years ago, the Chinese government banned 50 rude phrases from use by clerks and service-people in hotels, airports, and stores. Rudeness, it seems, is a global epidemic.

There has been a stampede of writers and analysts to examine this rudeness boom. George F. Will wrote a book, *The Triumph of Meanness*, and Mark Caldwell wrote another, *A History of Rudeness*. The latter was reviewed gleefully by the *New York Times*, whose only complaint was that the book didn't come down on rude people hard enough. And rudeness and the decline of good manners is a recurring theme in *U.S. News & World Report*, CNN, and *USA Today*.

Actually, despite all the hubbub, the supporting evidence for the increase of rudeness isn't really that clear. There's always been a general dissatisfaction among the older set about the poor manners of the younger generation. Way back in 224 B.C., comic playwright Plautus poked fun at his elders, who thought his generation's manners stank: "Mores deteriores increbescunt."

In fact, some have argued that, as a nation, we're actually becoming more polite, and in more important ways. For example, it may be true that not as many people know what that smaller fork on the left is for, but then again, most of us don't sit down to seven-course meals too often. It's a lot more practical to know when to step forward and when to defer in the deli line, or when to put your briefcase under your feet rather than in the overhead compartment. And while people may no longer say "ma'am" and "sir," they do ask permission before lighting a cigarette. Nor do most of us toss trash out of the car window.

Even with language, the case for the decline and fall of etiquette is not so clearcut. Were you and I shipped back in time to the 1920s, we would be appalled at the language used in an upper-class drawing room and vice versa. Our host and hostess would surely blanch if I slipped and said a curse word. But we'd be struck speechless over the number of horrifying and patronizing words for minorities sprinkled through the conversation. Could it be that, on balance, we're getting more polite in some areas and less polite in others?

That's exactly what's happening. We are seeing a redefinition of what politeness is, and by necessity, what rudeness is. Each new generation encounters new social situations for which there are no well-established rules or where the old rules no longer apply. For example, should I stand and give my seat on the train to a 50-year-old woman? In the 1920s, the etiquette was absolutely clear. But as we'll discuss later, 50 is no longer quite as old as it used to be. And in some situations and to some women, my offer would be received as the exact opposite of politeness.

Some consider it unspeakably rude to interrupt a conversation to answer a cell phone. But every restaurant and conference room are full of people who don't think it rude at all. In the same vein, we haven't quite sorted out the rules of etiquette for e-mail jokes or for splitting the check on a group date or even for asking someone out in the new workplace. It's not that we're rude, it's that we haven't had time to all agree on exactly what the new rules are. Each of us is making up our own set as we go.

But while rudeness may not be a trend, the increasing social unease over politeness is.

Implications

Expect the unease to grow. We will continue to see situations emerge where it's not clear just what polite behavior is. Expect us to continue to rapidly redefine etiquette and feel less and less secure about it.

Expect telecom technology to continue to create completely new social situations that demand new rules of etiquette. For example, is it rude of me to check e-mails while I'm on a conference call? Is it okay if I press Mute to hide the telltale click of computer keys as I do so? What over-the-horizon technologies will require new rules?

Expect time pressures to continue to reshape politeness. We are short of time and getting shorter. A few years ago, Pac Bell told its operators to stop saying "Please" to save time. E-mail is developing its own etiquette shorthand. I never listen to more than half of any voice mail before I rip on to the next one. As we continue to try to cram more and more communications in, conversations will continue to become more and more truncated, and we'll move farther and farther away from Jane Austen–type politeness.

But don't expect us to become comfortable with rudeness; instead, expect more effort expended to create and maintain a standardized set of manners.

The Opportunities

Businesses. This sounds a little odd, but if everyday politeness is so rare, why couldn't it become the next source of competitive advantage? As we'll discuss later in Chapter 7, "Consumer Trends," satisfying customers is going to be darn near impossible in the future. But being unfailingly polite, that's much easier. Use politeness to set your business apart from the herd.

There are more direct opportunities as well in the etiquette industry. Judith Martin, Miss Manners, is booked out for speeches years in advance. There are corporate training programs to teach salespeople proper golf course etiquette. A Greenwich teacher has teamed up with one of the large fast-food restaurants to give politeness seminars for tots. Organizations like Catalyst, the consulting firm, help clients define the rules of the polite workplace.

Individuals. Good manners are an opportunity because they're a real competitive weapon and one that's in good taste. You've got your Cal Tech engineering degree, your Harvard MBA, your flashy new suit from Joseph Banks, and a Tumi briefcase, and you still find 20 other job aspirants with exactly the same credentials in the interview room with you? Well, here's a way to get yourself noticed. Be polite. Be more than polite, be well mannered. Be exquisitely mannered. Unbutton your jacket when you sit, and button it when you rise. Let that woman pass through the door first. What the heck, let the guy she's with go through, too. Hold the Open button on the elevator door. (Don't look for praise when you are polite, that's a dead giveaway that it doesn't come naturally. Be casually formal.)

Okay, so that means you have to learn two sets of manners—the old one and the new one—but if you're smart enough to go to Cal Tech, you're surely smart enough to figure out how to use a soup spoon (scoop away from your mouth, and yes, you can tilt the bowl).

CHAPTER 7

Consumer Trends

If you're reading this book just for fun, you might as well skip the next two paragraphs. But if you're a pro, for instance, a planner at an ad agency or a strategy veep in a consumer goods company setting up a new products ideation workshop, you better read on.

It's time for a drop of definitional rigor. It is difficult to draw a clean, bright line between *societal trends* and *consumer trends*. Many trends could legitimately belong in either section, depending on how they are articulated and developed. What I have *tried* to do is classify as *societal* those trends that affect virtually all of us and affect our behaviors in multiple ways (e.g., how we spend our time, where we choose to live, with whom). I have labeled as *consumer* those trends that affect only some of us, usually one particular segment, and that only affect one particular aspect of that segment's behavior (i.e., how they buy).

It's not a clean split, but it is important to make the effort. Trend analysts often fall into a hole by looking at societal trends and trying to get more specific insights on purchase behavior than the data support, or even more commonly, making inferences about the market as a whole from trends that really affect only a single segment. To the extent that it is possible to keep these two sets of trends in neat, separate buckets, it makes them more manageable when the time comes to use them.

Whew. Enough of that. Now back to the show. In this section, we'll look at 11 trends:

1. *Peter Pan–ism.* This trend looks at boomers' outright refusal to age.

2. *Prematurity.* But that doesn't mean we think the world should be devoid of adults. We just don't want to be the grown-ups ourselves. In fact, we think adulthood is something to be tackled and gotten through as quickly as possible, which is why we're asking kids to get started earlier and earlier.

3. *Escalating expectations.* "I can't get no satisfaction." Nor can almost anyone else, it seems. Consumer satisfaction levels continue to fall, despite wonderful technology and growing affluence.

4. *Concrete consumer.* Well, perhaps then all of us marketers and businesspeople should just sit down with consumers and discuss this expectations gap? Fat chance. They're not listening, and nothing we do is going to make them.

5. *Faux authenticity.* We have a feel for real. Retro is raging. Old is on a roll. Antiquing is peaking. Ahem. Okay, maybe that last one went a bit too far. Many of us have a taste for products and experiences that we regard as genuine.

6. *Born to be wired.* We get technology like no generation before us, and expect it.

7. *Nibble and nap.* It used to be that you could set your watch by five events: waking up, breakfast, lunch, dinner, and bedtime. Now we've replaced those structured and well-defined daily events with dozens of impromptu snacks and rest periods.

8. *Buy now, pay never.* Consumer credit is not new. Even back in the olden times, like when Snow White lived, workers borrowed money. That's why those dwarfs were always singing "I owe, I owe, it's off to work I go." Or something like that. The difference was they paid it back, or the Sheriff of Nottingham showed up and huffed and puffed and blew . . . wait, that doesn't sound right. Never mind all that history stuff, debt is escalating and default rates are on the rise.

9. *Upscaling.* My mom wore a Timex. My daughter wears a Tag Heuer.

10. *The frugal rich.* It used to be the middle class went to Sears and the wealthy went to Saks Fifth Avenue. Now you see shoppers lugging Tiffany and Target bags in the same hand. Just because wealthy people have money, doesn't mean they intend to spend it.

11. *Plumposity.* I used to work with a 6-foot-7-inch genius named Benito Medero, who explained his ethnicity as two-thirds Uruguayan and one-third Mexican. When asked how that was possible (ancestry is usually expressed as one-half, one-quarter, one-eighth, etc.), he said he arrived in Mexico City 10 years before weighing 160 and was now up to 240. That same logic would make many of us two-thirds American and one-third Budweiser. We're gaining a pound or two.

That's it. Eleven trends that are affecting the way we shop and buy. Here we go.

Peter Pan-ism

The Trend

Like Peter Pan, we firmly believe that you only get old if you consent to. And we boomers don't. Ed is a top executive at one of the world's largest banks. When's he's not signing checks with 8 zeroes on them, he is at home with his wife and three sons, playing tennis at his club, or scuba diving with me in Little Cayman or Lake Michigan.

Ed has given up skiing for snowboarding and golf for tennis. He's even dyed his hair back to its original reddish blond. All of this is part of a deliberate program to act and look as young as he feels. As Ed explained his new hair color, "That white-haired guy in the mirror wasn't me. *This* is me." Ed speaks for us boomers all.

The best part of belonging to the biggest demographic group in history is that we control the media, which means that things are whatever we say they are. And we say old age is not us. We reserve the right to ride Razor scooters as long as we damn well please.

Factors and Factoids

The average response of 50-year-old Americans, when asked when old age begins, is 80 years old. Of course, like most things, there's some truth in it. In general, every generation is healthier and more active than the ones before it. Surveys say 40 percent of people over 65 say they have sex more than twice a month. Ten percent of health club members are over 55, and that number is expected to grow.

But the greater truth is that boomers just intend to follow Bob Dylan's advice and stay "forever young." We intend to look young, act young, and play young. Plastic surgery grew by 200 percent between 1989 and 1995, mostly eye jobs. Over half a million Americans over the age of 50 have gone back to college, and 15 percent of college students are over 40. This year, more than 15 percent of the 160,000 hip replacements went to boomers. That number will be 25 percent in a few years. Forty percent of stuffed animals are sold to adults for adults, and the market is growing. (Which could lead me to the Beanie Baby fad, but I'm not going to touch it.)

Implications

We will dress young and buy all manner of things youthful. Expect to continue to be surprised in the airport when that slim young thing in leather pants and leopard-skin halter turns around and you recognize your first-grade teacher, Miss McGillicuddy, who by now must be about 75. Expect her to be equally surprised to see you wearing Abercrombie & Fitch and riding a skateboard.

Of course, if we're going to dress and act like kids, we'll have to work harder to maintain the youthful illusion. In cars, it's not just the model year but also the mileage that determines the useful life of the vehicle. As it turns out, we may not be psychologically or even biologically old, but a lifetime of sunbathing, 5-kilometer races, skiing, and inline skating is taking its toll.

It's boomers or bust. Expect the antiaging industry, in all its manifestations, to continue to grow. What's in that bucket? Hearing aids, libido enhancements (like Viagra and penile implants), gum surgery, hormonal replacements (from estrogen for menopause to human growth hormone), hair replacements and colorants, all forms of plastic surgery and cosmetic dentistry, antiwrinkle treatments, joint replacements, weight loss programs, age-modified sports equipment (like cross bikes that are lightweight like road machines but without handlebars that require much bending at the waist), and a full battery of do-it-yourself medical diagnostics.

Expect the ghosts of the 1960s, 1970s, and 1980s to continue to dominate our culture. We are still the biggest demographic market for most things, and always will be, so programmers and advertisers will continue to pander to our version of what's hip. This is an awesome power, and one that we boomers have not always used wisely, as is evidenced by the fact that we still pack coliseums to watch grandfathers in Versace shirts play guitars and croak out songs about being street fightin' men. Sure, Mick, as long as the street fight finishes in time to make bingo. (A friend of mine read these last lines and called me up. He was livid and accused me of being an age bigot, having no taste in music, and being stupid. I still think, personally, that the idea of the Rolling Stones as grandpas is funny, but apparently, boomers are a little touchy on this subject. So let me be clear. It's a joke—it's just a joke. See "The Opportunity" section that follows.)

The Opportunity

If you make or sell products that go to the young, like Razor scooters or teddy bears, always be alert to the possibility of an adult version of the market. Vermont Teddy Bear Company says 90 percent of its products go to adults, at a couple of hundred bucks per. But don't forget that sometimes kid products have to be modified a bit to work for boomers, like the blue jeans of a few years ago that advertised a "skosh more room."

This might include some products and services that you wouldn't expect. Consider that in 1998 boomers sustained over 1 million medically treated sports injuries, which cost $18.7 billion to treat. (That's one reason the number of orthopedic surgeons grew by 10 percent in a 6-year span during the mid-1990s.)

Because of the high mileage, if you make products or sell services that used to go to the elderly, expect the market to grow faster than the growth in seniors. And if you're looking forward to boomers aging so you can market to them, you don't need to wait. You can start selling them those products right now. But be careful, boomers really don't like to be called *old*.

The name of the game for boomers will be to sell us the products our oldish bodies need without offending our youngish minds. Good news for brands and products that manage to stay hip. Bad news for any brand that gets tarred with the image of being solely for the elderly. Bye, bye Oldsmobile. When you advertise to a boomer, use Eminem, not Paul McCartney, to deliver the message. Dude.

Prematurity

The Trend

Now here's the irony: Adults expect to be kids forever. So what do we expect from kids? You got it. We expect them to act like adults, and we equip them accordingly:

- Palm recently donated 6,000 handheld organizers to 175 elementary school classes. The 8-year-olds plan to use them to track bluebirds for a science project, read e-books on presidents, and keep better calendars and to-do lists.

- A new toy named V-Mail lets 5-year-olds send and receive their own voice mails. Of course, they get their own personal identification number (PIN).

- For 2- and 3-year-olds in day care, IBM and Little Tykes have designed a sophisticated computer housed inside a multicolored plastic space pod. It's designed to be kidproof, with wires that can't be pulled out and keyboards that can take a cup of milk or two.

A couple of years ago, Kate Zernicke of the *New York Times* wrote a wonderful piece about one manifestation of this trend—formal preschool graduations. At one such event, held at Creative Beginnings Children's Center in Hartsdale, New York, the children march up to the podium to the sound of "Pomp and Circumstance," decked out in caps and gowns. They listen to speakers, receive diplomas and awards, and march down to the flash of cameras and applause. Kate says the only difference between this ceremony and the ones they'll attend in high school is that, in this case, the younger children are tied together with a rope. This is just the beginning for these kids. They face premature maturity.

Factors and Factoids

Whether it's clothing or toys or after-school activities, increasingly, younger and younger children are being treated like adults. There seem to be two factors driving this. First, of course, is the obvious one: We all want our kids to have a head start.

There's considerable evidence, for example, that starting the education process very early does give some kids an advantage over their peers. A 15-year U.S. study that tracked underprivileged kids who'd attended preschool found a 12 percent higher graduation rate and an arrest rate one-third lower than average. The French have long had very serious preschools. Every child enters one of the 19,000 écoles maternelles at age 3, and they are debating whether to start kids from less advantaged homes at age 2.

Extend that logic and you have kids beginning their preparation for the Ivy League or the professional soccer leagues as soon as they leave the womb and arrive home to lavish cribs filled with toys designed to instruct. These kids will move on to violin schools for toddlers and computer camps, dancing classes, and vocabulary flash cards. A friend of mine (and one of the most level-headed, laid-back people I've ever met) decided to home-school his little girl because the local school refused to allow her entry at age 4.

The second factor driving prematurity is that we can afford it. Gap clothes become Gap Kids and BabyGap. Toymakers can afford to put sophisticated electronics and learning modules into toys because parents can afford to buy them. Eleven-year-olds have cell phones so their parents will know when to pick them up from swim practice. Tony preschools now turn away up to two-thirds of applicants just like their more senior counterparts. What does *prematurity* mean?

Implications

Don't ever expect to hear the words *sir* or *ma'am* from a kid again. Instead, expect kids to adopt adult language and ape adult sensibilities. That's already happening on sitcoms, where it's common to see sage tots instruct their parents in life and love. My 17-year-old asked me yesterday if I could make it home to "do lunch" before my flight to Miami.

Expect a kiddie shadow market for almost anything and everything adults use, from facial products to clothers to sporting equipment cars. Expect tiers of products, with high-end, moderate and low-end offerings. It's also a bit of an oversimplification to suggest that adults will buy adultlike products for children. Richie Rich children will buy adultlike products for themselves, thanks to the rolls of cash they're given by parents and grandparents. Advertising to this new market will increase and become more sophisticated, fueling the children-talking-like-short-adults phenomenom.

Some experts are troubled by prematurity, with the attendant loss of childhood and traditional playtime. Not to worry. Yes, playtime has been replaced by instruction time, but at the same time official instruction time has become more playful. Middle and high schools now offer more and a greater variety of playlike courses, from ropes to drama.

And finally, other experts believe that's there's another price to be paid for lighting the candle earlier. They predict the end of innocence at any age, leading them to expect more problems like teenage alcoholism, credit card overload, and the current epidemic of teenage smoking. They expect more and more burned-out 30-year-olds and 20-somethings with midlife crises. By starting so early, kids may not only be accelerating their opportunities, they may be accelerating their problems. The jury's still out on this one.

The Opportunity

Well, somebody has to fill those empty after-school hours. The newest market will be services catering to children, and that includes everything from computers to etiquette. Entrepreneurs and small businesses are ideally suited to provide these services. The Strike Zone in Wilmette, Illinois, is a great example of the types of opportunities out there. They provide indoor batting cages complete with professional coaches to help tune up kids' swings before Little League tryouts.

Spotting product opportunities from this trend is easy. Just look around at what you own and buy, imagine it smaller and a brighter color. That should give you a start.

Escalating Expectations

The Trend

In 1981, Jan Carlzon became CEO of Scandinavian Airlines, which at that time was financially strapped, in part because of its well-earned reputation as one of the world's worst airlines. Within a year, he'd turned it into a moneymaker and industry star. His secret was simple: customer service. Just that. Forget strategic plans full of charts on barriers to entry and scale curves. Just focus on customers and meet *or exceed* their expectations, and everything will take care of itself.

It sounds a little dated today, but in the mid-1980s, every conversation in business circles was about cost, cost, cost. Executives found the idea that it was possible to build a great company through better customer service an epiphany. Soon every manager found himself or herself discussing "moments of truth," and reengineering his or her business to ensure that every employee was "either serving the customer, or serving someone who is." We talked about employee empowerment and ways to track service performance. And before long, every cubicle sported a little sign that read, "Always exceed customer expectations." Carlzon's ideas form the basis of every modern customer service program, from *Ama-* to *-zon.*

But there was something we didn't count on: mathematics. Customer expectations increase much faster than our ability to meet, much less exceed, them. Here's an example. McDonald's promised me my burgers right now and cheap. Burger King said I could have them "my way." Okay, now I want them my way, right now, and cheap. How can the poor guy behind the counter at McDonald's or BK exceed that expectation? What's faster than right now? Can he read my mind as I walk in the door and have it already bagged when I reach the counter? That might exceed my expectations for a trip or two, but then what happens the next time? By then, I'll expect him to meet me at the door, so to exceed my expectations, he has to meet me outside in the parking lot. But before long, I'll expect him in the parking lot, so he'll have to drop by the house with my order without me lifting the phone. You get the idea.

By almost any measure, products and services are better than they have ever been, and we're still not happy. And we're not going to get happy. Consumers today have escalating expectations, and no one is ever going to meet them, much less exceed them.

Factors and Factoids

Economists like Daniel Kahneman of Princeton call it the *satisfaction treadmill*. The more we make, the more we spend, the more we want. The faster we get it, the faster we want it. The more convenient it becomes, the more we realize just how convenient it could be. The more our unreasonable demands are met, the more unreasonable we become.

Take Nordstrom, the department store. They made their name on exceptional, at times even ridiculous, service. Nordstrom's legend has it that an irate customer once came in with a defective tire and demanded a refund, which Nordstrom promptly gave him. That was even though they'd never sold a tire in their history. Nordstrom's service once made them the highest rated of all department stores in the American Customer Satisfaction Index, a quarterly survey conducted by the University of Michigan business school and the benchmark used by many analysts and consumers. A book on the company, *The Nordstrom Way*, became a bible of customer service departments.

But Nordstrom's scores have dropped steadily over the last 5 years. By 2001, they were second to Costco in their category and just barely ahead of JCPenney and Target. A professor at Michigan explained the fall as being a case of escalating expectations. We now expect perfection from Nordstrom, and they cannot achieve it. (Although to their credit, they themselves make no excuses for the falling scores.)

Still, Nordstrom scores a 76. McDonald's got a 59 in 2000. That's not too good. Even the Internal Revenue Service got a 56 the last time they were measured. (Not surprisingly, the lowest score on record was an airline—53 percent.)

We consumers have become what comedian Rodney Dangerfield would call "a tough crowd." Well, how tough is it, Rodney? The crowd was so tough that . . . I won't even try my hand at vaudevillian humor.

Toughness has two sides: One side is being difficult to satisfy; the other side is being willing to act on that dissatisfaction. That second factor is high and growing as well. According to IDG, this year over one-half of all cell phone users will change their cellular providers. Consumers return over $100 billion dollars of products each year, 6 percent of all nonfood purchases. For the most part, not a single thing is wrong with the product. We're just not happy.

The Implications

Well, consumers aren't going to return to reasonableness. We can all forget that. Expect us to expect more.

Expectations will grow steadily. Service levels won't. Many of the gains from the new telephone and on-line technologies have already been realized. More expectations and the same service capability means a bigger gap—and more customer dissatisfaction. So also expect us to walk out, hang up, or click away from anyone who doesn't do exactly what we want right now, which will be everyone.

Opportunities

One opportunity is for high-end companies, like spa operators or high-end tour companies Backroads and Abercrombie & Kent. But the opportunity here is really for smaller companies. Personalized service can be the secret weapon. This doesn't mean consumers want a bit of a chat every time they walk in the store. Edward Jones, the St. Louis–based brokerage, has used its personal service touch to win 1,000 clients per month from Merrill Lynch. It does mean that when consumers have problems, they don't want to talk to a machine or try to navigate an absolutely impossible help menu. Personalization also can help you keep the customers you have by spotting problems before they walk away.

The Concrete Consumer

The Trend

Concrete is great stuff. It's too heavy to move. It's so hard a sledgehammer just bounces off. And if it's coated with one of those new high-tech polymer compounds, spray paint rinses away. Graffiti doesn't even stick. Concrete can't be moved or dented and messages don't stick. Hmmm. In other words, concrete is just like a modern consumer.

Factors and Factoids

Just about everyone in market research and advertising agrees: Marketing still works, but it sure doesn't work like it used to. Here are the numbers. Only 9 percent of television viewers can name the brand or even the product they just saw advertised on TV. That doesn't mean they forgot the commercial, just the message. At one time or another, we've all said something like, "Hey, I saw this great commercial last night, I can't remember what it's for, but in it this. . . .

This lack of stickiness is showing up in the way we purchase as well. The response to credit card offers is now 0.6 percent, one-half the historical levels. Click-through rates on Internet banner ads are also less than 1 percent. Paco Underhill's research says sales and markdowns no longer work—consumers aren't budged by come-ons like the post-Christmas everything-in-the-store-off pitch. He says less than 3 percent of paper coupons are redeemed.

Advertising hasn't gotten less compelling or less watchable. On the contrary, commercials now have million-dollar production budgets, Britney Spears in a halter top, and Spike Lee behind the camera. No, the real problem is that consumers have become marketing resistant. Why? We have had to learn to tune out for our own self-protection. There's just too much coming at us from too many different angles to absorb it all.

The typical consumer sees over 2,500 messages a day. There are 11 minutes 44 seconds of ads in every hour of prime-time TV programming. That's around 35 or so commercials. Those spots are pushing the 32,025 new products introduced into American supermarkets each year, 93.3 percent of which are absolutely duplicative of what's already on the shelf, according to Productscan. The typical U.S. household receives three credit card solicitations a month, more than 3.5 billion in total in 2000.

A taxi ride from the airport to the office is a gauntlet of messages. There are billboards for Tommy Hilfiger blue jeans, bus stop posters for Tanqueray gin, and signs on taxis for Broadway shows like *Rent*. I get 30 e-mail solicitations a day (mostly for Viagra, refilled toner cartridges, flowers, and debt consolidation—I can't even begin to imagine what market segment that must be).

Add in in-store signage, telemarketing calls, print, and radio. Two thousand five hundred messages per day begin to look a like an understatement. So rather than go insane, we've developed a knack for not listening, or listening very selectively. This acquired immunity means it takes more advertising dollars to get the same result.

Advertisers have tried to get around this with what is called *under-the-radar messaging* (i.e., advertisements that don't appear to be advertisements, like PR and product placements in movies). They've also searched out unusual places to put ads, hoping that will grab our attention the way an ad in the newspaper won't. As a result, pitches are now stuck everywhere, from women's restrooms (for face cream, and placed on the wall across from the mirror, printed in reverse) to the handles of gas pumps (tiny plastic cans of Coca Cola.) I even sat through a pitch once for crop art, a proposal to cut a client's logo into a cornfield on the approach path to the Kansas City airport.

It's not working. We've enlisted the help of technology in our efforts to block out advertising messages. In fact, there's a technological arms race going on between consumers and advertisers. TV commercials have become smaller and more frequent. Consumers retaliated with zappers and Tivo. There's spam e-mail and programs to block it. Advertisers took advantage of data mining and cheap telecommunications to establish telemarketing factories. Consumers cheerfully responded with answering machines and caller ID.

We're proud of our ability to ignore all this claptrap. In 1999, Ammirati Puris Lintas wrote this radio jingle for Ameritech's Privacy Manager product. It's sung to the tune of the pop hit "American Pie":

"Today I spent the day at home, without some sales guy on the phone
Selling something I don't need to own. Today's the day those phone calls died.
And I was singing, Bye-bye Telemarketing Guy.
I've got new Privacy Manager, now you're outta my life."

Bye, bye.

The Implications

Expect consumer marketing resistance to continue to build. We'll see more and more innovative tricks to try to slip the messages in, and more and more equally innovative ways to block them out.

Expect more attempts to reach young consumers who have not yet built up advertising tolerances. But since the Joe Camel controversy, regulators will closely scrutinize anything that steps over the line. Also expect advertisers to continue to try to just turn up the volume and blast messages Superbowl style. But don't expect any of these to work. Ad effectiveness is going to continue to decline.

Opportunities

The opportunities lie in finding ways to embed messages so that they can't be screened out, for example, sponsorship, such as the FedEx Orange Bowl and public relations. Admittedly, neither are ideal ways to get your message across. Public relations is uncontrollable, both in content and timing, and while sports announcers may say FedEx's name a few thousand times on New Year's Day when they talk about the Orange Bowl, they're still not saying why FedEx is better than the competition. But with concrete consumers, you take what you can get.

Think *TLC*—targeted, lean, and creative advertising. *Targeting* is important because consumers can turn off the concrete switch at will—if they think the message is important to them, they'll listen. Infomercials now bring in over $100 billion a year, up from $68.5 billion in 1995. Be *lean*—that zapper's ready. And finally, be *creative*. Of course, that means entertaining, but it also means taking risks. Forget the old advertising formulas unless you want your message just to go "splat" and slide right off that concrete smile.

Faux Authenticity

The Trend

Thunderbird is back. So are 1960s-style record players, art deco cocktail shakers, and gaudy Hawaiian shirts. Leather Harley saddlebags and bowl-shaped helmets sell like hotcakes. Perhaps to balance our affection for all things virtual, we now seek out authenticity, whether it's in television shows, in adventure vacations, or in antiques.

Factors and Factoids

Before we get too far into this, we need to define *authentic*, because the consumer definition isn't quite as stringent as the Merriam-Webster version. In the dictionary, *authentic* means genuine, real, bona fide. In consumer terms, *authentic* means genuine, real, bona fide, but it also means *sorta like genuine, real, and bona fide—only better.*

Genuine authentic stuff is usually old or made with older materials and technology. That flavor of authenticism mainly shows up in three consumption areas—architecture, food, and collectibles. Derelict theaters like the Chicago would have been razed in the 1960s. Now they are renovated. In Sydney, Australia, developers carefully erect steel scaffolding to hold up the limestone façade of old colonial era buildings, tear down the rest of the structure, and completely rebuild a modern building inside, without ever disturbing the authentic shell.

American Spoon Foods (ASF) makes fruit preserves and sauces very much like those that would have been available 100 years ago. They ship products nationwide. But you don't have to order from ASF, in Traverse City, Michigan, to get authentic food. What was completely unique when Justin Rashid started the company in the 1970s is now almost common. My local supermarket is stuffed with imported authentic products: Barilla pasta from Italy, Carr's biscuits (crackers to us) from England, and Macallan single-malt whiskey from Scotland, as well as all manner of products, from yogurt to tomato sauce, purportedly made the authentic way.

But the biggest focus of genuine authenticity is collectibles. eBay has 42.4 million registered users and sells over $5 billion worth of merchandise a year, much of it authentic originals of products like dolls, toys, and comics. Markets for collectibles exist for almost every item, period, and price point imaginable. Rare, vintage teddy bears sell for more than $100,000. Each year there is a car auction in Pebble Beach, California, where collectors come from around the world to bid on 1931 Cadillac V-16 Phaetons, pre-war aluminum Rolls-Royces designed for tiger hunting, racing cars that have won the Indy 500, and motorcycles once owned by Steve McQueen. (Bring at least $50,000 if you want to leave with anything.)

That's pretty interesting, but then again, there's this expanded consumer definition of authentic, what I'll call *faux authentic*. Faux authentic is the creation of products and services exactly like the original, or more often these days, exactly like the original only better.

Stores like Pottery Barn and Restoration Hardware are stuffed with modern devices with the look and feel of much older ones. Over Christmas, Restoration Hardware sold 25,000 boxy black-and-tan record players at $130 a pop. Encouraged by the success of Chrysler's PT Cruiser, carmakers have rushed to create a retro-Thunderbird, a new Mini Cooper, and a new Cruiser with wood side panels. Steiff makes a $275 teddy bear dressed in a turn-of-the-century police uniform with shiny brass buttons. Nor is faux authentic limited to products. There were 1,000 bed and breakfasts in 1980, and around 25,000 now. Hundreds of travel companies offer authentic wilderness adventures.

Most of these products, though, are really much better than the originals. The new two-seater sports cars, like the BMW Z3 and the Miata, start more reliably and leak a lot less than their 1960 ancestors, like MGB and Triumph. We spoke earlier about consumers expecting technology to be incorporated in everyday life, and we do. We want an authentic wilderness experience, but we also want the guide to carry a GPS and a radio. We want a rugged macho jeep, but we also need a place for the golf clubs. Hence faux authenticity.

Opportunities[1]

Play on your authenticity. Jim Koch, founder of Samuel Adams Boston lager, advertised the fact that he used his grandfather's beer recipe.

If you have a heritage, use it, albeit carefully. Heritage plays work particularly well with some sets of products. Take food for example. Food technology has become synonymous in consumers' minds with tasteless tomatoes and mad cow disease. The promise of old-time food plays well. And look at financial services. Consumers want to know your company has been around for 100 years, since it implies you'll be around for another 20 when they come to get their money out.

But heritage works much less well in technology products, including things like cars. Nobody cares that Zenith was once the leader in home electronics. And we once did some focus groups for a famous old auto brand who'd just made an advertisement that showed a beautiful woman with a long scarf driving a classic convertible in slow motion past one of the client's newer cars.

Consumers loved the spot—but they wanted to buy the old car. They kept saying, "Why don't you just make that car again?"

Born to be Wired

The Trend

In July of 2001, employees at the Blair Drummond Safari Park in Scotland were plagued by a series of heavy-breather phone calls. It turns out that the culprit was Chippy, a chimpanzee who'd swiped his handler's cell phone. Yes, this is where it has come to, folks, even chimps have cell phones.

Like Chippy, we are wired, plugged into more electronic devices than an extension cord on Christmas morning. As no generation has before, we *get* electronic technology. We have totally immersed ourselves in it, in ways that we do not even consciously think about.

Factors and Factoids

There are two components of being wired: (1) the incorporation of little tiny electronic brains in everything around us (remember "Itsy, Bitsy . . ." in Chapter 5?), and (2) the technology of wirelessness, which allows these little brains to follow us everywhere we go and communicate to other little electronic brains far away. It's interconnectedness on a micro-, rather than a macro-, scale.

Let's look at the little brain thing. There's one on your arm (in your wristwatch), four in your briefcase (laptop, calculator, Palm Pilot, and Blackberry), and another in your pocket (cell phone). Sure you've got a home computer, but there's a microprocessor in your TV, your VCR, your microwave, your coffeemaker, and your refrigerator. Odds are, in fact, you have 40 or 50 computers in your house. There's a couple in your digital camera, another in your HandyCam, and if you own a newer 35-mm single-lens reflex (SLR) film camera, one in there as well. Your scale may have a computer in it, as does the device that you clip on your bike or your waist to tell you how far and how fast you're going (and what your blood pressure is, how many calories you've burned, etc.). There are computational devices in your security system, the thermostat on the wall, and the Bose radio in the kitchen.

There are computers in your car that govern engine performance and tell you when to turn. There's one in your remote keying system. The newest phone answering services, like Wildfire and Webley, are very sophisticated computers complete with voice recognition and the ability to decide whether to put a call through based on your instructions. In Europe, Levi's and Philips sell a jacket with a half-dozen electronic devices built in. Intelligence is increasingly ubiquitous. Every year, 8 billion new little brains (better known as *microprocessors*) are born and go to good homes—like mine and yours.

But it gets even more interesting when you layer wirelessness on top of intelligence. Now one little brain can talk to another little brain. Imagine a day when you begin to go to bed and your living room sends a message to the bedroom to turn on the lights, drop the shades and warm the bed. Fantasy? That's exactly the same process that happens when you use your cell phone driving down the interstate. As you talk, your phone continually radios your location to the local station that is carrying the call. At the same time, that station is telling the next station along your route that you're coming and to get ready for the handoff. The technology to make your living room smart is already here, it's just cost that's the issue. With the ability to communicate among themselves, all of a sudden we're no longer living with computers, we're wired inside one giant computer.

Now you'd think this would scare the bejeezus out of us, that we'd have nightmares about electromagnetic radiation bouncing around, computers running amok like HAL in *2001: A Space Odyssey,* or freezing to death because a power station goes down and all of our devices are useless. We could all be frightened that some day we'll stand by, incapacitated and doomed, because we have lost even the most rudimentary survival skills like lighting a fire or adding a column of numbers. But it doesn't seem to scare us. My 70-year-old mother-in-law is taking computer classes, no more intimidated of this technology than I am of a kitten. We're born to be wired. We take all this technology completely for granted. We don't quite understand it, but we like it.

Implications

Expect us to expect things to think. Danny Hillis, the genius behind the Millennium clock, tells the story of giving a speech in the 1990s where he predicted that one day computers would be so cheap and so small that they'd be embedded in everything. Someone stood up and grabbed a mike. "Even a doorknob?" the questioner asked. "Absolutely," said Hillis. The audience howled with laughter. But of course doorknobs in hotels do now have computers inside. So do 60 percent of the new toys introduced last year, or at least they come with a CD-ROM or website tie-in.

Expect the continuance of what IBM calls *pervasive computing*. They're already trying to figure out ways to put computers in jewelry and to create geek glasses that will beam continual streams of information one-half inch in front of your retina. The Japanese are developing a toilet that will test your blood sugar and look for signs of cancer. If the computer guys are right, computers are going to get smaller and cheaper, wireless transmission more widespread and efficient, and visual displays less costly. So one day we will see Living Room calling his buddy upstairs, "Hey, Master Bedroom, get ready, here he comes. No wait, he's turning into Kitchen. Kitchen, head's up. Turn on the light. You say he's in the Oreo's again? Darn it, somebody better warn Scales."

Expect us to be completely comfortable with it. There's a small parochial school in Palo Alto that has *two* scanning electron microscopes.

The Opportunities

Gadgets are good businesses. Sure Iridium, the world wide network of satellites designed to allow phone calls from absolutely anywhere on earth failed. But the first personal digital assistant (PDA) failed, too. It's just a matter of time before we all wear Dick Tracy watch phones. Anything that intelligence can be put into, will have it. For example, remember TrapperKeeper notebooks in the 1980s? They're now obsolete, replaced by technology.

Even if you're not in the business of providing technology, you've still got to be able to work with technology and to talk it. Customers expect you to be tech savvy, and that ranges from having a useful Internet site to being able to answer questions about what you sell. So get smart or get help.

Nibble and Nap

The Trend

Work for a big snack foods company or sofa manufacturer and want to understand this trend? Head for Trend Central, the Winnetka, Illinois, Public Library.

Across the table from me right now, a woman reads *ValueLine* while she sips from a red grande Starbucks cup. Her husband is slumped down in his chair, head tilted forward, snoring softly. The librarian sees the coffee and doesn't even blink. No wonder—we've gone from eaters and sleepers to nibblers and nappers.

Eating used to mean one of three meals, eaten at specific times, and usually in a specific place—the kitchen table or dining room. Now it's a Nutri-Grain bar and a banana tossed in the bottom of a briefcase. Sleeping used to take place in bed, now it happens on an airplane or in front of a TV. These two basic functions used to take up large, carefully scheduled blocks of time. Now both have been broken up into more frequent but smaller ad hoc events. There are two things going on here: (1) replacement of large events with a series of small ones, and (2) an increase in flexible scheduling. These two combine to form a new lifestyle—"nibble and nap."

Factors and Factoids

In the 1980s, each of us averaged one snack a day. Now it's 1.6 per day. In 1977, we got 20 percent of our daily vitamins from snacks. Now it's 23 percent. Snack food is the fastest growing category in the supermarket. Entire stores like 7-Eleven are devoted to snacking. McDonald's does a booming business in milkshakes in the morning, the perfect food for the busy driver trying to eat with one hand and not make a mess. Eating has gone from three meals to many, from formal to informal, from communal to solitary, from dining to snacking.

Why all the snacking? We are a generation of multitaskers. We shave while we drive to work, talk on the phone while we answer our e-mail, and read the newspaper while walking on the treadmill. And we eat while we do everything, from driving to watching TV to riding the subway. Some have labeled our new approach to eating *grazing*. Like cattle, we just munch our way from one spot to another, chewing absentmindedly as we stroll. About the only thing we don't do while we eat is eat. The family dinner is an endangered species.

It is our growing affluence that makes this possible. We can now afford to buy portioned foods enclosed in expensive disposable packaging. A 20-ounce bottle of pop costs the same as a 2-liter bottle, because although the smaller bottle contains less liquid, it costs almost as much to package and distribute it. But we can afford the upcharge for portability. I am seldom without a small bottle of Poland Spring mineral water stuck in a pocket.

And since we all do it, eating in public has become so common that it is no longer seen as inappropriate or even unusual. Indeed, most public places provide food intended to be eaten on the spot, everything from a candy bar in a vending machine to take-out Chinese in the food court.

Just as we've broken big meals up into smaller meals, we've also broken up the traditional 8-hour block of sleep. Sixty-three percent of us sleep less than 8 hours a night, one-third less than 6½ hours. About the same percentage report we sleep less than 5 years ago.

However, there is one difference between the trends to nibbling and napping. When we skip dinner we make up the calories later. We try to catch up on sleep, too, either by binge sleeping on weekends or by napping, catching a few winks in the back of taxis, on airplanes, even on the sofa in front of the football game. Sixteen percent of workers say they are allowed to take a snooze on the job. But some of the lost sleep is simply gone. Many studies say a large number of Americans are chronically sleep deprived.

Implications

Expect sleep time to continue to shrink. Biology is about to take over. After age 50, humans begin cutting back on their nightly sleep naturally, averaging 3 minutes less sleep a year. (Does that mean that by the time I'm 130 I won't need to sleep at all?)

And also expect us to continue to graze, as manufacturers make more and more convenient food and it becomes easier to eat it. For example, cars already come with cup holders, but now minivans are starting to come with tiny coolers and even microwaves.

Expect us to continue to break eating and sleeping up into small, portable units.

The Opportunity

There are many ways to use nibble and nap to your advantage. If you're an employer, keeping ad hoc eating and sleeping in mind as you design your place of business can improve worker productivity. Really. Some employers have found that putting in popcorn machines makes office workers stay later. Fill up the kitchen with snacks and put in a microwave. Not only does it make for more satisfied employees, but it's good business. When the popcorn machines are taken out, the place empties out at 5.

The same logic applies to customers. The more comfortable they are, the longer they'll stay. Put a bowl of M&M's or apples and a carafe of water in the waiting room. Invest in comfortable chairs. If clients doze off, let them catch a few winks. (Well. . . .)

You know, I have a lot more to say on this one, but I'm exhausted. I think I'll just put my head down for a moment.

Buy Now, Pay Never

The Trend

My father-in-law raised his four children in a large rambling house on 117th Street in Roseland, an Irish et al. neighborhood on the south side of Chicago. Downstairs lived his brother-in-law, Barney, with Mary and another four kids. The two families lived together for 19 years before the two families could afford to move into their own homes.

But five of the nine children from the house on 117th Street had separate homes before their first babies were out of diapers. The difference? The parents were reluctant to go into debt. The children were comfortable taking on sizable mortgages. Not only do seven of the nine have a mortgage, but there are 22 cars (13 leased) and more than 50 credit cards among the families of the nine kids. We have a completely different attitude about debt and credit from our parents and grandparents.

In the last trend we talked about our increasingly ad hoc lifestyle. Well, this lifestyle's putting us *in hock,* too. We are all comfortable with credit. The problem is that some of us are a bit too comfortable and will never pay off what we have borrowed. To paraphrase a current car company promotion, it's a case of zero down and us having zero interest in ever paying it back.

Factors and Factoids

Consumers aren't going to repay their debt for two reasons: (1) They can't and (2) They don't have to. Household debt is now $7.5 trillion, double the level of the late 1980s. More than 14 percent of our income goes to service debt, and interest payments are more than 3 percent of income, up from around 2 percent in 1995, even though in 1995 interest rates were higher. For the first time, the average American family now owes more than a year's after-tax income. Sixty percent of us started this year with credit card debt. The average family now has a credit card balance of $1,700, versus $1,100 in 1989. (See Figure 7.1.)

It's going to continue to grow. Consumer debt was increasing at around 10 percent per year before the current recession, and although consumers have become a bit more cautious, especially since September 11, it's still growing. During initial months of the last recession, in the early 1990s, the average American household cut its debt by an inflation-adjusted $410. This time, each has taken on an average of $1,420 in additional debt.

Figure 7.1 **What Americans owe (trillion dollars).**

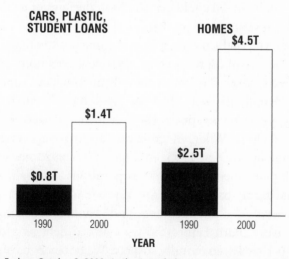

CARS, PLASTIC, STUDENT LOANS

HOMES

YEAR

Data Sources: Forbes, October 2, 2000; Author's analysis.

Consumer debt has to grow. Consumer spending accounts for over two-thirds of all economic activity. A sudden pullback in spending would cause not just a recession, but a worldwide depression, toppling economies around the world like dominoes. To increase spending, we must either save less, make more, or borrow. But savings is already around zero. That means we're spending all we make already, so to spend more we have to borrow.

Companies that are in the business of credit are pretty confident we will. Even though some credit card companies have seen their stock plummet due to bad debts, others continue to stuff mailboxes with credit card solicitations. Department stores still pay employees cash bonuses for getting customers to open a charge account rather than paying cash. Credit card issuers are even chasing college students, who now already carry an average of three credit cards. The Fed is slashing interest rates to encourage us to take the credit companies up on their offers, and at least some of us will. Debt will continue to pile up.

The question is whether it will ever get paid back. And the answer is some of it, but not all. Credit card charge-offs for bad debt are now more than 5 percent, near record levels. Personal bankruptcies run well over 1 million a year.

Both numbers should grow. One-fifth of low-income households are now heavily indebted. The number is lower among middle-class and upper-income households, but indebtedness among these groups is still high. All could get caught in the jaws of a falling stock market and shrinking job market.

Not repaying debt no longer carries much of a stigma. Perhaps that's because bankruptcy is now relatively commonplace on the evening news. Over the last decade, Kim Basinger, Toni Braxton, Dorothy Hamill, La Toya Jackson, and Burt Reynolds have all joined the list of bankrupts, a list that includes Larry King, Mark Twain, and Oscar Wilde. A governor of Arizona declared bankruptcy while in office in 1995. In 2000, 176 companies with assets of $94 billion filed. Admired corporations Swissair, Polaroid, Kmart, and Enron have all recently thrown in the financial towel.

Our views on indebtedness and bankruptcy have clearly changed. Those born before the war viewed debt as a dangerous trap, and perhaps even morally suspect. We boomers have shifted to an economist's definition. Debt is simply consumption accelerated. We figure there's no reason a medical student who will one day make 1 million bucks a year should wear rags today and Armani tomorrow, when it's just as easy to level it out a bit using credit tools. If occasionally we misstep, we tend to look at it as more a forecasting error than a lapse in responsible behavior. Nearly half of the individuals filing for bankruptcy were advised to do so by friends and family.

Implications

Expect continued easy availability of credit to almost every consumer. The variety and availability of credit tools will continue to grow. Don't be surprised to see increasingly aggressive credit offers from corporations looking to entice credit-saturated consumers. But also expect continued problems with indebtedness, and higher levels of write-offs and bad loans.

The Opportunity

There is a clear opportunity to help people find their way out of the jams credit helps them get into. Bankruptcy lawyers are booming. For the most part, they help people file under Chapter 7, which allows people to liquidate and still keep assets like their home. Seventy percent of consumer bankruptcies are Chapter 7.

But there's new legislation that will push people to file under Chapter 13, which allows people to keep fewer assets and forces them to enter a repayment plan. That should boost the credit counseling industry. Right now, the industry is one of the few not yet rolled up—another reason to take a closer look.

Okay, neither of these may be opportunities for you, but here's one for anyone with a business of any size: Assume write-offs. Build another 5 or 10 percent into the price to cover those who end up not paying. It's going to become more and more commonplace.

Upscaling

The Trend

Perhaps part of our debt problem is that somewhere along the way, we developed a taste for not just the good stuff, but for the very best.

Increasingly, we buy expensive, high-performance versions of even the most mundane everyday items.

Take the kitchen. Where there used to be a GE refrigerator, a Mr. Coffee, and a Panasonic radio, there are now a Sub-Zero, a La Pavoni expresso maker, and a Bose Wave. The cupboard that once held Corningware now houses Le Creuset. The Kenmore oven has transmogrified into a professional-grade Viking, and the simple pastel-colored Sunbeam mixer has become a huge, chrome Kitchen-Aid that sells for $500 and has what is called *planetary* action. (That means the beaters rotate around the bowl while it spins.) It's upscaling, and it's happening in almost every product and service category.

Factors and Factoids

Upscaling is ubiquitous.

- The average American home is now over 2,200 square feet, 50 percent larger than it was in 1970. That's even though the average family size has fallen by over 20 percent. Sixteen million of those homes have home theaters that cost more than $3,500. (That's one in every six households or so. In 1960, only 1 in every 200 homes owned a color TV.)

- Rolex sells 600,000 watches a year. (They also have another line, Cellini, with price tags that can exceed $1 million each, that grew steadily throughout the 1990s.)

- Ford sells around 1 million luxury cars and SUVs—Jaguars, Lincolns, Aston Martins, and the like. Dan Panoz recently launched the Esperante, an $80,000 hand-built sports car.

- Canyon Ranch, the luxury spa, has six locations across the country. Elizabeth Arden has 20.

Name the product or service, and there's a luxury version—blue jeans, dog food, tweezers, coffee, power tools, bicycles, picture frames, potato chips, and single-malt whiskey. And in most categories, over time, new, higher-end offerings leapfrog the old best-in-class to establish new niches higher up. In the 1960s, Smirnoff created high-end vodka. In the 1980s, Absolut displaced Smirnoff, and in the 1990s, Absolut was bumped down by Grey Goose and Ketel One. Chopin is now trying to scramble over those two to the top spot.

What's behind this? One factor is the growth of the mass upper class, a trend we discussed way back in Chapter 4, "Economic and Geopolitical Trends." Another is the easy access to credit, which we talked about in "Buy Now, Pay Never." And, of course, *interconnectedness* means the finest of everything is now only one click of a mouse away.

But there's something else going on here as well: an increasing appreciation of quality by the American consumer. Egad! We're becoming Europeanized. Like our French and German counterparts, we now appreciate quality and, more important, are getting comfortable paying for it.

Most of us have become connoisseurs by accident. That is, we didn't just wake up one morning under our Sears sheets, decide our lives were empty, and plot a course to the nearest Ralph Lauren store. Rather, we sort of inched into it, one Bon Appetit restaurant feature at a time. We learned about the advantages of high-end dog food from Iam's, and about professional cookware from Williams & Sonoma. Grey Goose has invested a small fortune in teaching bartenders to talk knowledgeably about the nuances of vodka, so they can in turn educate us. Catalog marketers sent us specialty catalogs on everything from clothes to reading lamps to gardening tools. Slowly, we became knowledgeable about not just individual premium offerings, but the entire premium and superpremium world. We come to understand that there is always a best of anything, and conclude it is often worth seeking out.

But there's another, more subtle process at work as well. Even those of us who have never read a single issue of *Travel & Leisure* or *Cigar Aficionado* have still moved upscale. For example, a Honda Accord is now 3 inches longer and has two more cylinders than it had 7 years ago. That little sedan didn't just take us to the grocery store, it took us upmarket as well. By allowing us to sample the benefits of individual seat warmers and CD players, Honda has prepared us to shop knowledgeably for Lexus and BMW. The step from very good to best is no longer as large or formidable as once it was. And once we've gone up, it's hard to go back down again.

The Implications

There is a market for the best in almost everything. And even if the economy stays down, that market won't go away. Luxury is hard for people to give up. Expect to continue to see more and more upscaling. Expect to see better products, like Michelob beer, squeezed to death on one side by improved versions of *good* (Budweiser) and on the other by *best* (e.g., Samuel Adams). Recessions are tough on airlines, but one survivor may well be JetBlue, all new aircraft, leather seats, and personal movies.

Opportunities

There is no such thing as the top end. There is always a higher rung. Be careful, it may be a very small market or, like Iam's, take a long time to build, but it's there. Somewhere out there is someone willing to pay $1 million dollars for a pair of nail clippers with a laser guidance system. If you can find them.

Of course, as we'll see in the next trend, there's always a bottom rung, too.

The Frugal Rich

The Trend

Sounds like it's tough to be a marketer these days. Earlier in this chapter, we said consumers have ridiculous expectations and ignore everything advertisers say to them. That's just the half of it. They're harder to predict, too.

Take Suzy and Mike, a very successful young couple who own a handful of boutique hotels. They have two kids, a Mercedes, an SUV, a city home, and a beach house. Suzy has accounts at any number of stores, including Saks and Neiman Marcus. But she does most of her shopping at Target, which she pronounces *Tar-jhay*, with a phony French accent and a wink.

She's not alone—the Target parking lot has more than a few Benzes and Beemers. Call them the frugal rich, wealthy who are flocking to Old Navy, outlet malls, and to discount fashion houses like Hennes & Mauritz on Fifth Avenue in New York.

Factors and Factoids

A few years ago, Roper Starch surveyed households with incomes of more than $100,000. It found that 81 percent had shopped at a discount store in the last year, over twice as many as had spent money in a designer store like Chanel. Ninety-four percent of those said the most important factor in their purchase decision was whether the product offered good value for the money, three times as many as were worried about things like prestige. In part, this reflects a trend to more decorum and understatement around discussions of money. In 1981, people were twice as likely to admit they bought their cars to show status as in 1996. But it also reflects more *shopping down* (i.e., the well-off hunting the off-price).

What's behind this? Is what Debra Goldman calls the "consumer republic" getting more egalitarian and less materialistic? No.

There has been a lot of talk about downsizing and simplicity. Yankelovitch says three-fourths of Americans want to simplify their lives. But cut through the hype, and there's no evidence at all that people are turning their backs on the material world. As we discussed with the trend to upscaling, more people drive luxury cars than ever before, own $10,000 watches, watch large-screen TVs, and live in "McMansions" with whirlpools and SubZero refrigerators. Even Oprah's magazine, which espouses simplicity, says tea tastes better when sipped from a $135 Tiffany teacup.

Well then, is the frugal rich trend just more proof that *rational consumer* has become an oxymoron? As we've already discussed, there's clearly some odd consumer behavior out there. We've talked about some of these consumer contradictions already—environmentalists in SUVs, young oldsters and old youth, overweight people who want to be thin, and the whole concept of natural cigarettes. Is frugal rich more of the same? Nope.

Whenever we see a "contradiction" in consumer behavior, one of two things is happening. Sometimes it's not really a contradiction, say because we have mistakenly lumped two very different market segments together, and we're trying to reconcile two different behaviors into one. But more often, we've found a situation where consumers are trying to balance inherently conflicting objectives. For example, the peer pressure to smoke coupled with the belief that natural products promote health and long life, has led Generation Y consumers to an odd compromise, American Spirit natural cigarettes.

But the frugal rich trend isn't about rejecting materialism, muddled segmentation, or compromised objectives. No one here is compromising. The rich simply no longer seem to feel a need to shop for upscale products at upscale stores to prove they're wealthy.

The reason? In this time of millionaires next door and easy credit, carrying a Tiffany's bag or driving a BMW no longer says much about wealth. Anyone can drive one. Well, perhaps not anyone, but many. Spending is less and less an indicator of wealth or even success. That disconnect changes consumer behavior in two ways. One, it takes any stigma out of being seen in Target, since no one who sees Suzy's car in the lot is going to take from it that she's unsuccessful. But even more than that, being frugal about everyday purchases like household items and even some clothing is in an odd way reverse-chic. It's a wink between those in the know that says wealth is about more than just brand-name toilet paper.

The Implications

We marketers are going to have to rethink our approaches to defining markets. For decades, we have divided the world up into A, B, C, and D groupings based on household income. We've then tried to sell expensive products to the rich and cheaper ones to the poor. But now all that's forgotten. Top-end department stores and designer shops will increasingly find themselves chasing customers in suburban malls. Value-for-money store propositions like Kohl's and Wal-Mart will continue to fare better than upscale and midmarket stores, even when the recession ends.

Expect prestige and image pitches to only appeal to the most unsophisticated consumers. Most consumers will not be swayed by swank commercials pitching consumer goods as tools to show success. Instead, make the pitch about performance, style, or value. (Remember though, value is not about cheapness. A Rolex may be a good value because it keeps time better, lasts longer, and has higher resale, but it's not cheap.)

Opportunities

The breakdown of the tyranny of A-B-C-D marketing is great news for marketers. Every market is now bigger. If you make more mundane products, think of how to do a *Tar-jhay* and bring them to the attention of the segment of the wealthy. If you make more upper-end products, don't assume that just because a consumer household's income bracket says they can't afford it that they can't. And if you market everyday products, don't assume away the upper-end market.

Plumposity

The Trend

In poor countries, the starving end up in a hospital. Here they end up on *Friends*. (I apologize for that. I know anorexia's not really funny.) But I'm trying to make a point here. In poor nations, the rich are fat and the poor are thin. In a rich country like the United States, the rich are plump and the poor are even plumper. But in poor countries fat is chic. In the United States, fat is bad, bad, bad.

Factors and Factoids

Sixty-one percent of Americans are now officially overweight, up 5 percent from a decade ago. Eighteen percent of the country is now morbidly obese (i.e., fat to the point where it may adversely affect health). Each year, 430,000 Americans die prematurely due to tobacco. Obesity currently causes 300,000 premature deaths per annum, but the number is growing and the two lines may cross in a few years.

There are two main reasons for this trend to tubby, push to pudge, path to portly, fad to fat.[2] First, of course, is the increasingly nonphysical world we live in. Economists report a strong correlation between a tendency to be overweight and a lack of physical activity in one's job. As we discussed earlier in the technology section, not only do we no longer depend on muscles to work, we no longer depend on them to do even the simplest of tasks. We have machines to do everything, from digging ditches to chopping carrots. People used to be paid to sweat, now we pay gyms for the privilege.

It's not just us adults who have slowed down. Our children no longer change clothes after school and run outside to play tag. Now they spend those hours in front of the TV playing a video game. We simply don't burn many calories as we go about our daily business.

But even if we all made our livings pounding stones into gravel, we'd probably still be chunky. The basic problem is that we're just too darn good at food production. Ten thousand, 1,000, and even

100 years ago, humans ate anything they could find and at every opportunity. And despite this constant appetite, it is very unlikely that anyone in a Cro-Magnon family carried a few extra pounds. That's because until the last 100 years or so, food was pretty hard to come by.

However, food is now abundant and cheap. A hyperefficient food production system means that one American farmer now feeds over 100 other people, 20 times more efficient than a century ago. In relative terms, restaurants literally give the stuff away, through oversized portions and additional food at a small upcharge (e.g., McDonald's Supersize option). As our food production system becomes more and more efficient, cost per calorie will continue to drop.

Not only is it *how much* we eat, though, it's also *what* we eat. We no longer consume mastodon jerky, roots, and berries. Instead, we fill up on desserts and snacks, foods particularly rich in fats and sugar. Just as we have a genetic predisposition to big appetites, we have a genetic love of sugar. That developed when a little sugar rush could make the difference between outrunning a predator or ending up as lunch. But the Neanderthal could only get tiny, weak hits of sugar, for instance, from the occasional handful of berries. We can practically mainline the stuff, and do.

So here's the arithmetic: Cro-Magnon appetites plus a Neanderthal's sweet tooth plus a twenty-first-century food production system equals pudge.

Do we like this newfound substance? No, we do not. We have become a bit more politically correct about how we talk about fattiness, but we still don't like it. About a quarter of us openly admit that fat people are less attractive than thin ones. Even the rest of us want to lose a few pounds. Actually, it's more than a few pounds. Sixty-two percent say we'd like to lose 20 pounds, up from 52 percent in 1990.[3]

To help, we're turning to drugs, gym memberships, exercise equipment, surgery, and special meal systems in huge and growing numbers. Diet books fill a whole section of the local Barnes & Noble, and there are always one or two fad diet how-to's on the *New York Times* Bestseller Lists. We're even buying strange devices that shock our stomachs while we sit in front of the TV. But we're still gaining weight.

Implications

Expect us to continue to celebrate slimness. Our mantra will remain "You can never be too rich or too thin." And expect the weight gains to continue. According to *Fitness* magazine, 64 percent of women say their "ultimate fantasy" is to be able to eat as much as they want and not gain weight. Unfortunately, despite all the technology and dieting, at this point we're still putting on the pounds.

Over the next decade at least, the pudge problem will likely increase. Excess weight tends to peak between 55 and 64, the age band where boomers are headed next.

The Opportunity

Obviously, there's a huge opportunity in helping people to reduce their weight. Subway, a chain of sandwich restaurants, has driven sales through the roof using the stories of customers who have used its products to slim down.

But the fresher and more intriguing opportunity is helping consumers come to terms with the reality of heaviness. Today, there's a real gap between advertising and clothing manufacturer fantasy and consumer reality. In dress shops, sizes 4 and 6 are called "regular." Regular for whom? The average American woman is a size 14.

Stores that provide full ranges of attractive clothes like Lane Bryant are expanding. Tommy Hilfiger and the Gap are adding larger sizes. Magazines like *Mode* are using models who look like real people. (Well, plus-size models sort of look like real people. They may be a size 10, but they're still drop-dead gorgeous with cheekbones you could hang-glide off of.)

Business Trends

The good news is that there are lots and lots of business trends. The bad news is that there are a plethora of journalists and consultants all out there scrambling around for the next big thing and touting what they find as the next *big* thing. Literally, tens of thousands of articles on business trends are written each year. It's easy to get a bit jaundiced. But don't. This is important stuff.

The 11 I've picked run the gamut, from established and powering on to just starting, and suggest opportunities for everyone from individuals to small businesses to Fortune 500 to not-for-profits. They are:

1. *The death of demography.* If Bob Dylan sang in Madison Avenue coffeehouses, he'd be singing "The marketing times, they are a changing." The media mix is shifting away from demographically purchased media, and that's changing the whole process of marketing.

2. *Niche picking.* Jack Welch was wrong. It's not "be number one or number two in every industry in which you compete." Often times, the number two position in an industry is about as safe as the passenger seat in a 1962 Corvair. Instead, the new mantra is "Be number one or number ten in every industry."

3. *Experience this!* We've moved from selling goods to providing services to creating experiences. Customers like it, and so do employees, which means shareholders will as well.

4. *On the brandwagon.* More brands have been created in the last decade than in all the hundreds of decades that have come before. From large industrial conglomerates like GE to tiny hole-in-the-wall restaurants, every one is climbing on the brandwagon.

5. *A la carte business models.* It's now possible to assemble companies as easily as it is to build a LEGO fort, and it works exactly the same way—by taking off the shelf pieces and popping them together.

6. *Reintermediation.* Remember all the talk about disintermediation? Forget it, intermediaries are never *dis*placed, only *re*placed.

7. *Strange bedfellows.* All the corporate mergers and strategic alliances are creating unlikely collaborators. Sometimes it's a key customer; other times, it's an archfoe.

8. *The price is wrong.* Take-it-or-leave-it pricing has left the building.

9. *Gotcha tactics.* To make money, companies are increasingly resorting to more aggressive marketing and the imposition of fee for service. Consumers and their watchdogs are howling "Trickery!"

10. *Mass personalization.* The problem with one-to-one marketing is there's one marketer and a million customers, so how can we make it work? The answer: mass personalization.

11. *A pound of risk to go.* We now buy and sell bundles of risk like bags of potatoes, and it fundamentally changes the price of just about every single thing on the planet.

The Death of Demography

The Trend

Marketing based mostly on demography is dead, and it's time to bury it. Marketing is changing before our very eyes. Gray-flannel ad agencies with the names of legendary founders on their doors are finding themselves slowly losing sway in the marketing department, replaced by upstarts from management consultancies and direct marketing organizations.

What's happening is we're seeing the industry's equivalent of a tectonic plate shift, a trend that will culminate in the creation of the third great age of marketing. (The first two, FYI, were the age of geography and the age of demography, and I'll talk a little bit about them in the "Factors and Factoids" section.) This trend is the art of crafting ads for—and delivering them to—very small markets, even smaller than individuals. I'll call this new age the *age of singularity,* for lack of a better term. (This is not a very good name for a great age, but there's a lot of heat around this topic. Other terms all come with some sort of baggage and mean different things to different people. So I'm going to start with a clean sheet here.)

Factors and Factoids

Let's put a stake in the ground. Marketing as we know it started in Philadelphia in 1841, when Volney B. Palmer opened the first ad agency. It wasn't a modern-style agency, with creatives, artists, and account executives, it was just a little office where Volney bought newspaper space for clients. (The full-service agency would have to wait a few decades, until J. Walter Thompson came along.)

Today, it may not seem like much to build a business on. But remember, this was in a day when every single community had its own paper, communication was costly and slow, and much of the market growth was in the distant hinterlands beyond Ohio.

And consider this: Volney not only invented the ad agency industry, he also made it possible for retailers and consumer products manufacturers to become huge, branded corporations. Instead of simply relying on customers to wander into their stores, merchants could now use advertising to go out and find new business. This meant companies could get big and buy more newspaper and radio space (after 1922) and get even bigger. I call what Volney started the *age of geography,* because the secret to successful marketing was finding the right space in the right newspapers and on the right radio stations to reach the right communities.

The second great age of marketing started on October 27, 1946, when Bristol-Myers sponsored the first commercial television program. Television was soon a national medium, and it was no longer sufficient to be able to aggregate communities—TV reached all of them at once. Instead, competitive advantage came from skillfully picking programs that appealed to different demographic groups. Call this the *age of demography*. TV proved so powerful a medium that marketing companies began spending 10 times as much on marketing as they did on product development.

And now we're entering the age of singularity. This age is all about targeted marketing to very small markets, like households or individuals. (See Figure 8.1.)

Enough history, let's look at this at a very personal level. Down the street from me lives Dan. We live in houses of the same size in the same community. From a geographic perspective, we are identical. Both of us are 48-year-old Caucasians and have been married for over 20 years. I have two children; he has three. We have had

Figure 8.1 **Media usage in the three great ages of advertising.** **Definitions:** *geographic media:* **radio, newspaper, Yellow Pages;** *demographic media:* **magazines, broadcast TV;** *singular media:* **Internet, cable TV, direct mail. (*Note:* Outdoor is not included, although it is a geographic medium. Cable TV is both a demographic medium and a singular medium.)**

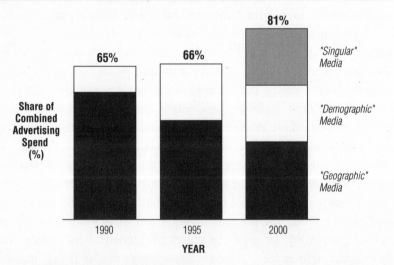

Sources: McKinsey Quarterly, *analysis by author.*

similar careers. We watch the same TV shows. On a demographic basis, Dan and I are identical.

But here's the rub. We don't buy much of the same stuff. I drive a Honda; Dan drives a Mercedes. I wear Italian suits and French ties or cheap khakis; Dan doesn't wear suits, and buys expensive khakis. He drinks Miller Lite; I drink Heineken. So at the level that matters here (i.e., what we buy), we are far from identical.

Now suppose BMW wants to offer a free test drive in its latest sedan to people who are likely to buy it. If the company tries to make this offer on a geographic basis, for instance, in a newspaper ad, it hits me and a lot of other people who aren't too interested. It's a waste of BMW's time and effort. Okay then, what if they try a TV ad on Sportscenter? It's probably better, but it still hits me along with 10 million teenage males, and we've already decided that I'm a waste of time. But if a marketer could understand that Dan's a target and I'm not, and send the ad message just to him, wouldn't that be more efficient? Yes.

We've already talked about the three trends that make singularity possible: (1) down in the data mine, which allows marketing technicians to track the purchase behavior of consumers as individuals and to tailor offers by household; (2) interconnectedness and the declining real cost of personal communication, which allows marketers to cost-effectively communicate to individuals; and finally (3) the trend toward the concrete consumer. If you remember, that last trend talked about the ability of consumers to selectively tune out advertising, which means, increasingly, messages must be very targeted to register on a consumer's consciousness.

But consider the impact of all of that on the way marketing is *done*. First of all, it changes the media mix toward more targeted vehicles, like cable TV, direct mail, and e-mail.

It also changes the process of marketing. When the process is built around TV commercials that cost $10 million to develop, $2 million each to produce, and $1 million per airing, the emphasis has to be on a lot of upfront work to get it right. When the process is built around an e-mail that costs $10,000 to develop and 5 cents each to send, the emphasis shifts to trying lots of things and seeing which ones work. For example, Crayola recently developed 72 messages for an e-mail campaign and tested 16 at once. If those 16 hadn't worked, they would have tried 16 more, and so on. Just 15 years ago, the best marketers in the world would have considered that approach insane.

Implications

There are many things that could slow this trend: tougher privacy legislation; growing consumer resistance to direct mail, e-mail, and telemarketing; and the improving efficiency of old-style, demographic marketing. Right now, however, it doesn't look like anything will.

Expect to see more and more singular marketing. Union Bank of Norway has begun using analysis of behavioral data to target micromessages to individuals. They've gotten a response rate of 60 percent, 12 times the historical uptake of 5 percent.

Expect to see more and more ready-fire-aim marketing, and a gradual decline in old-style, carefully planned megacampaigns.

Expect to see the margins on traditional market research, especially attitudinal research, grind down to zero. Once testing is cheap and fast, it's easier just to test a new idea than it is to ask people if they think they might like it.

The Opportunity

In some ways, this is a war between the old and the new, and in a war the arms merchants are the ones who win. There are some really exciting new marketing tools coming along. Modem Media analyzes web traffic; Manna produces analytical software; Marketing Analytics develops algorithms for analyzing sales data; Verbind stores consumer transaction history and predicts behavior from the record; EntertainmentBlvd.com analyzes past entertainment purchases to predict potential products customers might like, (à la Amazon and its book recommendations). Gerald Zaltman of Harvard has developed ZMET, a technique to tease out buying biases people may not know they have. If it all sounds a bit techy and analytical, it is. (That particular opportunity is for the quants out there.)

But what if you're an old-style classical marketer? Well, if you're up for it, learn to use the new tools and keep on marketing. But if you're not, don't despair. In the next chapter, we'll talk about the trend to retooling. There's hope yet.

Niche Picking

The Trend

Ever heard of Dennis Cwik? His business, Private Autopsies, Inc., performs postmortems for questioning families and unconvinced insurance companies. The Chicago-based company averages three a month. He thinks that he can build the business up to 10 times that size, and at $3,000 per autopsy, turn it into a nice, million-dollar niche business.

This particular niche may not be the niche for you, but Dennis's strategy is right on the mark. The trend is niche picking.

Factors and Factoids

We're seeing more and more niche picking, driven in part by economics—the natural consequence of any large, technologically sophisticated and interconnected society to specialize. The United States is already the largest, most technologically sophisticated and interconnected economy the world has ever known, and it's getting more specialized every day. (See Figure 8.2.)

Figure 8.2 **Growth of specialties.**

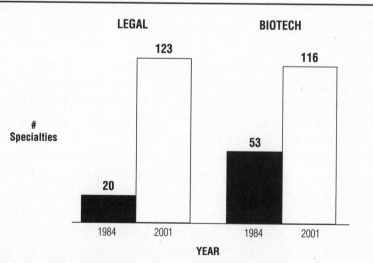

Sources: *Washington Post, Martindale Hubbell Legal Directory, Cornell University Report,* interviews, *CORPTECH Directory of Technology Companies,* author analysis.

It's getting harder and harder for a generalist to serve the whole market. Over time, some customer groups get large enough that someone can afford to focus on just their needs. Like an amoeba, part of the generalist business splits off to service a certain type of customer, with a certain type of product based on a certain technology. Over time, that business grows, and a niche splits off from that. And so on, ad nauseum.

Let's look at a very mundane example. Fifty years ago supermarkets carried salt. Now they carry salt, iodized salt, ice cream salt, salt for sidewalks, margarita salt, sea salt, and gourmet salt. As the salt market grew, it turned from a single homogenous market to a large market surrounded by many niches. This process has been accelerated by the rise of the Internet, which has created true national and international markets for even the smallest and most arcane specialties.

And small, medium, and even largish businesses need to be specialized, because world-class competition is coming to a street corner near you. If you're a local ad agency in Portland, Oregon, you can easily now find yourself pitching against giant firms from New York and San Francisco. And vice versa. The local bank has to compete with Citibank, and the local limo service with Boston Coach.

This is true, even for the smallest and most local of businesses. Twenty years ago the cable television industry was made up of thousands of tiny, family-owned companies. By the time this is written, three companies will likely control almost two-thirds. Waste Management and other large companies now fight for small-town garbage collection contracts. The local radio station competes head-to-head against Clear Channel, a San Antonio firm that owns 1,200 stations and prepares the programs for 47 stations at once. The local gas station is up against Mobil and Jiffy Lube. The local coffee shop has to fight for customers with Starbucks.

You name it—hardware stores, maid services, florists, funeral homes, pest control, video stores, car washes, realtors, used car lots, laundromats, concert promoters, sandwich shops. In every one of these industries, what used to be a local, not-very-competitive business is now a war of local Davids versus large, corporate Goliaths.

Giant competitors usually mean midget margins. Niches mean midget markets, but giant margins. Take the aluminum canning industry. It's a big industry, with companies fighting fiercely to supply Coke, Pepsi, Bud, and Miller. There are multi-million-dollar contracts for aluminum sheet, for high-speed canning lines, and for transportation of empty and filled cans. But the most successful company in this giant industry? A tiny firm in Ohio that makes the machines that wash the cans before they were filled. This is too small a niche to interest the giants, but it's safe, dependable, and highly profitable.[1]

And niches are not just a place to get a toehold on the way to the big time. The reality is that nichedom is almost always a better place to be than number two or number three in industry. Miller Beer was a very profitable number 12, but has been a consistently unprofitable number 2. Providian Financial was considered the best financial institution in America when it was small and focused, and has been a disaster as a top-10 credit card issuer.

Implications

Expect the small generalist, no matter the industry, to become an endangered species. And don't count on being a sorta-big generalist, either. Remember "Be number one or number two in every industry in which you compete?" Be careful, number two is no guarantee of success (e.g., DEC the computer manufacturer and Winston cigarettes). In those same categories, niche suppliers like Sam Adams, Sun, Southwest, and American Spirit have thrived. The industry leader will win, and so will those in profitable and defendable niches.

The Opportunity

Niching is scary. It's putting all your eggs in one basket. And a small one-egg basket at that. Still, there's a mathematically infinite range of opportunities for niche businesses. Take my business, management consulting. LEK could have slugged it out toe to toe with BCG and Bain; instead, they chose a narrow market (investment bankers) and a limited product line (due diligence on acquisitions) and built a great business that has survived for decades. Z-S in Evanston, Illinois, focuses on salesforce realignment for pharmaceutical companies. First Manhattan targets strategy and cost reduction in the financial industry. Jay Alix just does turnarounds, and mostly works on the borrower side. Integral takes the ideas of academics and works with real-world clients to implement them.

Right now, the overall consulting industry is in the doldrums, and small, generalist firms are dying like flies. But niche firms like these are thriving.

Find a niche. Own it.

Experience This!

The Trend

At DMB&B, I worked with Jim, a senior executive in his mid-50s, very fit, well off, and by his own admission, an obsessive collector. But Jim didn't collect stamps, rare books, wine, or cars. He collected experiences.

Every year for his birthday, his wife would give him a new experience. When he'd finished it, he'd write a long letter about the experience and circulate it inside the agency and to his circle of friends. One year it was baseball fantasy camp. Another time it was an aerial dogfight in MIGs over the North Atlantic. Once it was a wilderness trek. His letters were terrific, full of enthusiasm and detail, and for months afterward people would drop by his office to ask questions and offer up suggestions for his next big adventure. Many of us have now begun to collect experiences, from whale watching to white-water rafting. But that's only half of the experience trend.

But "experience this" is more than that. At Disney World, the summer ticket takers are told they're cast members and all part of the big show. The Geek Squad comes to fix your computer dressed in short-sleeved white shirts, thin black ties and thick-rimmed black glasses. And yes, of course, they wear pocket protectors. At Ed Debevic's restaurants in Chicago and Los Angeles, the wait staff all wear costumes, and from time to time climb on the tables to dance and belt out a song. Companies have decided that entertaining customers is good business and are telling us to "Experience this!"

Factors and Factoids

Joe Pine and Jim Gilmore first spotted this trend, or at least first brought it to our attention. Their argument is that there's a natural progression from goods to services to experiences driven by competition.

Here's how it works. Companies start out selling unique and differentiated products, but over time competitors catch up, and product differentiation is no longer an advantage. Good companies then add a measure of service. For example, American Airlines started its AAdvantage program to provide a whole suite of extra services to its best customers. It worked, but not for very long. Now every airline has its own frequent flyer program, and AAdvantage is no longer unique. So the next step in the progression is experience, which is where Southwest Airlines excels.

Pine and Gilmore argue that most companies can create an experience around their offerings, and the best ones do—from restaurants (Planet Hollywood) to selling cars (Land Rover's rugged on-site test track) to insurance claims adjustment (Progressive). Experiences are very different from both goods and services. They are hard to copy, memorable, and best of all, employees like providing experiences. Making coffee is work. Providing a coffee house experience is show business. So companies are beginning to embed experiences in whatever it is they make and sell.

And of course, back to where we started this discussion, there are also some companies that skip the first two parts of the progression (product and service) and sell nothing but the experience. For example, in addition to the run-of-the-mill karaoke, parasailing, bungee jumping, tandem parachute jumping, jetboating, and white-water rafting, there are the following:

- *Fan conventions for every sports franchise.* In Chicago, these include ones for Bears, the Bulls, the Cubs, the White Sox, and the Blackhawks. If you don't get enough, there's always a winter cruise around the Caribbean with Sox skipper Jerry Manuel, some of the guys and their wives. Or if you're from the other side of town, there's a tour of Wrigley Field on summer Sundays when the Cubs are out of town.

- *Tank and submachine gun rentals.* A company in England rents World War II tanks for a spin around the Bedforshire countryside. A shooting range in Atlanta specializes in automatic weapons.

- *Extreme sports samplers.* Backroads takes 40-somethings on 200-mile bicycle jaunts across Southern Utah. Club Med Bali offers trapeze training.

- *Weird stuff.* There is even a scuba diving trip into a mine near St. Louis. (The attraction of this is supposed to be a few moments of perfect blackness. One of my friends who went calls it an eternity of perfect terror, since floating in the dark made her lose her sense of up-and-down. She ended up clinging to the rope for dear life and praying for the lights to come back on.)

Implications

Just like purple is the next black, experiences are the next services. That is, more and more companies will go from just thinking of service as a series of programmed steps to a broader definition. For example, part of Jiffy Lube's success is that by providing comfortable waiting areas, coffee, and viewing window, they've made auto maintenance a far less awkward and intimidating prospect.

The Opportunity

Add a measure of fun to every transaction. Think Playland at McDonald's. Put in a reason for customers to keep coming back. Here's a way to start: Go outside the front door of your business, close your eyes for a moment, turn around, and walk back in—in slow motion. Pretend that you're attending a play. What is going on stage? And what *should* be going on?

On the Brandwagon

The Trend

There's a nasty custody battle going on in Minneapolis. General Mills admits he's not the birth parent of Doughboy, but since his marriage to the Doughboy's mom, Pillsbury, he's now come to love the little fellow as his own. But the government wants to take custody away from the General, and place the Doughboy in a foster home with a neighbor, International Multifoods. General Mills has offered to give the Multifoods family visitation rights through a licensing agreement, but the Federal Trade Commission (FTC) worries about the effect of all this change on the offspring, and whether he'll do well in a split parenting situation.

Twenty years ago, brands were no big thing, something for trademark attorneys working for companies that make laundry soap to worry about. Now everyone's on the brandwagon.

Factors and Factoids

In 1998, the financial services industry created 7,076 brands, as measured by trademarks and service marks. That's more than the 6,908 the industry registered in the entire decade of the 1980s. And it's not just happening in the newly deregulated banking sector, either. (See Table 8.1.)

Here's one more way to get an idea of the rate at which the creation of brands is accelerating. In 1930, there were 110 trademarks registered in the auto industry. By 1960, it had grown to a total of 952. By 1990, it was up to 10,391. Since 1995, more trademarks have been created in the auto industry than in the entire century before. Most of those new brands were extensions of previous brands, but there were a significant number of completely de novo brands as well.

The brand explosion really started in 1987 in the United Kingdom, when Grand Met put the brand value of a new acquisition, Smirnoff, on its balance sheet for roughly $1 million. This wasn't the first time acquired brands had gone on the balance sheet—Rupert Murdoch had been doing it for several years with Australian media properties. But it was a very high-profile move by a high-profile company in a major market. Now this didn't create a rush to go out and stick brand values on balance sheets, but it did spark intense interest in the whole area of valuing intangible assets and brand equity. (Professor David Aaker probably deserves the title of Father of brand equity.)

Table 8.1 **New Brands Registered**

	1990	1998
Insurance and finance	1,642	7,076
Wine and spirits	429	1,534
Staple foods	1,628	5,213
Vehicles	910	2,622

Source: Chris Lederer analysis of CASSIS data.

And as business strategists really began to think about brands, they came to a startling conclusion. Brands are in many ways the ultimate strategic asset. They are ownable, competitively defendable, infinitely scalable, and very flexible. GM and Harley-Davidson turned brand licensing into multi-million-dollar profit centers. Procter & Gamble used the Vicks brand to get into home vaporizers, a new category for them. Brands, an afterthought for many managers in the 1960s and 1970s, became important in the 1980s and came to dominate the strategic agenda of the 1990s.

At a more nuts-and-bolts level, brands are springing up from several sources. First, of course, are new products and product extensions, which as we discussed in "Instant Obsolescence," now number in the tens of thousands each year. Many of these are being created in the services sector and would have gone unbranded before. The second source is branded features and attributes. Du Pont and Monsanto have been doing it for years, but Intel's recent success has driven a new spate of what are known as *ingredient brands*. Finally, there are changes to corporate names. In 2000, 2,976 U.S. companies changed their names, about half due to mergers or acquisitions. Add in the 155,141 new businesses started in the United States each year, and that's another source of brand growth.

Implications

Expect the number of new brands being created to continue to grow, although at a less frenetic pace than the last few years of the Internet "brandgrab." Brands have a unique property for business: the more intense the competition, the more they're worth. That means that even when the current wave of hype recedes, brands will still be important.

Expect more and more brand recycling. We're literally running out of good brand names. That's one reason for the increasing use of manufactured words such as *Claritin* and *Questar*. And one thing the dot-coms proved: One Superbowl commercial does not a respected brand make. The alternative? Recycling. Packard Bell, the name of the computer company, was actually the name of an old line of radios made by Teledyne and purchased by two Israeli entrepreneurs for $100,000. Schottenstein Stores paid $68.6 million for the

Bugle Boy jeans trademark. Other recently recycled brands include 1980s-and-before icons Converse, J. Peterman, Joan & David, and Adrienne Vittadini.

The Opportunity

The Bible says "A good name is to be chosen above great riches." In the world of business, you don't have to choose. A good brand name leads to great riches, be it personal or business, and if you already own a great one, think about how to use it in new ways (e.g., to sell new products or reach new markets). (For a great book on branding, you might try the *Infinite Asset: Managing Brands to Build New Value,* written by Chris Lederer and yours truly.)

A la Carte Business Models

The Trend

Remember 40 minutes ago, when I said the dot-coms were right about three things, and the importance of ownership to employees was number one? Here's number two: *à la carte business models.* What this means is that companies can essentially assemble a business à la carte. For example, a biotech pharmaceutical company could start up tomorrow with nothing more than a patent, a cell phone, and a bank account, and be in business next month.

Factors and Factoids

The biggest change in manufacturing during the last 20 years has been the outsourcing of major elements of production and service. Electronics companies now outsource 73 percent of their manufacturing. For example, Nvidia sells Microsoft the graphics chips for its Xbox game machine. But they just design them. The manufacturing is contracted out to Taiwan Semiconductor Manufacturing Company. A few years ago, Sara Lee, the company that produces cheesecakes, sausages, handbags, and hosiery, considered getting out of manufacturing altogether. Gibson Greetings actually did.

Contract drug manufacturing is a $30 billion business. Two-thirds of U.S. auto manufacturing, half a trillion dollars, is outsourced. And it's not just manufacturing, companies also outsource virtually everything from logistics and shipping, to payroll preparation, to employee benefits management, to PR, to IT systems development, to facilities management, to customer service and inside and outside sales. Procter & Gamble's board just authorized the company to investigate outsourcing $10 billion in back-office functions (e.g., HR, accounting, and IT). Smaller companies even outsource things like marketing and financial management. Overall, outsourcing grew by 18 percent in 2000.

A company really only needs to own three things: (1) a brand, (2) a set of customer relationships, and (3) a core set of intellectual capital. Everything else, theoretically, can be sourced out.

What's behind à la carte business models? One major driver is interconnectedness. With better communications and transportation, it's possible to create almost seamless virtual companies.

The second key driver is specialization. In the old days, Ford and GM made almost everything they used, from the steel to engine blocks to auto electronics. But it is very hard to be great at everything, and over time specialists whittled away any task that was not absolutely essential to the carmaking process. That means the automakers keep design, assembly, marketing, and salesforce management mostly in-house, and look to specialists for everything else. That same process is now underway in every industry.

Implications

In a model with à la carte business models, expect instant competition. Our earlier example of the biopharmaceutical company is not strictly hypothetical. Companies now do spring up overnight. The key barrier to entry for most industries is no longer production, but room in the sales channel and establishing a brand.

Expect scale to be less important. For a start-up, low volumes can mean high production costs and ruinous margins. (A new semiconductor plant costs $1 billion or $2 billion.) However, by outsourcing to a contract manufacturer who's making similar products, it's possible to borrow a bit of scale. (Scale is often misunderstood. For example, in most industries, it's not necessary to be the largest volume or the low-cost producer, as long as you're close. If you're just starting up and making 10,000 widgets versus the industry leader's 10 million, your costs won't be close. If you can get a contract manufacturer who's already making 1 million widgets to make your widgets for you, then you'll probably be in the ball park.)

Expect generally accepted accounting principles (GAAP) to be completely rewritten. Our accounting rules were written in a day when tangible assets like factories and trucks went hand-in-hand with intangible assets like patents and brands. Because of à la carte pricing models, there's been a decoupling of the two. That means that the market value of companies is often 5 or 10 times their asset book value. But almost all accounting systems and auditing processes are designed around keeping track of book assets. There's got to be a major overhaul of accounting to catch up with reality and prepare for an even larger gap in the future.

The Opportunity

There are two opportunities here. The first is if you run a start-up, or even an established business in which you're doing everything yourself, take a hard look at everything you do. Are you world class? Is staying world class in everything taking time away from other things that are more important to you? Michael Rourke built a box to help handicapped people control their environment. But after 10 years, he found himself spending all his time managing inventory, and none on his first love, research and development (R&D). So his company, Quartet, found someone to manage 95 percent of their inventory, cutting the time required to manage inventory down to 1 hour a month.

I just struck a deal with a terrific consulting firm in Boston, Integral, to take over providing consulting services to clients interested in my new approaches to quantitatively modeling brand portfolios. I *could* do it, but it requires large teams and global reach. It would have meant spending all my time recruiting and training a team, two activities that I don't like and that I'm not very good at. Better to find a partner.

And the second opportunity is to provide outsourcing services. But be careful. Over time, companies always squeeze their suppliers. By the way, outsourcing as a trend is here to stay, but this does have a cyclical element to it. If you're a contract manufacturer in a high-growth industry that is starting to mature, beware. Often when high-growth companies find their growth falling, they look close to home to boost margins, and often that means bringing things back in-house. So that means don't forget to build your own brand and sales channel relationships as you go. You may need them someday.

Reintermediation

The Trend

I can see it now. It's 2030, and I'm sitting out on the porch in a rocking chair with four kids at my feet.

"Were you in the revolution, Great-grandpa?" asks little Susie.

I pause, then answer truthfully. "Yes, I was, honey, just like everyone else. I grabbed my sleeping bag and barricaded myself in a start-up, writing business plans, and printing up stock options to hand out to the new recruits. They just loved them," I chuckle. "Used to walk around talking about how much they were worth. It was so sweet."

"Were you a dot-communist, Great-grandpa?" asks her younger brother George.

"Well, everybody was a dot-communist in those days, Georgie. We were going to build new on-line communities where Internet service would be free and equal, break the hold of the media conglomerates over content, and put those damn middlemen out of business."

"What's a middleman, Grandpa?"

"A middleman is an intermediary, like a car dealer or a travel agent or a stock broker or a publisher," I say.

"Did you do it, Great-grandpa, put those old middlepersons out of business?" Susie asks softly.

My voice cracks, and a tear rolls down my wrinkled cheek. "No honey, we sure didn't. Instead of getting rid of the middlemen, we created more of them, and at least one ginormous one—eBay. Every generation, from the Romans on, has said the middleman has to go, and he's still here."

I hear my granddaughter's footsteps coming. "Kids, are you pestering your Great-grandpa? Let him nap, now. Come on, it's time to go watch Great-grandma compete in the street luge at the Senior X-Games. Susie, tuck that blanket around his legs. Bye, Gramps. You get some rest now."

Factors and Factoids

An intermediary is anyone in the supply chain between the manufacturer and the user of a product. In goods, wholesalers, distributors, and retailers are the intermediaries. In services, they are the brokers and agents (e.g., travel agents and insurance agents). In theory, as supply-and-demand chains become more efficient, it should be possible to displace intermediaries, which is known in the financial services industry as the D-word, *disintermediation*. That's where the Internet comes in. At least that's what Bill Gates had in mind in his 1995 book, when he promised a "friction-free" economy.

Many Internet business plans were built around some sort of disintermediation. The logic was simple: A CD costs 25 cents to make; $9.50 to ship, distribute, and retail; and sells for $17. That's somewhere between $9.50 and $16.75 that could be taken out, and presumably split with the consumer.

In most industries, the intermediary's cut isn't as dramatic. In travel, real estate, and brokerage, it's under 10 percent. And for big commercial companies doing huge transactions like bonds or grain trading, it's down in the 1 to 3 percent range. Still, if a large company like GM could save even 1 percent on its materials, that totals to hundreds of millions of dollars a year. And for a farmer, who lives on razor-thin margins already, a percent here and there is a lot. They jumped at the chance to buy chemicals more cheaply on-line, and sell grain through Cybercrop.com at lower commissions.

But intermediaries weren't displaced by the Internet, and it's become clear that it is unlikely they will be. This should not surprise us—they do add value. Carrying inventory, moving products, coordinating logistics, making markets and setting prices, collecting data on customers, and disseminating information to customers about new products—all those functions are valuable. Those who have tried to just stop doing these activities have found out just how valuable they in fact are. Nike worked with i2 to create a streamlined supply chain management without intermediaries, and soon found inventories ballooning and orders going unfilled, which in turn contributed to Nike's poor quarterly result in early 2001.

But the other reason why intermediaries aren't being displaced is because they have something to say about it, and they aren't interested in being cut out. Intermediation is a tough business, and those that succeed in it are pretty darn tough. Look at how intermediaries have responded to the Internet. Some have embraced it. The leading headhunting websites are run by traditional executive recruiters.

Others, however, have fought it. Auctioneers are trying to force eBay to take the licensing exam in every state where it operates. Chrysler dealers in the Northwest have refused to service cars sold over the Internet. Car dealers in 12 states have pushed through laws making it almost impossible for manufacturers to sell cars directly. And last year, the American Association of Travel Agents (ASTA) filed a complaint with the Justice Department to try to block the launch of Orbitz's travel site. If we're ever going to displace intermediaries, it's going to take a lot more than a slick business plan and a portal concept.

Implications

Don't expect disintermediation. Do expect reintermediation, the replacement of inefficient intermediaries with more efficient ones. Booking a flight through Travelocity or Expedia isn't disintermediation, it's just dealing with a travel agent that's a lot more efficient than most. An intermediary still handles our packages, it's just Mailboxes Etc. or UPS instead of the U.S. Postal Service.

Expect those intermediaries who base their business on easily available information, simple facilitation, or on holding in-market inventories to struggle. For example, the number of insurance agencies has fallen from 70,000 in 1980 to just more than half of that, 36,000 today. Half of an insurance agent's job is active selling, and the other half is simple facilitation—order taking (and the order-taking half is going away). Travel agents have lost business to Expedia and Orbitz, and have begun to downsize and even go out of business. Optometrists have lost out because of mail-order contact lenses.

Expect the big, successful intermediaries to get bigger and more successful. Interconnectedness will actually allow them to extend their reach and roll their model out more extensively. For example, grocery distributors and wholesalers have struggled, except for Supervalu, the most sophisticated and streamlined in the industry. The same is true in academic journal distribution and similar industries.

The Opportunity

There's a great opportunity here if you are already an intermediary. The Internet allows you to reach levels of efficiency never before dreamed of. While the rest of the agents and distributors are down at the statehouse fighting change, spend your time thinking of ways to use it to make your business the winner when the smoke clears.

Also, look for suppliers and customers that seem to be encroaching on your space. Try to understand the underlying customer needs or changing economics that are pulling them into your backyard, and find a way to respond, even if it means partnering with them.

If you're not an intermediary today, think about whether you should be. We're moving to a service economy, and many services are really just intermediation (e.g., personal concierge services), or they have huge amounts of intermediation embedded in them (e.g., interior decorating). Disintermediation? Forget about it. Look for new opportunities to intermediate.

Strange Bedfellows

The Trend

"Misery acquaints a man with strange bedfellows," William Shakespeare said. And so does competition. We now live in a business world where your fiercest competitor in one arena is your business partner in another and your customer in yet another.

Factors and Factoids

There are two factors driving this trend, and they're both related. First is the epidemic of mergers and acquisitions. There were less than 1,000 deals in 1981. Today, there are around 10,000 each year. Most big mergers are based on synergies, which almost by definition mean most companies try to buy direct competitors, where synergies are greatest. Even when companies continue to run the businesses separately, there usually is at least some sharing (e.g. in R&D and design). It's no accident that the new Jaguar looks a lot like a dressed-up Ford Taurus. Underneath the sheet metal are many of the same parts.

But what really puts the strain in strange bedfellows are strategic alliances. That's where two companies team up to attack a new market or develop a new product together. Strategic alliances have exploded over the last 5 years, almost doubling from 5,200 in 1996 to over 10,000 today. The typical large (more than $2 billion) corporation has averaged initiating one new strategic alliance every other week during that span. Some examples:

- American Airlines and British Airways (BA) are founding members of the OneWorld Alliance, an agglomeration of those two plus a half-dozen or so others (e.g., Finnair and Sabena). The basic purpose of the alliance is to provide end-to-end travel for business passengers. For example, BA will bring a businessperson from London to New York, and American will carry him or her on to Kansas City. But American and BA also compete head to head on the same trans-Atlantic routes.

- Amazon.com has 8,000 marketing partners that refer business to it and receive a commission on the sale. Many of these partners are authors, publishers, and bookstores that also sell books themselves.

- Ericsson and Sony are teaming up to make cellular handsets, even though Ericsson is a major manufacturer of cell phones.

- Pfizer is teaming up with Microsoft and IBM to make and sell software to doctors, even though Microsoft also has a formal strategic alliance with WebMD. WebMD is already trying to develop the same products and has agreed to use Microsoft technology in its new software. (Microsoft is the Madonna of the strategic alliance world. It has alliances with Ford, Starbucks, and hundreds of others, including archfoes Apple and Corel, maker of WordPerfect.)

Implications

Expect to see lots more combinations, and some really strange ones. A few years ago Sainsbury announced a strategic alliance with British Airways, based on the logic that one was "Britain's favorite supermarket," and the other was the "world's favorite airline."

Expect to operate in a world of constrained competition, what Barry Nalebuff calls "co-opetition." A change in classic corporate culture will be required to pull this off. Once I asked an executive of one of the two big cola companies for his strategic goal. He answered, "I want to put those SOBs out of business, to have them lose their jobs, and to make their children go hungry. I want to pour salt on their fields and drive their cattle into the sea." A little too Biblical perhaps, but I got the message. For him, it was total competition, no holds barred, and I would *never* find a can of the competitor's product in his rec room fridge. (And by implication, since I was his consultant, he better never find a can in mine.)

But that level of clarity and ambiguity doesn't work in a world of strange bedfellows. Microsoft even has an executive in charge of helping alliance partners compete against themselves. Don't be surprised to bid against someone one day, and the next week see him or her sitting at the national sales convention, or to read in the *Wall Street Journal* that your company has just signed an agreement with Oracle to develop that same new piece of software that your team's been slaving over for 3 years.

Expect a bumpy road. The most common alliances are where one side wants technology, and the other wants market access. But what happens a few years down the road, when each has gotten a good idea of what it is the other one knows? The answer is often a dispute over who now owns what. In 1982, Intel licensed AMD to build its 8086 chip. Four years later, they changed their mind. But AMD had used the intervening time to build up their own manufacturing and technical expertise, and they immediately went into business against Intel. In 1999, Priceline discussed a merger with Expedia. The two shared strategic plans and exchanged technical information. Talks broke down, but the next year Expedia rolled out a suite of products very much like Priceline's. Priceline sued, and the two sides settled. Expect a fair proportion of alliances to end up in court.

Opportunity

If you're a large company, picking the right bedfellows can create new growth and allow you to enter new markets with minimal risk, to protect competitive flanks, and to create the mass of a megacompany without the capital investment. If you're a small company, the trend to strange bedfellows is going to provide lots of AMD-like opportunities, chances to partner with much larger firms to bootstrap yourself into the big time.

Be careful to keep track of who brings what to the party, because if the whole thing falls apart, the opportunity changes to one of getting paid for what you put in.

The Price Is Wrong

The Trend

Priceline.com may have faded, but the idea of negotiable prices is back. Savvy travelers feel no embarrassment haggling at airline counters and hotel desks. We're back to a world of dynamic pricing and on-the-spot negotiation.

Factors and Factoids

If you're a seller of goods, what's the definition of pricing heaven? That would be where you know the price every customer is willing to pay, and no customer knows what the other has paid. And the definition of pricing hell would be just the opposite: a world where the customer knows exactly what you will take for it and what everyone else is paying. Today most retailers and sellers of product live in pricing hell, and the three people who put them there are Richard Sears, Bob Crandall, and Vinton Cerf.

Richard Sears was, of course, the founder of Sears, and he's the man who introduced transparent pricing to America. The turn of the last century was the heyday of rampant price fixing and gouging. By offering a catalog of products with fixed prices, Sears essentially established national prices and put a ceiling on what local merchants could charge. The merchants didn't like transparent prices, but they liked what came from transparent pricing even worse: price wars, discounting, and cyclical promotions. By the beginning of the 1990s, retailers lived in a pricing world that most didn't think could get much worse.

Enter Bob Crandall, former CEO of American Airlines. In the late 1970s and early 1980s, Crandall's company invented something called *yield management*. Actually, the basic principle of yield management has been around for centuries. The idea is that the price of perishable products should drop as they get closer to their expiration date. That's why there's a bin of discounted fruit in the supermarket. But Crandall implemented it on a grand scale. The hundred economists and programmers in American Airline's Decision Technologies Group created a system that would offer to sell the same seat on a flight for a different price based on your willingness to commit in advance, or to be flexible at the last minute.

The system works by analyzing how many seats remain unfilled and changing the price almost continuously to attract price-sensitive travelers. (American claims to check its inventory and prices 30 million times a day. That is over 300 times a second.) It turns out that yield management has filled planes but not boosted profits for airlines.[2] That's for two reasons.

First, yield management systems have taught consumers that every price is really negotiable, and that if they're willing to book early enough or wait long enough, they can get the lowest price. For example, in the cruise industry, there is usually a huge rush of bookings just before sailing, the result of savvy retirees waiting until the very last minute when prices begin to plummet. Consumers have learned to game the system.

There's more. Now consumers have their own technology tools to work with. And that happened when Dr. Cerf and Dr. Bob Kahn invented the Internet. Voila! If you're a retailer, welcome to the pricing nightmare on Main Street. Consumers are ready to haggle and are armed with the world's best technology to help them.

Last week in New York, I booked a room through my travel agent and paid $265. Brian (yes, the same Brian) booked his through the Internet and paid $125. This week my agent is booking mine through the Internet and I'm paying $155 ($135 to the hotel and $20 to the agent for her trouble). The yield management system may be selling an extra room at $125, but it's giving me a discount of $130 over what I would have otherwise paid. Dodgy economics at best for the hotel.

Implications

Expect dynamic pricing and yield management to continue to spread, now that customers are used to it. Hotels and cruise lines have already climbed on board. Next stop: anything that has very peaky capacity utilization, such as restaurants and tollways. New Jersey has already experimented with higher tolls at peak times. And the new budget for New York City projects $800 million in 2006 from congestion pricing.

Expect also to see some version of dynamic pricing for all perishable goods. For example, the prices of magazines will drop as they get closer to replacement. Computer programs will set weekly prices of electronic products, playing off sales channels, inventory left in the warehouse, and time to the next release.

Expect haggling to become commonplace. Not confident in your hondling (i.e., bargaining) skills? Not to worry. A software company has created Haggleware, a program that helps consumers create a bidding war with sellers of products over the Internet. And at Hagglezone.com, a software algorithm will haggle for you—bargaining with software algorithms in yield management systems. (Am I the only one a little scared by this aspect of the trend—computers battling computers at the checkout counter?)

The Opportunity

Expect to haggle and be haggled with. Know your costs and how low you can afford to go. Make your pricing scheme as complex as possible, just in case you ever have to explain to a customer why somebody else got his or her fence for 50 percent less.

Gotcha Tactics

The Trend

Sounds like companies are defenseless against the new, informed consumer-haggler? Perhaps not. There's always the opportunity to make money through what Connecticut Attorney General Richard Blumenthal told CBS's *Sixty Minutes* was "competing by cheating." Cheating is too strong a word, let's call them *gotcha tactics*.

Each of us sees gotcha tactics every day. For example:

- For months, my charge card company added an unexplained charge of 50 cents to my bill, until I finally got annoyed enough to have my assistant inquire. Jane never did get an explanation, but the charge went away as mysteriously as it appeared. Still, they managed to get that 50 cents each month for years before I caught them. Got me.

- Recently in a convenience store franchised by a leading gasoline company, I saw a consumer fill his tank with gas, pick up a gallon of milk, and offer the clerk a coupon. The coupon said that the milk was half-price with a fill-up. The customer stared incredulously as the clerk pointed to microscopic print on the bottom of the coupon that said the offer wasn't valid in this store. The customer walked out, leaving the milk on the counter, but he couldn't return the gasoline for a refund. Got him.

- It's almost impossible to make a local call anymore, because phone companies have carved up geographies into so many area codes that everything becomes a toll call. Got me again.

Welcome to gotcha sales tactics—the art of fine print, hidden fees, signing up customers without their permission, and tacking unexpected and even false charges onto the original price. The trend here is not that consumers are being cheated. (That's been around forever—there were probably shady Pleistocene-era cavemen offering time-shares in caves infested with saber-toothed tigers.) The trend is that companies accused of gotcha tactics used to be low-rent telesales outfits based in Nevada. Now the accused are blue chips like AT&T, Providian Financial, Citibank, and Qwest.

Factors and Factoids

There are three factors driving this trend: (1) the price squeeze we spoke about in the last section, (2) unbundled pricing, and (3) outsourcing.

First, let's talk about the price squeeze. The problem is companies have to make a profit, and if prices fall to a point where a profit is out of the question, they have to look for new ways to bolster the top line. Those ways often involve charging excessive fees in one area to make up for losses in another, or in sneaking additional charges onto the bill. For example, since the breakup of AT&T and the introduction of competition into long distance, long-distance rates have fallen by 49.7 points. But local rates, which are seldom competitive, have risen by almost the same amount as long distance has fallen: 45.2 points. (Fascinating factoid: 9 percent of U.S. local markets are now competitive. If you adjust the 45.2 number to reflect just the 91 percent of markets that have no competition, local rates have risen by 49.7 points, *exactly* the amount long-distance rates have fallen.) Now that local phone companies no longer have the revenue from long distance, they're making it up somewhere else.

The state of Connecticut is also suing AT&T for adding on unjustified charges, like a universal connectivity charge and a national access contribution. The same state recently ordered Acme Rent-a-Car to stop tacking speeding fines onto rental bills. The way it worked is this: Acme used a global positioning system (GPS) system to track its rental cars and every time a driver exceeded 79 miles an hour for more than 2 minutes, it automatically debited $150 from their credit card for "wear and tear" to the vehicle. One driver got hit with an extra $450 on his rental bill. Citibank just agreed to pay $1.6 million to 26 states to settle complaints that their contracted telemarketers tricked people into buying products and services. As companies try to backfill for lost revenues due to cuts in list price, they increasingly move to gotcha techniques.

Ironically, the second factor leading to gotcha tactics have been moves intended to protect consumers, like the implementation of the Truth in Lending form that mortgage companies are required to provide to consumers as part of their closing. Another form means more paperwork, and more places to hide gotchas.

For example, in 2000, 22 states cracked down on auto leasing companies that advertised "No Money Down," but charged hundreds of dollars in up-front acquisition fees. Also in 2000, the Better Business Bureau received 2,902 complaints about mortgage and escrow companies. Many of these were for things like hidden fees and changing the amount of points between loan initiation and closing. (The difference between 3 and 4 points doesn't sound like much to an excited first-time homebuyer, until they realize that each point is 1 percent of the total purchase price.)

And the final factor is outsourcing. Many larger, reputable companies have now outsourced their telemarketing and customer acquisition functions to subcontractors. Qwest Communications recently settled a suit because a contractor forged the names of customers to switch their phone services from another company. Fly-by-night travel companies scam $12 billion a year from consumers, and often these tricks involve reputable companies. For example, over the last 5 years, hundreds of Wisconsin couples have been offered free cruises on a brand-name cruise line. However, once they arrived at the dock in Miami, the travel companies charged them hundreds of dollars in fees to get on board. Vacation luggage in hand, many of them forked over the cash. Add all three factors up, and it's a case of "Gotcha."

Implications

Expect gotcha tactics to continue. Unfortunately, even reputable merchants will continue to use gotcha. First of all, additional fees are here to stay. For many banks, much of their profit now comes from transaction fees. And disclosing them too openly puts the honest at a disadvantage. For example, car dealerships that put honest, fully loaded prices in their newspaper ads will lose traffic to those that put stripped-down, less-than-honest numbers in theirs. We're caught in a gotcha cycle, where the honest companies almost have to gotcha to keep up with the less honest.

Expect serious brand damage to blue chips who get caught. Providian's stock plummeted when it got hit with class-action suits over its gotcha pricing, even though the suits covered a relatively small percentage of its business. And expect companies that cheat to get caught. If it's not consumer protection organizations (who caught AT&T) or the media (who caught Providian), it will be their own employees (Enron) or even competitors who turn them in. Recently, Coca-Cola was investigated by the European Commission for anticompetitive behavior. The whistle-blower? Pepsi.

Expect a resurgence in packaged pricing, especially for low-ticket items. In 2001, actress Jamie Lee Curtis pitched customers on cellular pricing plans with no gotcha's. Consumer uptake so far has been strong.

The Opportunity

Any time flimflam artists roam the land, there are many opportunities for honest businesses with solid reputations. There are three rules to follow:

1. Avoid gotcha tactics.
2. Patiently explain the differences to the customer.
3. Rat on your competitors to regulatory agencies at every turn. Sorry, that sounds ugly. However, when gotcha behavior is

allowed to run unchecked, it stains the whole industry, including your business. So turning in deceptive competitors is not just a good short-term competitive tactic, but it is also an investment in the long-term health of the industry.

Mass Personalization

The Trend

When I was Chief Marketing Officer at Booz-Allen, part of my job was to package ideas to be presented to the press and clients. One day I got a call from one of my partners in the financial services practice. He wanted my help marketing a new approach his team had developed for companies with large customer service units. They called their methodology *industrialized intimacy*. Great idea. Great name for a Philip K. Dick novel—bad name for a consulting product. (Maybe that's the reason the team's work never really got the recognition it deserved.)

The partner's argument was that we've entered a time of industrialized customer service, with 3 million people working in call centers. But we expect the same personal touch from a giant American Express (AMEX) call center as we are used to from the corner travel agency. And that expectation changes the way customer service must be delivered. It creates a need for industrialized intimacy, or better said, *mass personalization*.

Factors and Factoids

If mass personalization were a movie, the brief description in the Sunday paper would read "Service Economy meets Mass Customization. Classic feel-good love story. Four stars."

As we have moved to a service economy, we have not just become greater consumers of services, we've also changed the way we buy them. For example, the number of child care workers who come to a person's home will fall from 275,000 to 250,000 during the decade from 1996 to 2006. But the number of child care workers overall will leap from 830,000 to 1,129,000 over the same time period. We're consuming more child care services, but instead of buying it from an individual, we're going to purchase child care from a child care center, which is in effect a small service factory.

In that swap, we've gained lower cost, more consistency of delivery, and increased convenience, but we've lost the personal touch. It's much more difficult to effectively provide intimacy in an industrial setting.

New technologies like data mining are allowing companies to track, develop products for, and market to individuals, an approach known as *mass customization*. These technologies, properly deployed, also allow companies to put the personal touch back in services. For example, the person with whom I am speaking at AMEX has never spoken with me before. But he knows all my little details and preferences. He knows that I like aisle seats on flights of less than 3 hours and window seats on longer flights. He knows all my frequent flyer numbers and what status I have on each airline. And he even knows that I would rather walk to Atlanta than fly there on one particular airline. What makes that possible is he's looking at a computer screen that contains all that information and arrays it in a way that he can take a 10-second glance at the screen and sound like he's my new best friend in the whole world.

That's the most common way to actually implement mass personalization, through what is known as customer relationship management (CRM) software. Companies now buy $6.5 billion in CRM software each year from companies like Siebel and SAP.[3] The consulting firm of PricewaterhouseCoopers alone does more than $1 billion each year in CRM consulting. Currently, 25 percent of Fortune 500 companies have installed CRM software, but next year 38 percent of large companies plan to spend more. Even more interesting, 41 percent of midsized companies and 28 percent of small companies plan to invest in CRM.

The promise of CRM is a single file with everything the company knows about any customer. And while data like my height and hobbies are nice, what they really want to capture is every interaction I have ever had with the company, every purchase, every phone call, every e-mail, and every meeting with a salesperson. It's a terribly difficult challenge, both technologically (should an e-mail from sam_hill@heliosconsulting.com go into Sam I. Hill's customer file?)

and culturally (salespeople do not like to file call reports, although with PDAs and laptops, it's becoming less of a chore every day). But when we finally get there, the end will be completely seamless, fully realized mass personalization.

Implications

Expect a CRM system to become the new backbone of company IT, linking everything from the call center to the accounts payable system. Expect scaled-down versions of these programs to be used by the smallest of companies, and when it does, expect service to improve.

The Opportunity

If you're an individual or a tiny company, just because you're not ready to pay PWC $1 million to install an SAP system doesn't mean you can't profitably adopt the principles of CRM. Software like Now Contact Manager can provide much of the same functionality, and it is easy to learn. The key is simply installing the organizational discipline to use it.

The payoff, though, is pretty high. Saying to a key customer, "John, the last time we spoke you wanted me to find a metric meter, and I think Donna called Saturday to tell you it's in," sounds a lot more professional than, "Who is this? Oh, and remind me again, what was I supposed to be looking for? Who told you it was here? Was it me? Are you sure?" And adding that last little touch (e.g., "And John, how did Lucy's play go?") might be the little extra that creates the next sale.

A Pound of Risk, to Go

The Trend

The only test I failed at the University of Chicago was on the mathematics of risk. And now 20 years later, I'm going to try to explain the trend of unbundling and trading risk. Hmmm. This should be interesting. (Well, it *is* one of the big 60 trends. I can't just ignore it.)

Let me start at a level I'm sure I understand. When you buy a house, it comes with all sorts of risks. There's the risk that it will burn down; the risk that the mailman will trip on a loose flagstone, break his leg, and sue; and the risk that the price you end up selling it for will be less than what you paid for it.

Now most of us are pretty selective about the risks we take.[4] We're willing to risk $200 on the blackjack table on the cruise ship, but we're not too interested in risking our $200,000 home. So we pay someone to take as much of that home risk as possible. Insurance companies will take some of the risks from us, and the rest we're stuck with.[5]

The same thing is true at the commercial level, although companies have long been able to sell off more kinds of risk and to a broader group of investors than an individual homeowner. Until very recently, however, there were some risks no company could sell and even Lloyd's of London wouldn't buy. For example, there was no way to guarantee stock prices.

Here's the trend: Over the last 20 years, we have seen an explosion in the types of risks a company is able to get others to assume, and an explosion in the tools to bundle and sell off those risks. Companies that buy and sell risk are not just insurance companies, but a host of trading firms. Almost every type of risk now has its price, and companies essentially buy and sell pounds of risk, just like they used to sell potatoes.

Factors and Factoids

Corporations are even more conservative than people. They don't want any downside risk if they can help it—fire, flood, employee injury, quality control mistakes, executives being kidnapped, a mistake by the board of directors. You name the catastrophe, they buy insurance to protect against it. In 1995, Fortune 1000 corporations spent $18.2 billion on insurance, around $6.49 per thousand dollars of revenue.

To handle the business risks that insurance companies won't take, corporations turn to banks and investors. For example, for years companies have engaged in factoring, or selling off, their receivables to reduce the risk of late or nonpayment. And since the middle of the nineteenth century, companies have tried to manage the risk of the price of raw materials by buying and selling commodities futures. The Kansas City Board of Trade began selling wheat futures in 1876. The Chicago Butter and Egg Board became the Chicago Mercantile Exchange and began selling dairy futures in 1919. There are futures boards for grains, dairy, oil and natural gas, sugar, cotton, coffee, cocoa, soybeans, metals, and silk.

That's old. Here's what's new. In the 1970s, governments stopped regulating things like exchange rates, creating all sorts of new risks and opportunities to manage them. Around the same time, mathematicians and economists developed new models to more effectively price risk, like the Black-Scholes options pricing formula (in 1973). Finally, interconnectedness allowed bundles of risks to be traded across borders, creating bigger, global markets over which to spread risk. The result is new exchanges have developed to sell financial futures (i.e., tools that allow a company to lock in exchange and interest rates for some period of time) and options (which can be used as insurance against the price of a security going up or down).

In fact, the size and number of financial exchanges to trade these instruments haven't grown, they've exploded. The Chicago Board Options Exchange started trading in 1973, and 11 years later was the second most active exchange in the world [after the New York Stock Exchange (NYSE)]. There are now 60 exchanges around the world selling options and futures: the BM&F (Brazil), founded in 1983; MEFF (Spain), in 1989; SAFEX (South Africa), in 1990; the New York Board of Trade (NYBOT), in 1998; and also in 1998 came CX (a joint venture between the NYBOT and Cantor Fitzgerald.)

Of course, risk is tricky business. The objective is to end up with less risk, but often companies using these new instruments don't quite know what they're doing. Anyway, the temptation to gamble a little can be hard to resist. Ask Procter & Gamble. They lost $102 million in 1994, which seemed like a lot until the Orange County government lost $1.7 billion 8 months later. Barings lost £900 million in 1995, and the Enron bill is still being tallied.

Apart from these growing pains, the real story here is the ability to parcel and price risk, all types of risk, and move those risks around the world. Through the use of creative combinations of instruments and markets, there's virtually no risk that can't be bought and sold. Even mortgage companies and insurance companies now bundle up their risk and sell it off.

Implications

Expect risk markets to continue to expand, notwithstanding the occasional Enron. One day you will be able to buy a new house and, for a small consideration, buy insurance that the price won't fall when you sell it. Or buy a policy on your vacation home that the lake level won't rise. Perhaps you'll even be able to ensure your degree, say guaranteeing your first 5 years of earnings to ensure you'll make enough to repay the one-quarter million dollars you borrowed to finance 4 years of undergraduate and 3 years of med school.

As people get more and more comfortable with the idea of risk, look for far more sophisticated financial planning tools for individuals. (Unfortunately, the whole day trading fiasco was part of the learning process.) Look for personal financial portfolios to hold 100 shares of IBM and 30 risk units of the financing for a new megadam on the Yangtze River.

The Opportunity

For large and even small businesses, it's worth learning more about risk instruments and what they can and cannot do. For example, they can't get you a guaranteed risk-free after-tax return of 10 percent. (See Procter & Gamble's situation, discussed earlier.) But they can take some of the risk out of holding a large inventory or serving a new customer in Caracas.

CHAPTER 9

Workplace Trends

For Americans, the workplace is sacred ground. Russia may be the land of the worker, but the United States is the land of work. Our nation is composed of people lured from around the world with the promise that we would find them a job. In the United States, work is our salvation. From hard work, all good things flow. It is our central ethic. The closest optimistic America can come to defining *hopelessness* is to show the faces of Depression-era people in endless job lines.

We hold ourselves out as the "land of opportunity," with the clear understanding that the road to opportunity is through hard work, a fair wage for a fair day's effort, and advancement on the basis of merit, not nepotism or favoritism. We believe almost unanimously that work is a necessity, essential both to feeding our stomachs and our self-esteem.

In short, work is important to us, and trends that affect the workplace affect us at a particularly profound level. In this chapter, we will look at our final nine trends:

1. *D-I-V-E-R-S-E.* The clear trend is toward a time when race, sex, and religion are irrelevant once we step inside the door of the workplace. It's a bumpy road, but the progress is undeniable.

2. *Paraprofessionalism.* You name the profession and I'll name the paraprofession. For virtually every highly skilled job that

requires multiple degrees, there is a scaled-down technical equivalent or two, like paralegals or physician's assistant. Paraprofessionals are the factory floor workers of the service economy.

3. *What, me work?* Work may be sacred to us, and the work ethic our national credo, but the truth is we don't really like to work all that much. If Tom Brokaw is right and our parents were the Greatest Generation, perhaps his book on us will be entitled the *Laziest Generation.*

4. *The last job review.* Legal actions are making honest job reviews obsolete. The day is coming when *direct feedback* will be a workplace oxymoron.

5. *Celebrity CEOs.* Can I have your autograph, Mr. Welch? Sign right here next to Sammy Sosa, Brittney, and that woman who took off her shirt at the Laker's game.

6. *Mercenary management.* What ever happened to loyalty of companies to workers and workers to companies? It's gone, replaced by a world of mercenaries who work for the highest bidder. And it's not all bad.

7. *24/7/365.* We are a round-the-clock society, and 24 million people work at night keeping that clock wound and ticking.

8. *Retooling.* You don't see many classified ads anymore for typesetters or cobblers. As the economy changes, so do the key skills it requires. Many individuals find themselves with 20 years of career left and an obsolete set of expertise. So the answer is to *retool,* returning to school to gain a new set of skills, and relaunching your career.

9. *In a land far, far away.* I live in Chicago. My clients are in Miami, New York, Amsterdam, Dallas, and Phoenix. The consultants who work for me live in Palo Alto, Boston, Park City, Chappaqua (NY), and Manhattan. Call it extreme tele-working, something as far beyond telecommuting as video-phones are beyond two tin cans and a string.

That's it, the final 9 trends of the 60. Grab the wheel with both hands and stomp on the accelerator, we're turning onto the home stretch now.

D-I-V-E-R-S-E

The Trend

Earlier in this book, we spoke of TV sitcoms as being the laboratories where we conduct our social experiments. Well, when it comes time to move from the lab to the real world, the first place the experiments are transplanted to is the workplace. And no social experiment there has been more widely implemented or more wildly successful than diversity.

The American workplace is now the least racist, sexist, homophobic place the world has ever known. That's right. The world. Ever. And it's getting better.

Factors and Factoids

In 1940, before diversity, the typical woman in the workforce earned only 58 percent of what the typical man did. Black males' earnings were well under one-half of those of white males. By the end of the 1990s, both blacks and females earned around 75 percent of what white males do.

The gap has narrowed because women and minorities now have access to better jobs, and some level of confidence that once they're in the workforce, they will be allowed to succeed. For example, consider the different opportunities available to black women today. In 1940, 6 of every 10 black women worked as domestic servants. Today, only 1 in 20 is a domestic servant.

This is not just a cosmetic change (e.g., taking off the maid uniform and donning one with a golden arches logo). This is real progress. In 1940, even though African Americans represented 12 percent and women more than one-half of the U.S. population, only 8 percent of physicians and 4 percent of attorneys were female or black. Today, over 30 percent of both physicians and attorneys are black and/or female. Fifteen percent of engineers are black or female, up from less than 1 percent in 1940. In the acting industry, in 1997, African Americans won 14.1 percent of the roles.

Most major corporations now have a diversity program, and all have a policy of recruitment and advancement without discrimination. This is not to say that racism and sexism in the workplace are dead. Both are still there. (On the day I wrote this, American

Express settled a class-action suit brought by thousands of female employees.) And many more prejudices (e.g., religious intolerance, agism) are still relatively unaddressed. Still, overt displays of bigotry are simply not tolerated in the workplace.

Or if they are tolerated, there's a price to be paid. And it's a biggie. On November 16, 2000, Coca-Cola agreed to pay 2,000 current and former employees $113 million, part of a $192.5 million settlement. The settlement was in response to a class-action suit alleging racial bias in hiring and promotion. It was the largest such settlement in history, beating out Texaco's $176.1 million in 1996. (A senior Texaco official still wins the "Most Obnoxious and Costly Single Quote by Someone Who Should Know Better" award. Even though Texaco had well-documented equal opportunity guidelines, African-American employees felt like they were bumping up against a glass ceiling where blacks could never get promoted. It turned out that they were right. One high-ranking executive was secretly taped talking about "uppity" Jews and "nigglas."[1])

Implications

Expect the workplace to continue to lead the way as the social engine of America. There's still plenty of room to improve, for example, in promoting women and minorities to the executive ranks. American Express, Lucent Technologies, AOL Time Warner, Kraft, and Hewlett-Packard (HP) are the exceptions, not the rules.

When Catalyst studied 48 firms who represent just under one-half of all securities industry employment, they found that 75 percent of executive-level jobs were held by white males, 19 percent by white women, and 6 percent by men or women of color. Only 28 Fortune 500 companies have female chief financial officers (CFOs). In a study of the boards of directors of major corporations, one-half had no or only one female or minority board member. Those numbers suggest huge potential upside.

Expect race relations overall to continue to improve. Intolerance of intolerance will continue to trickle down from the workplace and schools back into society as a whole. With more opportunity comes less frustration. There were 36 race riots in the 1960s and 1970s, 2 in the 1980s and 1990s.

The Opportunity

The workplace is integrated. The rest of the America is not. Researchers say the average white person lives in a neighborhood that is 80 percent white, down from 85 percent in 1990, but still relatively homogeneous. That means the new workplace is a different place from where all of us grew up, and from where most of us still live. So we need help understanding it and fully realizing its potential.

There's a huge business opportunity helping to create that understanding. ProGroup in Minneapolis produces calendars providing information on religious holidays. Sales almost doubled in 2001 to 200,000. Catalyst consults with companies on diversity programs. Work/Family Directions develops diversity training kits for the children of Xerox employees.

Paraprofessionals

The Trend

Once upon a time, there were doctors and there were nurses. The doctor and nurse worked together with a secretary in a little office, and they took care of everything that came through the door, from a stubbed toe to schizophrenia.

Now, that little office has become a city-block-sized group practice with dozens of physicians. The badges of the people who work there read not only *doctor* or *nurse,* but also *nurse practitioner, licensed practical nurse, nurse's aide, physicians' assistant, emergency medical technician, x-ray technician, pharmacist,* and *pharmacy aide.*

Similarly, there are now lawyers and paralegals, accountants and tax preparers, engineers and engineering technicians, advertising creatives and account planners. For almost every profession, there is now a shadow or paraprofession.

Factors and Factoids

The paralegal career emerged in the late 1960s and early 1970s. By 1998, there were 136,000 paralegals, four times as many as in 1980. Only computer-related occupations grew faster over the time period. By 2008, that number will almost double, growing at almost four times the growth rate of lawyers. That's not all. There were 237 physicians' assistants practicing in 1990 and 31,000 in 1998. That number is expected to double in the next 5 years.

What's behind the paraboom? The fundamental driver is the growth in services. Professional services have moved from luxury goods to mass-market products, the same revolution that the automobile industry underwent a century ago. And the production process for a high-volume product is very different from the process to make a low-volume product. For example, the first cars and motorcycles were made in a workshop. (There were literally hundreds of automotive workshops in the early part of the last century. Even Briggs & Stratton, the lawn mower engine company, made a few cars along the way.) There a master, along with an apprentice or two, turned out a new car or motorcycle every 4 to 6 months. Each vehicle was unique, custom built to order, and expensive.

But as the demand for cars grew, the workshop model didn't make sense anymore. If Henry Ford wanted to make twice as many cars in his workshop, he needed twice as many masters and apprentices, which meant it would take him literally years to double production. So Henry adopted and refined the idea of the assembly line. He broke up a master's massive knowledge base into a thousand small parts, and created a thousand specialized jobs. This way, it was possible for a new worker to learn a job in an afternoon instead of a decade. He could train thousands and thousands of workers, expanding production exponentially. This mass-production approach was more efficient, cheaper, and enabled his company to produce huge volumes of new Fords every year instead of a handful.

We're now doing the same thing with professional services, industrializing them. Instead of asking a nurse trained as a generalist to perform 20 highly specialized tasks, better to carve that specialized knowledge up into 20 discrete parcels and teach each parcel to a single person.

And of course, specialist technicians are a lot cheaper than masters. For example, before paralegals, secretaries and young lawyers often did more routine tasks. But secretaries had to be trained on the job, which was costly and slow. The alternative was to use a new recruit. Younger lawyers are less expensive than older lawyers, but they are still a pretty pricey way to tackle relatively mundane tasks.

(Senior partners at law firms bill $500 per hour and up, and associates $200.) It's a lot more economical to have the young lawyers supervise paralegals who cost only $100 per hour.

Universities and technical schools have begun producing more and more specialized technicians to support professionals. This is great news for professionals. Even the most basic task in a doctor's office requires a highly specialized vocabulary and familiarity with complex, intricate procedures. It even takes training to *understand* a physician. For example, many doctors dictate notes as they do their rounds, notes that must be transcribed correctly to ensure proper patient care and to minimize legal exposure. It's much better to have medical transcriptionists, specialists trained to understand the terminology and shorthand of clinical medicine, type up the notes, rather than to have a speedy typist with no knowledge of the field do it.

Implications

Expect generalists to become extinct, at least in the professional services sector. Increasingly, new workers will specialize not just by industry, but by task (e.g., an oncology nurse). Many of these specialized jobs will be filled by paraprofessionals. Within the next 2 decades, virtually every profession will have a flotilla of paraprofessions floating around it.

The Opportunity

Specialize. Early. That's the standard advice Professor Ben Shapiro of Harvard, now retired, used to give his MBA students. He was right. He still is. In a specialized world, the specialists get secure jobs (well, what passes for secure in this chaotic world), and the generalists live on the vulnerable edge.

What, Me Work?

The Trend

One thing almost everyone seems to agree on is that the American work ethic is sick or dying. Are they right, or is this another one of those perpetual trends (like rudeness) that every generation complains about?

They are right, the famed American work ethic is dead. Or if it's not dead, it's clearly retired, wearing plaid pants and playing golf in Arizona.

Factors and Factoids

Oddly enough, the whole idea that there should be a work ethic is pretty much an American concept. Sometime around the end of the nineteenth century, work and virtue became inextricably linked in our national mind. In 1904, economist Max Weber gave it a name, the "Protestant ethic," which over time became the "Protestant work ethic," and finally just the "work ethic."

And the whole concept of working hard remains pretty much an American quirk today. In the rest of the world, the objective is to work as little as necessary to get by. In the United States, the idea is to make as much as possible within the available work time window. Europeans find it perverse that 25 percent of us don't even use up all our vacation, especially since we only get half as many vacation days as they do in the first place.

Americans work 137 hours a year more than the Japanese, 260 more than the British, and 499 hours a year more than Germans. Over the decade of the 1990s, Americans added 36 hours per year, moving up to around 1,979 hours, and passing the Japanese for the first time. Some of those extra 499 hours come from our miserly approach to holidays. (See Figure 9.1.)

Our extra annual hours are also a function of our commitment to the full work week. In most of the industrialized world, the work-week is well below 40 hours, and work hours are decreasing. For example, France now has an official 35-hour workweek. In contrast, Americans work about 42 hours per week, and that number has been creeping upward pretty steadily since World War II.

On the face of it, there might seem to be an argument that the work ethic is alive and well, not ill and in retirement. But this is one of those cases where the numbers lie. What the aforementioned statistics fail to capture is that work over the last few decades has become decidedly less worky. For example, in 1965, the typical employee took 1 hour per week of personal time (e.g., making phone calls, reading papers, attending birthday celebrations for

Figure 9.1   **U.S. and world's perspective on work.**

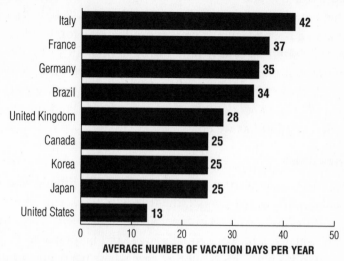

Sources: World Tourism Organization.

fellow workers, giving blood, selling Girl Scout cookies). In 1985, that number had increased to 6 hours per week.

With the Internet and e-mail, the number has probably continued to rise. Taking out all that unauthorized personal time, the average workweek is not really in the forties, but rather down in low thirties. Those quick trips to Sportsline.com may not seem like much, but they add up.

In 1975, in fact, the average worker took 200 hours of personal time per year at work. In 1985, that had grown to 300. If that trend has continued, the number is now 450 hours per year. That means one day a week is devoted just to goofing off. So we spent an extra week a year *at work* in 2000, but we *actually worked* for more than 2 weeks less, for a net decline of 64 hours a year. Even then, 55 percent of us still say we're overworked.

In sum, we just aren't as sure about this work thing as we used to be. We start work later in life than our ancestors (19 years old versus 13), retire earlier (60 versus 66), and do our best to work less in between. Yes, some of us worked 80 hours a week in the dot-com days, but it was only with the understanding that this was a temporary thing, say for 3 years, until we made $20 million and retired to our yachts.

There *is* a little bit of a perpetual trend to this. People have been complaining about declining worker productivity for awhile. Daniel Defoe (of *Robinson Crusoe* fame) wrote a book in 1726 about the decline of work ethic *and* manners called *Insolence and the Insufferable Behavior of Servants in England*. But this time, the decline's for real. We don't work as hard as our parents, and our children won't work as hard as we do.

Implications

Expect the work ethic to continue to weaken. The official workweek may ebb and flow, but overall, the true workweek will continue to shrink. Recession or no recession, expect good talent with a strong commitment to hard work to be scarce, and be prepared to pay a premium to keep it. This is another case where we're going Euro.

The Opportunity

The very old and MBAs. That is, every employer wants to staff his or her business with the most productive and hardest workers around. The older the worker, the more likely that they'll come with a definition of the workweek that calls for more than 40 hours and minimal phone breaks. And MBAs in their first 2 years are notoriously ambitious and hard working. Look for pockets of hard workers like these and find a way to use them.

The Last Job Review

The Trend

The head of the engineering department at the General Foods plant in Kankakee, Illinois, gave me my first formal job review. He called me into his office. "Well, Sam, I'm giving you a raise. But I have to tell you, there are three things about you that I don't like."

Back then, I hadn't yet given up on the idea of self-improvement, so I carefully balanced my pad on my knee and readied myself to write down his important words.

"One, you're too intense and you make everybody nervous," he said. I wrote down, "Too intense."

"Two, you're an arrogant jerk," he said. I didn't write that down. My wife had already brought this to my attention several times in our still young marriage, and she didn't really use the word "jerk," either. She was, eh, even more direct.

"And three, you better find something else to do, because you can do anything in the world once, and nothing in the world twice." I understood perfectly well what he meant. Successful engineers are those who learn how to do repetitive tasks in the easiest and most reliable way, and then have the discipline to stick to their methodology. If I do the same thing 10 times, I do it 10 different ways. On my pad, I wrote down, "Finish application for B-school, ASAP."

True story. Today, I would never be lucky enough to get such a wonderfully frank and useful course correction. Because the honest job review is an endangered species.

Factors and Factoids

In January 1999, Jacques Nasser instituted a new performance review system at Ford. Two and a half years later, Mr. Nasser was pushed out as CEO, at least in part because of his performance review system. He left behind a half-dozen lawsuits, including two class actions, that alleged everything from agism to subjective application to a bias against white males.

What was so wrong with Mr. Nasser's system? His intention was to force managers to stop giving everyone high marks and automatic raises. To do that, his system required every nonunion employee be rated A (top achiever), B (achiever), or C (improvement required). To make sure the system was honest, Nasser said only 90 percent of the 18,000 employees could receive an A or a B, and that those who stayed in the C group for two successive years would be considered for dismissal. But employees who were used to years, even decades, of soft evaluations cried "Foul." And then they called their lawyers.

Ford's certainly not the only company using what's known in the human resources trade as *up or out* or *rank and yank*. Intel, Cisco, McKinsey, Enron, Hewlett-Packard (HP), Microsoft, and Conoco all use forced rankings. In fact, 25 percent of the Fortune 500 uses these types of systems. And a lot of them are getting sued, just like Ford.

There are two problems with forced rankings. One is simply that people don't like to get C's. Instead, people want to work in Lake Woebegone, where everyone is above average. (I wish I'd made that line up, because it's great. But it's a paraphrase of a comment made by Dick Grote to *Fortune* magazine reporter Matt Boyle.) When they do get a bad grade, they don't view it as an honest evaluation of performance, but as an insult. This turned out to be particularly insulting at Ford, where some employees had gone 25 years without ever receiving a tough appraisal.

Nor do supervisors like giving C's. Often, negative appraisals don't improve performance, they just create a disgruntled employee who sulks until next year's appraisal. Smart managers long ago learned an easier way to deal with the hapless and the hopeless: Give that loafer an A on his annual appraisal and pawn him off an another department.

But even if managers would give them and employees would accept them in good spirits, there are still problems with creating a fair and unbiased grading system. On-the-job appraisal systems are very subjective and grading is very difficult. Are there extenuating circumstances? Is it fair for a good person on an excellent team of 10 people to be rated lower than a those on a poor team loaded with duds? Are subtle cultural biases sneaking into the evaluation?

Take this topic of unintentional bias. Management consulting and law firms have long had up-or-out systems. They apply them with great impartiality and careful checks and balances. Still, they have found that males and females with essentially identical performances can receive very different ratings. For example, a male taking time off for family can be credited with *appropriate lifestyle management,* whereas a female can be labeled *not serious about a long-term career.* A male can be called *passionate and intense,* which are good, whereas a woman can be labeled *emotional.* And so on.

The subjectivity does not appear to be conscious on the part of those doing the rating. And such biases, although hard to spot on an individual basis, show up like Day-Glo hotpants under a black light when all promotions and grading are subjected to the scrutiny of statistical programs. When biases do pop out, they create an instant basis for slam-dunk class-action suits.

Even individuals who are fired for cause often demand and receive large severance packages, by threatening legal actions that will require washing the company's dirty laundry in public. (Such severance packages typically involve a gag order on why the individual was terminated, which allows rogues to build entire careers doing what one headhunter friend calls *falling up*.)

Maybe there is a perfectly fair performance appraisal system, but it appears that no one has yet found it. Or at least no one has created one that seems fair to those who lose out.

Implications

Expect to see forced ranking systems to fall out of favor. Anyway, there's a better alternative. It's more expensive in the short term, but cheaper than losing a large class-action suit. It's called *reengineering*.

Sure, reengineering is supposed to be about improving efficiency and workflows. But it also works pretty well to get rid of nonperformers. Just park them in nonjobs, and periodically sweep the nonjobs out with a reengineering study. Admittedly, it's costly. It's also a pretty blunt tool. Lots of pretty good people go out in the flush. Still, it works, and that's why we will continue to see every large company in a perpetual restructuring mode.

The Opportunity

If you have an idea for an appraisal system that is demonstrably fair, truly measures performance, is liked by managers, and can stand up to lawsuit scrutiny, put down this book and get to work. There's a billion dollars out there to the one who gets it right.

The Celebrity CEO

The Trend

In 1999, Carly Fiorina became CEO of HP. Hired to turn around the stumbling giant, she spent her first 6 months making appearances on national TV talk shows, traveling around the world on a Gulfstream IV jet, giving speeches to HP employees, and offering interviews to the local media in each country. She immediately launched a $200 million TV ad campaign that showed her standing in front of the famous garage where HP was born. Welcome to the age of the celebrity CEO, superstars who get superstar billing, superstar contracts, and who endure superstar expectations.

Factors and Factoids

CEOs are the American equivalent of nobility. In 1996, according to *Time* magazine, 7 of the 10 most powerful Americans were CEOs. Originally, the CEO elite was made up of company founders like Andrew Carnegie, J. P. Morgan, Henry Ford, and their modern-day peers—Steve Jobs (Apple), Bill Gates (Microsoft), Larry Ellison (Oracle), Phil Knight (Nike), Michael Dell, Jeff Bezos (Amazon), Andy Grove (Intel), and Herb Kelleher (Southwest Airlines).

However, there's a new breed of CEO celebrity emerging, managers who rose through the ranks, became CEOs, and leveraged their CEO position to create a personal brand that extends beyond the walls of their companies and the Rolodexes of headhunters out to the man or woman on the street. Call them celebrity professional CEOs: Lee Iacocca (Chrysler), Jack Welch (GE), Roger Enrico (Pepsi), Lou Gerstner (IBM), Michael Eisner (Disney), and Phil Condit (Boeing).

What's it like to be a CEO celeb? Pretty good, actually. Every year, *Forbes* magazine does an article on what CEOs make. In the 2000 issue, the top 800 CEOs had a combined compensation of $5.8 billion. That's an average of $7.5 million each per year. In 1999, the average CEO earned 107 times the pay of the average stiff on the factory floor, twice the ratio of a decade ago.

And that's when they're working. These days, even when a celebrity CEO leaves his or her post, they still don't do too badly. Sometimes, in fact, they get paid more to go than to stay. Jill Barad of Mattel had an employment contract for $21 million. When she was fired for making a ruinous acquisition, she left with a package worth $47 million. That included 5 years' salary and bonuses ($26.4 million), forgiveness of a home loan ($3 million), money to pay the income taxes on the forgiven loans ($3.31 million), and her office furniture (technically, she bought the furniture—for $1) Doug Ivestor of Coke walked away with $166 million, about $6 million for each of the 25 years he'd spent with the company. At the end of his first year on the job, Bob Annunziata was paid $16 million to leave Global Crossing.

Of course, Virgin Records recently paid Mariah Carey $49 million not to sing, and several NBA franchises have paid Steve Kerr not to play. So maybe it all makes sense in a loopy celebrity-logic sort of a way.

Why this emergence of the celebrity CEO? Several reasons, most of which derive from the fact that in a modern corporation, there's not really that much a CEO can do as a day-to-day manager. The businesses of a large corporation are so far flung and so complex that few CEOs can master all their details. Even strategic decisions often require a level of understanding that only those deep in the business units possess.

That's why the CEO is surrounded by an inner circle of very highly paid professional managers who worry about the tax status of that electric motor plant in Guangzhou, the details of the latest union contract, or the market's reaction to a spin-off of the plastics division. And that's why Walter Wriston, former celebrity CEO of Citibank, says the CEO's role in the 1990s was redefined from being a manager to being "a cheerleader, a motivator, and a leader." Carly Fiorina takes that one step further, saying, "leadership is a performance."

These days, surveys suggest that 45 percent of a corporation's reputation is driven by the CEO. Bob Crandall, former CEO of American Airlines and a notoriously bottom-line-oriented executive, viewed his celebrity as a tool, "We were trying to transform the image of American. A successful public position is in effect the equivalent of an advertising campaign." Bill Gates spends one-tenth of his time with the media, and flies selected groups of reporters to his private family compound for weekend retreats. For awhile, Andy Grove bylined a newspaper column. Jeff Bezos appears in commercials.

And in a world where the operations of large corporations are so complex that no investor can really understand what's going on inside the company, corporate reputation and CEO charisma are often critical factors in determining the success of a new initial public offering.

Implications

Expect the cult of personality around CEOs to continue. Media coverage of CEOs has risen by 53 percent over the last decade. Why? More people own stock and thus are interested in business, and personal stories are the easiest to understand and have the broadest appeal. (The old newspaper adage says a few people will understand an article about an idea, most people will understand one about an event, but everyone will understand a story about people.)

Expect it to be very hard to keep talented second bananas. The payoff for being the CEO of a major corporation is huge, *huge*. Michael Dell is worth more than Michael Jordan. Phil Knight is worth more than Gladys Knight (and the Pips.) Bill Gates is worth more than Bill Clinton, and possibly worth more than Arkansas. (Lest I offend someone in Little Rock, that was a little joke. In truth, Arkansas is almost three times as large as Microsoft.[2]) The best and the brightest are going to head for the corporate suite, and it's going to be hard to keep them down in the organization when bigger opportunities beckon.

The Opportunity

How can you profit from this trend? Either plan on becoming a CEO or support others' efforts to get to the corner suite.

If you're going for the job yourself, here's a tip: Every up-and-coming young vice president with CEO aspirations should have a personal marketing plan and a marketing team that includes a PR expert and a blue-chip headhunter.

Start out by marketing yourself internally. Be relentless, but subtle. There's a story I was told about former Apple CEO John Scully. According to legend at Pepsi, where he started out, he'd write his board presentations weeks ahead of time. Once every week before the meeting, he'd grab two or three young managers and go through the presentation. He'd probe them on what worked, and ask them questions to make sure they understood his meaning. The next week he'd grab a different group and try again. Not surprisingly, Scully had a reputation as a brilliant presenter, clear, compelling, and ready for every question. If you want to be a CEO, what better segment to market to than the Board? And how better to do it?

And if you're not an up-and-coming young VP, consider all that advice from the other side. Become part of the marketing team. Write the PR plan. Become the indispensable number two.

Of course, there's an even easier way to profit from this trend. Sarah Teslik of the Council of Institutional Investors told the *Wall*

Street Journal to "sell short any company whose CEO appears in *Town & Country.*" She *said* she was joking.

Mercenary Management

The Trend

David Newkirk, senior vice president in charge of strategy for Booz-Allen & Hamilton, explains the explosive growth of the consulting industry by arguing that today's CEOs are in the same situation as barons in the Middle Ages. Those feudal lords couldn't afford to keep a large standing army, but never knew when they might need one. Their solution: a small standing garrison of highly paid, highly competent loyal soldiers supplemented by mercenaries.[3] That's the way modern corporations work, too—a loyal core supplemented by bands of paid mercenaries—individuals and teams of people who resemble the rent-an-army of the Middle Ages, willing to fight on any side of any battle, loyal as long as the checks keep coming.

Factors and Factoids

In 1998, *Fast Company* journalist Daniel Pink wrote a book in which he claimed there were 33 million *free agents* (i.e., self-employed freelancers renting themselves out to corporations and dot-coms starved for talent). Then came the dot-com meltdown and corporate retrenchments, and many of the free agents bolted from their corner offices at the local Starbucks to fill out applications for real jobs. So here's one trend that was all hype, eh?

Not at all. Pink was right on. And free agents are only one type of corporate mercenary. For example, those numbers count free-lancers or individual consultants filling roles that would tradition-ally be handled by a full-time hire, and they capture executives working under specified-term employment contracts. But they don't capture the mercernary armies provided to systems departments by companies like Accenture, Computer Associates, and the Global Services Division of IBM.

Last week I sat in a strategy summit for a major corporation. Ten of the people in the room were employees of the corporation. The other 10 of us were mercenaries. Two were freelance consul-tants, and the rest were members of my firm and a top-three strategy consultancy. I've been on a team of 200 charged with writing the plan for a new business where 80 percent of the team were mercenaries from eight different consulting firms.

There is a set of fundamental factors that mean mercenary management is here to stay. First, of course, is the high variability of the workload in a corporation today. One big acquisition means that there's suddenly a need for 60 people who understand how to integrate systems. In today's lean and mean corporate environment, no one's got 60 good information technology (IT) types sitting in a room playing rummy waiting for an assignment. Instead, call Accenture, Deloitte's, or PricewaterhouseCoopers (PWC), and order an army.

There's also portability of skills. Over the last century, the managerial toolkit has become more standardized. Accountants all use the same systems, MBAs the same frameworks, and programmers the same languages. Gone are the days when companies had their own executive training schools to produce managers with skills tailored to the processes and procedures of one corporation. Now GM hires from Chrysler (Bob Lutz), and Chrysler replaces him with executives from Mercedes and Ford.

And finally, there is a set of managers who are comfortable with being free agents. Free agentry isn't for everyone. When the cutbacks come, mercenaries are often the first to go. The pay's all over the map—sometimes better, and often worse. And there is that little issue of working for people you don't necessarily like very much. Still, mercenaries can live wherever they please and have flexibility in things like setting their work schedule.

Implications

Expect mercenary management to change the role of the line manager. In a mercenary world, inside managers need a whole new set of skills. Instead of supervising employees who plan a career with the company, whom they must both develop and nurture, they supervise a team whose loyalty is to a completely different entity. Managers of mercenaries don't need to be able to explain the company's career path manual, they need to understand the legal enforceability of noncompete clauses in consulting contracts. Managing mercenaries means you don't fix problem workers, you replace them. And finally, those medieval kings may have slept better with a mercenary army in the courtyard, but you can be darn sure they had a trusted soldier keep a discrete eye on all those armed pros all the time. Managing mercenaries means keeping an eagle eye on scope documents, project schedules, and invoices.

Expect the emergence of a whole new set of mercenary office etiquette. When a mercenary gets an e-mail invitation for John's retirement party, does she go? It's going to cost the client $200 an hour for him or her to lick the frosting off his or her fingers. How does a mercenary handle it when the client supervisor slips her resume into his briefcase. Mercenaries fall into an odd never-never world between vendors and employees.

Expect the mercenary management trend to ebb and flow. In the short term, expect the use of the bottom end of the mercenary force, temporary staffers, to flatten out. In 2000, Microsoft lost a lawsuit brought by a group who claimed they were actually Microsoft employees just kept on the payroll of temp agencies to keep wages and benefits down. It turned out that 35 percent of Microsoft's U.S. workforce was in fact *permatemps,* mercenaries not by choice. Involuntary free agency, or forcing people to work just outside the company boundary to keep costs down, may not stand up to political pressure.

But expect the number of higher-end, voluntary mercenaries to continue to grow.

When I was a kid, I was enthralled by reruns of old black-and-white westerns like *Sugarfoot, Cheyenne,* and *Yancey Derringer.* But my favorite was one in which Richard Boone played an urbane gambler who also rented himself out as a gunslinger. His business card read, "Have gun. Will travel. Wire Paladin. San Francisco." We're going to see more and more business cards that say things like: "Know marketing. Will travel. E-mail Lambert. Park City."

The Opportunity

There are opportunities everywhere here. There are, of course, opportunities to be a free-agent mercenary. But before you quit your day job, be sure you have one of those portable (and sustainable) skill sets I spoke about. If your skill set is very specific to a single company, you may do well early, but find business winds down as your knowledge goes out of date. Examples of portable and sustainable skill sets include programming languages, knowledge gained through positions in industry associations, and expertise that is externally focused (e.g., marketing).

There are also opportunities to help connect these modern soldiers of fortune with potential employers. Temporary staffing services have taken a beating in the post-dot-com meltdown, but specialized agencies, like Paladin, which provide hired guns for marketing departments and ad agencies, are still doing well. The Brenner Group rents out dozens of CFOs. And turnaround firms like Jay Alix of Detroit are still providing temporary CEOs to businesses wobbling due to the recession.

There are opportunities to help support mercenaries. Pink talked of the "seven pillars of free agency," pillars like Kinko's. In truth, mercenaries need everything that any small business needs, but configured to be hassle-free and to be compatible with the systems and procedures of their larger, more sophisticated clients. That is, my company is a tiny firm, with only a dozen or so employees, but we need the same graphics software and bibliographic databases that our clients and bigger mercenaries like Accenture use.

Finally, if you're a small business, bite the bullet and hire a professional CFO for the final two weeks before the IPO. You can get a million-dollar name for $3,000 a day. Mercenaries cost money, but then again, they command those prices for a reason.

24/7/365

The Trend

In 1971, Denny Strickland was arrested at 2 A.M. for loitering in the laundromat in Blackshear, Georgia. His excuse was that he couldn't sleep. The mall and stores all closed at 8, the Dairy Queen at 11, and the television stations stopped broadcasting at midnight. Desperate for entertainment, he took a load of clothes (colored) and a box of Tide down to the local laundromat. He put everything in a front-load washer, dropped in a few quarters, and pulled up a chair to watch the clothes slosh around. That's where they found him an hour later, sitting in front of the washing machine holding a handful of quarters, which he would have used up had they not hauled him away.

It may not surprise you to learn that Denny had issues. Specifically, he had a history with the law, mostly relating to possession of illegal hallucinogens. But the issue that got him busted this time was trend-related: He was a man born before his time. Denny was a 24/7 guy in a 9-to-5 world.

The *city that never sleeps* has become the *world that never sleeps*. In 2000, Random House's *Webster's College Dictionary* included 24/7 for the first time, formally recognizing that we have become an around-the-clock society. An estimated 24 million people work at night to keep that clock wound and ticking.

Factors and Factoids

There have always been some people who work outside the 9-to-5 world, but traditionally these were factory shift workers, entertainment industry workers, and emergency services personnel (e.g., police, nurses, and security). But according to Circadian Research, quoted in the *Wall Street Journal,* the number of people who work at night has moved steadily upward over the decades and now includes one in every six workers or so.

The increase in night workers is actually the last in a series of dominoes falling on the road to 24/7/365. The first domino fell when the 9-to-5 workday began to break down. In an interconnected world with company states, more people must occasionally work outside traditional office hours. Nine to 5 in Washington is still 9 to 5 in Singapore, but when it's A.M. in one place, it is P.M. in the other. There's a 1-hour overlapping window of normal business hours between Chicago and Paris, none between LA and London, or Moscow and New York.

Professionals and managers increasingly find that the end of the day isn't a crisp, clean line drawn at 5 P.M., but a fuzzy one, depending on the burning issues of the moment. For example, cell phones have turned the evening commute time into meeting time, effectively extending the workday. And just staying in touch with European colleagues means that someone's going to have to take the occasional 10 P.M. or 7 A.M. call, either at this end or the other.

The second domino in the 24/7 story is the increase in extended retailing hours. Fifty years ago, when everyone left work at 5, the post office, bank, and grocery store could all close at 5 or 6, and perhaps 8 P.M. 1 day a week. But now many stores are open until at least 9 P.M. and on both weekend days. Some are even open around the clock, like groceries and pharmacies, convenience stores, restaurants, casinos, and even hardware stores. And this has set off a chain reaction. Consumers now expect to be able to transact business at any hour of the night or day. And this expectation of 24/7 creates its own momentum.

The third domino is technology, which has made 24/7 easy to do. From good lighting to climate control to keycard entry to secure buildings to call forwarding and remote access to computer systems to cable TV, it's simply technically easier to operate a 16-, 17-, or even 24-hour day than it has ever been before.

Which has caused the fourth domino to topple—the rise in workers of the night. Someone has to answer the phone at Citibank, manipulate the register at Walgreen's, hand over the copier key at Kinko's, and get down sheets of plywood at Home Depot. And those workers don't just work an occasional late night, but start their workday when the rest of us are winding down. And part of the reason they're willing to do these jobs goes back to the technology factor mentioned in the preceding paragraph. For example, technology has also made working off hours less onerous. A VCR means that night workers aren't stuck watching *Scooby Doo* reruns and soaps all day. Last night's *Law and Order* is just a button push away.

Implications

Expect economics and technology to continue to push us to a round-the-clock society. It's simply more efficient to spread the use of infrastructure, be it factories or interstates, over as many hours as possible. And it makes a lot more sense to work on that interstate at 3 A.M. than 3 P.M. Also expect to see more night service workers, as consumers come to expect 24-hour availability for virtually everything. There are some professions that are naturally suited to operating outside the 9-to-5 window—executive recruitment, home maintenance, telemarketing, routine medical care—and sooner or later, that's when they'll be.

Expect to see the coming of the standard 12-hour day for white-collar workers. This doesn't mean that every professional will work 12 hours each day, just that offices will standardize around 7 to 7, and within that frame allow some degree of flexible working hours. There are some obvious benefits.

First, it provides a much larger window of overlap for companies with offices in multiple time zones, which increasingly is all of them. Second, it is a nifty compromise that allows employers to roll back flextime and remote working, both of which took hold in the talent-strapped 1990s, without looking like jerks. "Back to the office, Bill, but let's set a schedule we both can live with," sounds better than, "Be sure to punch in no later than 9:05."

Expect also a continued move to 24/7/365, especially as we increase our flexibility around religions. And finally, expect the Midwestern early dinner to die out, to be replaced by a more European go-home-and-nap-and-then-go-out regimen.

The Opportunity

Anything that day workers need, night workers need. The most glaring and hottest opportunity is day care. In 1993, Ford built a 24-hour center for the children of its night-shift workers. In 2001, it opened the first of 13 more. The new center has five applications for every opening. Hospitals are adding 24-hour day care to attract nurses. Casinos are building them to lower employee absenteeism. In Florida, the number of off-hour child care centers is growing at 7 percent a year and is now more than 1,500.

But no matter what your business, customers expect to be able to transact business any time. That means you should think about extending your hours or finding an after-hours partner to cater to all those night owls out there. Travel agents now sign up with national service bureaus so if their customers get stuck in Dallas-Ft. Worth at midnight, they can get help with flights.

Retooling

The Trend

Joan Marroso of Flint, Michigan, tells the story of agonizing over whether to resume her studies once her youngest started school. She asked her mother-in-law for advice.

"Pete and the kids are all in favor of it, but Mom, I'll be forty when I get out of school," Joan said.

"And how old will you be in four years if you don't go back to school?" her mom asked.

Joan returned to school, got her law degree, and recently retired after a distinguished career as a family court judge.

Products aren't the only things that become outdated way too fast. Extraordinary changes to our economy have resulted in huge groups of midlife workers with the wrong skill set. So they're now retooling themselves.

Factors and Factoids

In all, one in three Americans over the age of 50, approximately 23 million, were engaged in some sort of adult education last year. That's twice as many as were involved a decade ago. Fifteen percent of college students are now more than 40 years old. One hundred thousand MBAs graduate each year, many who are adults retooling from careers as engineers and credit analysts to careers as management consultants and investment bankers.

One reason adults are retooling in such numbers is that their existing jobs end, for instance, because it's one of those jobs designed to end at a certain point. For example, there aren't many job openings for 40-year-old football or baseball players, or infantry soldiers. These people reach a point where they are no longer physically able to meet the requirements of the job.

More common, of course, is retooling as a response to retrenchment. In the first quarter of 1989, around 10,000 people had their jobs eliminated. In the first quarter of 2001, that number was around 410,000. Often, for those who have been retrenched, simply finding the same job somewhere else is not an option. For example, the number of bookkeepers is falling while the number of data entry clerks is climbing. What's happening is that automated bookkeeping systems fed by data entry clerks are replacing bookkeepers. Bookkeepers must be retooled to work in the new environment.

But not everyone is retooling or else. A piece of this trend is about people who are finally doing what they've always wanted to do. Finally, they reach a point in life when they can afford to do whatever it is. For example, there are 153 nuns in Sister Moms, an organization for nuns who have joined orders after having raised, and often are still raising, children. Some even have grandchildren.

Some people even retool for retirement. There are 272 Institutes for Learning in Retirement. Perpetual Learning and Teaching Organization (PLATO) was founded by UCLA 20 years ago; 56 percent of its 375 students already have masters and doctorates.

What do people retool to become? Everything. MDs become high school English teachers. Geologists become website designers. Tool and die makers learn computer programming. Some retool several times throughout their life, like my former colleague, Dave, who has degrees and short careers in medicine, management consulting, and law. (At 40, he's now decided to become a playwright.)

Implications

Expect to see more and more resumes with a Grand Canyon–sized split right down the middle: managers from GM with 20 years' experience applying for entry-level positions as quality control consultants.

Expect the death of early retirement. Instead, you'll see more and more tiered careers. The first 20 years will be spent on a high-paying, high-pressure tier like law; the second in a very structured but less remunerative job like teaching; and a final stint in a very low-paying, flexible, and low-pressure job like the starter at the local golf course.

Expect to see more and more diversity at schools and universities. That guy with the gray hair may be the professor, or just some freshman lost on the way to the student center.

The Opportunity

There are huge opportunities to provide the education and training required to retool. University of Phoenix, a for-profit university designed for working adults, now has 84,000 students. (You have to be over 23 to apply.) Both start-ups and established learning factories are rushing to get into the distance or e-learning business. In 1999, 15 percent of colleges offered accredited degrees through on-line courses. Last year, that had climbed to 34 percent. The list includes Stanford, Duke, and Seton Hall. Jones International in Englewood, Colorado, is fully accredited and only offers courses on-line.

There's another opportunity as well. Thirty percent of new students in on-line universities drop out. Other studies of retoolers at community colleges have found an even higher rate. The reasons? There are many, but one is that some of those who would profit most from retooling do not have the home support and transportation infrastructure to enable them to go to classes and to study. The opportunity? Day care centers next to evening MBA programs or places where people taking on-line courses can come, drop off their kids, sit down at a computer with high-speed access, and do their studies.

In a Land Far, Far Away

The Trend

Phil's office is in Chicago. His house, wife, and collection of antique racing cars is in Maine. It's called *extreme teleworking*, living hundreds or even thousands of miles from where the office is.

Factors and Factoids

First of all, let's draw a clean line between telecommuting and extreme teleworking. *Telecommuting* was a 1990s fad fueled by the confluence of a number of short- and long-term phenomena: shortage of talent, well-intended efforts to keep women in the workforce during their childbearing years, the declining cost of electronic interconnectedness, and increasing commute times that result from suburban sprawl. At its peak, an estimated 16.5 million people worked at home at least 1 day per month. That's 12 percent of the workforce.

But working at home is a mixed blessing. That dining room table stacked with unfinished work detracts from home as a place of rest and refuge. Telecommuting can easily turn a home into the virtual sweatshop, where there is no end to the workday.

Not only that, but it's often inefficient. There are constant interruptions. It's easy to tell when my client Alan is working from home. Every few minutes he covers the speaker with his hand and stage whispers, "Not now, Emmy, Daddy is working. Go see if Mommy can take you potty." Few home offices are as well equipped as real ones. And even e-mail, as wonderful as it is, is no substitute for wandering down the hall and catching up.

All things being equal, employers prefer employees where they can see them. With the current glut of talent, those willing to live near where they work and come in every day will have a clear advantage over those who won't. It may take a while for baby-boomer, X, and Y generations to get the message, but we've seen the peak of the telecommuting fad.

Extreme teleworking, however, is something else altogether. We've always had a few extreme teleworkers. But they were very few and limited to professions that are by their very nature solitary. Ernest Hemingway could work in Key West and Ketchum, and Zane Grey did much of his writing at night while spending his days fishing off the Bay of Islands in New Zealand. For them, distance made their work easier. Most professions don't need isolation and perfect quiet, they require constant communication with other people. So, traditionally, people lived where they worked. Even the great tycoons and robber barons at the turn of the twentieth century went into the office every day.

Now though, a whole raft of people has adopted extreme tele-working. We've already met Phil from Maine, who's a management consultant. His argument is that even when he lived in Chicago, he never spent more than 1 day a week in the office. Instead, he was always out with the clients. Now the office in Chicago is just one more stop on the weekly circuit. My agent lives at the very tip of Long Island and goes into the city once or twice a month. My writing coach lives out on Cape Cod, and I haven't seen her face-to-face for at least 5 years. Gene lives in Lake Forest, Illinois, and runs a company whose office is smack-dab in the center of midtown Manhattan. Steve sits in Houston developing software for his company in Kansas City. Alan, a star radio deejay in Boise, lives in San Diego and has never been to Boise. None of these people have solitary occupations. Far from it, each of them spends a major portion of the day working with other people.

We are seeing the rise of extreme suburbs full of extreme tele-workers. San Diego is the unofficial capital of the motivational speaking industry. Dozens of professional speakers live there, commuting to sales meetings around the world during the spring and fall seasons. Tiny Park City, Utah, has a thriving community of traditional extreme teleworkers—artists, writers, and actors, along with a set of the new breed of long-distance workers, management consultants like George and Alex, mutual fund managers, venture capitalists, and investment bankers.

The key enabler here is interconnectedness. Park City is completely interconnected. Alex can make two conference calls to New York, head out for the slopes at midmorning, and be back in time to work the phones in the afternoon. He can receive huge, complex reports over his high-speed DSL line, edit them, and shoot them back to his teams in Washington and Auckland. If he does need to do some face time, there's a major airport less than an hour away. Still, he's thinking about buying a new videoconference system for $12,000, the cost of a half-dozen airline tickets.

Implications

Expect to see those who can get by with it move to an extreme teleworking model. Perfect candidates for teleworking are those who work on projects, who commit less than all of their time to a single project, and who have a long track record with the company hiring them. The typical path for an extreme teleworker will be to start their career in an urban center, building contacts, a client base, and a specialized base of expertise, and then migrate to extreme teleworking over time. Cities like San Diego and Park City that offer exceptional lifestyles and great interconnectedness will be extreme teleworking hubs.

The Opportunity

Extreme teleworkers depend on interconnectedness, so anything that makes interconnectedness smoother is a big winner. Oh, and here's another opportunity: tax accounting services. States are just beginning to pick up on this extreme teleworking thing and the implications for tax leakage. And teletaxes are coming. Stewart, who lives in upstate New York but works for clients in Florida, Texas, and Arizona, filled out four state income tax forms last year.

* * * *

And ta da—that's it. Sixty trends in 60 minutes. New let's talk about how to use them.

Trendblasting

Ready to go trendblasting? You may feel blasted already. (Take a look at the bibliography. I think you'll be impressed at all the ground you've covered in the last 60 minutes.) Still, so far, all we've done is prep work. Now the fun starts. Let's regroup for a moment and put everything in context.

The Trend Analysis Methodology

When I study a trend, I always ask myself four basic questions:

1. What is really changing here?
2. Why is it happening? Is it just a fad that will come and go, or is something more fundamental going on?
3. How and when might it play out?
4. What sort of opportunities will arise if it does?

I have a specific methodology to try to get at each question. To answer "What's changing," I observe very carefully and systematically. To answer "Why," I study the trend in depth and from a number of perspectives. To answer "How and when," I extrapolate, projecting the trend and its impacts into the medium term, for instance, 3 to 5 years. And to answer "What opportunities," I create, combining several trends and all I've observed about similar changes in other industries or arenas have played out.

You've probably noticed by now that the discussion of every trend in this book is structured exactly the same way. That's a direct result of the process I just laid out. It's not just the way I write about trends, it's the way I think about them.

If you're a more intuitive type, here's a mnemonic device to keep the process straight. Create a mental image of a toolbox. In that box are four scopes: a periscope to observe what's changing, a microscope to study why, a telescope to extrapolate how and when, and a kaleidoscope to create opportunities. When you spot a trend that you think deserves closer analysis, it's time to reach for your toolbox.

Perhaps this is one of those analogies that's clearer to the writer than the reader, so let me try to sum it up:

QUESTION	METHODOLOGY	OUTPUTS	TOOLBOX
What's changing?	Observe	Trend	Periscope
Why?	Study	Factors and factoids	Microscope
How and when?	Extrapolate	Implications	Telescope
What's the opportunity?	Create	Opportunity	Kaleidoscope

I have found that the best way to answer the first two questions is to work alone or with a small, focused team. Typically, that takes weeks, even months, as the team talks to experts, digs up facts, analyzes data, and reformulates the trends. Answering the last two questions is a much faster process. I've found the best way is working with my colleagues in a short, sharp, focused interactive session. I call those sessions *trendblasting workshops*.

The Trendblasting Workshop

Creating opportunities from trends is like a nuclear reaction: you need a critical mass of the right materials. Here's the trendblasting equation:

$$O = (T * B)/t$$

O stands for opportunity, T for trends, and B for brains. The t stands for time. To create the explosion we're looking for, we need

30 trends and a dozen or two good brains, and we're going to compress all of that together into a few short hours. With luck, we'll get a big bang at the end.

A trendblasting workshop is a half-day or full-day conference where a team of people come together to create business opportunities from trends. It is a disciplined and structured process with three discrete activities: (1) brisk presentation of a large number of trends as thought starters, (2) breakout sessions with smaller subgroups focused on a few of the more relevant trends and tasked with specific deliverables, and (3) a free-ranging discussion among the larger group to test and refine the results from the small groups.

Getting Started

To conduct a trendblasting workshop, you'll need four things: (1) a suitable place, a team of smart people, a trends basebook, and a workshop facilitator. (Oh, and you should probably bring some toys to scatter around on the table: LEGOs, Play-Doh, Nerf balls, Slinkies, and stuff like that. If you bring *simple* toys, you'll find people less likely to stand up and pace, or play computer games, or do other things that take them physically or mentally out of the team dynamic.)

I've done workshops in big rooms and small rooms, with breakout rooms and without, off-site and on. Here are my preferences: one big, big room off-site. I say "big, big" because you're going to want to break the group into smaller teams and task them, and they're going to need some private team space to do that. But I think a corner of a big room works just as well as a breakout room. There's something that just feels right about having five teams of five people each working around a flip chart, but doing it all in the same room so everyone can see each other and peek at the other team's thoughts.

Having said that, I don't think one room versus several breakout rooms is a big deal. I do think on-site versus off-site is. You just never get the same quality of thought or focus inside corporate walls as outside. Take your team away and lock them up. If you can get away with it, confiscate their cell phones and pagers (but promise them lots of phone breaks so they don't go into voice-mail withdrawal).

Whom should you invite? My best experiences have come with 15 to 30 people. Much smaller and it's hard to form teams. Much larger and not enough people get airtime. When you prepare the invite list, go for two qualities: (1) diversity and (2) smarts. By diversity, I don't mean sexual or ethnic diversity. Instead, I mean *professional* diversity—people from different functions within the organization, from different businesses and units, and ideally from different geographies.

The more diversity you have, the greater the breadth of the resident knowledge, and the more likely you are not to get stuck by an unanticipated question like "Is the chronosynclastic infundibulum market really growing?" If the group is broad enough, *somebody* will know. I even like to go outside the organization and invite two or three (absolutely no more) from the ad agency, the company consultant, or a distributor.

Do prepare a trends basebook ahead of time. Have a team invest some weeks compiling a list of trends, digging on those first two questions and pulling things together in a coherent, interesting form. The better the prep, the better the day. One question I often get is "Should we circulate the basebooks ahead of time?" My answer is usually yes. It doesn't save any time to send them early—you still have to cover the material in real time because not everyone will have prepped. It's just more courteous to those participants who do like to prepare.

And finally, get a facilitator and an aide. A good facilitator will keep things moving, make sure everyone stays involved, and pull stuff together at the end. An aide can take messages, and sort out coffee, new projector bulbs, and all the other logistical details. Both will free you and your managers up to think.

Running the Workshop

Here's a typical agenda for a trendblasting workshop:

8:30 to 9:00	Introduction
9:00 to 9:30	Trendblast
9:30 to 10:30	Breakout working session: implications
10:30 to 11:00	Telephones, coffee, whatever break

11:00 to 12:00	Report back by teams
12:00 to 1:00	Lunch, more phone time
1:00 to 2:00	Group discussion: most interesting implications
2:00 to 3:00	Breakout working session: opportunities
3:30 to 4:00	Telephones, brownies, Klondike bars, coffee break
4:00 to 5:00	Report back by teams
5:00 to 5:30	Wrap-up/tasking

You'll see that I planned a 9-hour day, but with a generous 2 hours devoted to breaks. It's your call, but I find 9 hours is the absolute max a group can take. I also find that when the scheduled breaks are too short, people start self-scheduling, and by midafternoon someone ends up running around like a border collie on shearing day, trying to round up the team. And even in a group of smart people, there's always somebody that doesn't realize that just because checkout time is officially 11 A.M., that doesn't mean they have to leave the meeting and check out at 11 on the dot. Might as well give them a scheduled break. Anyway, I think break time is not really time wasted. People still mull over the issues as they sip their coffee.

Here's how each of the major sessions work. The trendblast is a quick survey of between 20 and 30 relevant trends. Here's a hint: Stick to 90 seconds or less per trend. This is called a *trendblast,* not a *trendplod.* You'll probably find 90 seconds per trend pretty hard to do. After all that hard prep work, the temptation to take 10 minutes to present each trend is almost impossible to resist.

So don't try. Give someone a stopwatch and have them time the presenter. If you stick to between 60 and 90 seconds, the presenter will find all he or she has time to do is tell the group what the trend is and what's behind it, and give a factoid or two for illustration. And that's all you want. Believe me. I've almost killed workshops by presenting page after page of dense analysis. You handpicked a room of smart people. They'll get it.

After you're done with the blast, tell each team to pick two and go discuss them. In an hour they need to come back with two pieces of flipchart paper, one for each trend they picked. For each, have them discuss why they picked it, who it will affect, and how it might play out. Someone from each team will present the two pages to the group. After everyone has presented, take an hour for group discussion to decide which two or three trends are the most important. There are lots of ways to do this, from acclamation to walking around the room and voting. I don't think it matters as long as you come out with a couple of winners.

For the next breakout, assign each group a trend. Ideally, every trend will be assigned twice. (Nothing like a little subtle competition to keep everyone's juices flowing.) Their task this time is to talk about opportunities—what the opportunity is, who would buy it, what it will take to realize it, and *what we still need to know before we could write and pitch a business plan to a venture capitalist.* The mental image of standing up and asking for money seems to bring people down from the stratosphere to the realm of the real pretty quickly.

At the end of the day, take a few minutes to thank everyone, summarize the key points, and agree on next steps. Don't leave the room without a list of who's doing what by when!

That's it. There are almost endless variations on the day (e.g., making it a half-day session). It seems like I've tried most of them, and I keep coming back to the agenda I laid out at the beginning of this section. (If you do something else and it really works well, drop me an e-mail.)

There Are Two Sides to Every Story . . . and to Every Opportunity

Well, that's how to do a trendblasting workshop in detail—too much detail, probably. If it's not, maybe I'll put up a place on my website where people can learn more and exchange ideas.

But before we get out of this chapter, I want to tell a story about a truck, a 1994 Dodge Ram to be exact. Here's the background. By the early 1990s, pickup trucks were moving toward a more carlike ride and smooth-sided, subtle carlike styling. Every pickup, no matter who made it, looked exactly alike. Two players, Ford and Chevrolet, held most of the full-sized pickup truck market. Dodge Ram, made by the Chrysler Corporation, had less than 7 percent of the market.

Determined to claw their way back into a major position, Dodge executives told designer Trevor Creed to create a truck that didn't look like anyone else's, that is, a design that consumers would notice. He took them at their word. The 1994 Dodge Ram featured bulging fenders and an in-your-face grill, a design that some said looked more like a miniature semi than a pickup truck, and one that Minneapolis auto writer John Gilbert called *bizarre* and a *monstrosity.* (And he *liked* the new truck.)

When Dodge tested the new design with consumers, as the story goes, the result was startling: Eighty percent of consumers absolutely hated the 1994 Ram, and 20 percent absolutely loved it. Dodge executives were fascinated. They were used to traditional designs that provoked narrow preferences and less extreme emotions. The new design seemed to leave no one in the undecided box. But these unusual results forced a major marketing decision: Could Dodge afford to launch a new design that 80 percent of the market would never even consider buying?

But then again, Ram market share in 1993 was only 7 percent. If only the new Ram could tap into that 20 percent who loved the new design, then maybe it was worth the gamble. Chrysler President Bob Lutz, now over at GM turning things upside down, gave the thumbs up. The strategy was a runaway success. Ram sales immediately shot up from 70,000 vehicles in 1993, the year before the introduction, to 200,000 in 1994. The new design took North American Truck of the Year honors. The following year, the truck sold more than 250,000 vehicles and market share topped 15 percent. In 1998, Dodge sold almost 400,000 full-sized pickup trucks, its highest level ever.

Here's the moral of the story. There are two sides to every opportunity: There was an opportunity making trucks that looked like cars, and there was an opportunity making trucks that looked like trucks. To paraphrase Clyde Fessler of Harley-Davidson, "If the competition goes right, you can always go left." As you analyze trends and discuss them in your workshops, always be on the alert for the *other* opportunity. There's always one there, and as often as not, it's not getting nearly as much attention as the obvious one.

CHAPTER 11

Final Thoughts

My editor says that I need to make sure readers walk away from this book with my vision. In a way, I think that's cheating. I mean, I thought my job was to write the book, and your job was to read the book and discern the vision. Division of labor and all that. But I've now learned when to argue with editors, and when to wave the white flag. This time I can tell from the steely glint in her eyes and the twitching muscle in her jaw that's she's serious, so I better get to work.

When you stand nose to canvas against a Georges Seurat painting in the Art Institute, all you see are dots, little dabs of paint. But as you step back, forms start to emerge, and eventually an entire scene of a park on a Sunday afternoon appears. As you have read this book, I hope the same thing has occurred. Standing close you saw a lot of factoids, but as you stepped back, you saw trends; as you stepped back even further, you began to see a larger scene of trends interacting and playing off one another on a huge canvas.

And that's my vision, one of a world with many important trends and countertrends, interacting in complex ways to create opportunities and threats in numerous, and often unexpected, ways. For marketers, the broader business community, and individuals, it is critical to not just see one little piece of the canvas, but the whole panorama. That is, it's important to know about the Age Wave, and it's important to know about the information revolution, but it's more important to know how the Age Wave interacts with the information revolution and all the other things that are going on in the world today. From that broader and deeper understanding comes opportunity.

Or said more simply, life is like a surfing contest. (I can't help thinking of Forrest Gump as I write that line.) The way a surfing contest works is this. Two surfers paddle out together for a set amount of time. During that time, they can ride as many waves as they wish. Each ride is scored by judges. The surfer who scores more points moves on in the tournament, while the other is finished.

The winner is not always the best surfer, but usually the surfer who that day picks the best waves. Wave picking is largely skill and a little bit good fortune. Sometimes a great rider will make one of the three cardinal mistakes of wave picking: (1) missing a good wave, (2) picking a wave that he or she doesn't have the skills or equipment to ride, or even worse, (3) picking a wave that doesn't go anywhere but down (what surfers call a dumper, which is pretty self-explanatory). Meanwhile, a less accomplished surfer 100 yards away will paddle onto something that doesn't look like much, but turns into a perfect pipe. He or she is the surfer who takes home the big trophy.

In business and life, just like in surfing, no matter how good you are, very little happens if there's no wave to carry you along. To succeed, you need to pick a wave. But not just any wave. Some waves are dumpers, some have already passed, and some won't be right for you. You need to know which wave to climb on, and which ones to let pass by.

This is a very simple metaphor, and it makes it seem a little too easy. The truth is that in real life it's even harder to tell when and how waves are going to break. And it's getting harder. Every day there are more waves, coming from more directions, crashing into each other, and creating more chop and foam. There's also at least one more big difference between surfing contests and life: A surfer can always decide that he or she doesn't like any of the waves, just paddle in, and come back next week. We can't.

As individuals, we must decide where to live, what career to build, what to wear, how to look, where to go to school. As businesses, we must decide on which markets, which technologies, and which business models. And as marketers, we must decide on which segments, which positionings, and which media. [Once, at DMB&B, someone did a calculation and decided that a $50 million fall ad budget could theoretically be spent in a quadrillion different ways (e.g., broadcast versus cable, primetime versus dayparts).]

The key to making the right decisions will be to make them based not on things as they are, but as they will be. That is, by understanding the broader picture of trends and the world they are shaping, we can make decisions ahead of the curve rather than behind it. That is, you *can* pick the right wave. I hope that this book will give you both the tools and the inventory of trends to create a perspective that reflects the specifics of your business, your markets, and your life.

Now go hang ten.

Andrew Jaffee and the good folks at Wiley have been after me for years to do a project together, but due to one circumstance or another, it's just never worked out. Finally, last summer, Andrew called just as I was finishing a 2-year grind producing *Infinite Asset*.

This time, he suggested a book based on an article on trends that I'd done for *Fortune Small Business*. I wasn't really ready to start a new project, but Andrew and my agent managed to convince me that this would be an easy book: 200 pages, wide margins, no new research, just write down what was already in my head. And shoot, the article was already written. How hard could it be?

Now I know why my wife glares at me when I describe our son's birth as *easy*. There is no such thing as an easy birth, easily passing a kidney stone, or an easy book. My little 200-page book with no new research turned into a much longer one that involved months of digging, writing, and rewriting. If anything, this book was *harder* because everything had to be rewritten over and over to pack all that content in without making it unreadable.

If I ever use the words *easy* and *book writing* in the same sentence, I hope someone smacks me upside the head with a brick.

Nonetheless, this was easier than it might have been due to the kindness and help of several people. Kirsten Sandberg at HBSP, which held the option on my next work, graciously gave me permission to work with Wiley. Thanks to Hank Gilman and Josh Hyatt of FSB for working with me on the original article, and to Josh for helping me structure the original outline for this book. Josh and I were going to write this together, but we couldn't get our schedules aligned. He's a great writer, and it would have been a much better book if he'd been able to take it on.

The fact that it turned out as well as it did is in large part due to the efforts of my long-time editor and writing coach Regina Fazio Maruca, who helped clean up my passive sentences and florid prose. The book also profited greatly from the careful editing and suggestions of my team at Wiley: Airié Dekidjiev, Emily Conway, and Jessie Noyes. Thanks also to the marketing team at Wiley, especially Michelle Patterson for her enthusiasm and hard work. (Was it seven covers or eight?) And, of course, to Tom Laughman and North Market Street Graphics.

Special thanks to Brian Fischer for reading and correcting the technology section, and to Steve Silver, who did a similar task on the "Death of Demographics" trend, and to Liz Upsall, who was the first to read and comment on the completed draft.

Creating this book involved months of research. Most of that was done by myself and Rachel E. Hill. Rachel is brilliant, diligent, hard-working, discerning, and funny. (She's also my daughter, and it was a wonderful treat to work together on this.) When both Rachel and I were completely stumped, we turned to a pro, Bill Loughner of the University of Georgia. In 25 years, I have yet to come up with a question he can't answer.

Also contributing to the research were my team here at Helios: Carolyn Yoch, Rebecca Clement, Margaret Russell, Donna Donovan, and Jacqui Levine, as well as the reference desk at the Winnetka Library: Juli Janovicz, Dorothy Szczepaniak, Jill Brasseur, and Raymond Kearney.

The Dodge Ram case study is based on a write-up by Mark Heber of Dodge, provided to me with the permission of Jim Schroer.

Thanks to my clients, especially Christopher Ainsley and Bill Patzarian, for their patience during the final 4 months when I was working on their businesses by day, and writing furiously to meet my deadlines by night. Except for a few comments by Christopher about me being a bit punchy, they were remarkably tactful about my bleary eyes and occasional disappearances.

Finally, the charts and exhibits for this book were done by my long-time collaborator, the outstanding graphic artist Randy Johnson.

Chapter 2

1. Arthur Lieberman, quoted in "The Patent King," *Fortune* magazine, 14 May 2001.
2. *Chronosynclastic infundibulum* is a term invented by Kurt Vonnegut.

Chapter 3

1. True story. On June 10, 1848, the *California Star* newspaper ran an editorial deploring the huge exodus of people headed for the goldfield, and the empty towns left behind. Four days later the paper closed, as the entire staff left to become prospectors. That's the thing about fads like gold rushes and internet start-ups, once caught up in them even the most level-headed have trouble thinking straight. The source of this story, www.despair.com, is full of this and similarly intriguing anecdotes, facts and observations. They also publish a great calendar.

Chapter 4

1. In the name of full disclosure, my wife and I have a small investment in this venture. It is not publicly traded.
2. For the other two times, see the "Brandwagon" and the "A la Carte Business Model" trends in Chapter 8.
3. *Kyrgyzstan* is in Central Asia; *Kiribati* is in the mid-Pacific at the intersection of the Equator and the International Date Line; *Myanmar* is in Southeast Asia (formerly known as Burma); *Zebrano* is not a real country

but a type of imitation wood in Cadillac autos; *Azerbaijan* is in Southwest Asia; *Eritrea* is in East Africa; *Tuvalu* is in the Southwest Pacific.

4. Examples the *-stan* states include Uzbekistan, Tajikistan, and Kyrgyzstan.

5. This is not an actual estimate, but is probably conservative, given Nigeria's population, literacy rate, and number of people employed in agriculture.

Chapter 5

1. I promised to avoid footnotes to the extent possible. But the data for this analysis are the work of Michael Cox of the Federal Reserve Bank of Dallas, which each year produces an absolutely fascinating annual report on topics like technology and changes to the workforce.

2. The movement of African-Americans northward in the mid-twentieth century constitutes another major migration, although the numbers of people involved are far smaller.

3. The term *pharma-space* is not to be confused with the software marketed under the name *PharmaSpace*.

4. You have my word of honor that I am not making this up. See "Nanotechnology and Complexity: Consequences for Computing," speech presented at the University of Aston, United Kingdom, January 1996.

5. There actually are several ways to do it, but the way I have described it translates very directly to the formula that mathematicians use: $S = n(n+1)/2$.

6. This estimate and several of the statistics in this trend are from Moore and Simon.

7. In the data, diarrhea is tracked as an infectious disease, not merely a symptom.

8. This is one of those trends that could belong in Chapter 6, "Societal Trends," as well, but because I believe the next step, antiaging, will be technology-driven, I've elected to leave it here.

Chapter 6

1. I apologize for doing that. I needed a way to end that section, and the song seemed like a good idea, but now you'll be stuck humming it for days—just like I am right now. Here are the next few lines, that's the least I can do: "All of them had hair of gold, like their mother, the youngest one in curls."

2. A Harris Poll question, quoted in the *New York Times,* 3 June 2001.

3. However, the proportion of people who can read effectively may be as low as two-thirds, according to some estimates.

4. I really struggled with this title, tempted to honor Johnny Cash by calling the trend "A Country Named Sue." But I was afraid the pun might be

obscure to some readers. Still, the preceding trend in this book is "Instant Polling." In that spirit, log onto our website, www.heliosconsulting.com, and vote for Warren Zevon if you like the current title or Johnny Cash if you don't. If Johnny wins, we'll change the title of this trend when the book goes into paperback.

5. This comparison is from the *Journal of the American Bar Association.* The American Bar Association (ABA) is a *little* touchy on this subject. They point out, quite correctly, that you get very different results if you measure law degrees, admission to the bar, and lawyers without bar qualifications who still practice (illegal in the United States). All of those make the United States look less out of whack with the rest of the world. However, others argue that the U.S. number is even higher than the number I've used, so on balance, I think my number is fair.

Chapter 7

1. Note to the reader: This isn't a typesetting error. I just didn't feel like doing a separate "Implications" section for this one. It felt like I was getting a little mechanical. So I decided to mix it up a bit. Remember, it was Ralph Waldo Emerson who purportedly said, "Foolish consistency is the hobgoblin of little minds."

2. Strictly speaking, plumposity is a trend, not a fad.

3. This is a surprisingly close number to the 61 percent cited earlier, the proportion of Americans that scientists say are overweight for their age and height.

Chapter 8

1. This is a very dated example, but to be honest, most of the successful niche players I've worked with have asked me to keep their successes quiet, for obvious reasons.

2. This is actually a contentious point. American Airlines claims to have saved $1.4 billion from 1989 through 1992 through yield management. For a host of reasons, that assertion should be looked at skeptically. What is not open to question is that profitability of the airline industry has fluctuated wildly during the 1980s and 1990s, and has been below reasonable levels for much of the period.

3. In the spirit of full disclosure, I have spoken on this topic at several SAP forums.

4. Some would argue we're not as selective as we should be. There's some form of gambling in every state, except Utah and Hawaii. Thirty-one states have casinos, and 36 have lotteries. Gambling in the United States is a $30 billion industry, and that doesn't even count day trading.

5. In this section, I'm going to talk about companies buying risk. *Buying risk* means the same thing as *selling risk protection.* I think *buying risk* is less awkward.

Chapter 9

1. When reviewing the tape, it sounded as if Treasurer Robert W. Ulrich had said the *n*-word. One former Texaco insider suggested that had to be wrong, maybe the word was *nigglas.* [sic]. (Of course, there is no such word, and I find this feeble explanation pathetic.) This note is based on an excerpt from the book by former Texaco employees Bari-Ellen Roberts and Jack E. White, quoted in *Time* magazine.

2. Arkansas's Gross State Product in 1999 was $64.8 billion. Microsoft's revenues in 2000 were almost $23 billion.

3. Mercenary knights were called *paladins* in France and *ronin* in Japan.

General

Caplow, Theodore, Louis Hicks, and B. N. Wattenberg. *The First Measured Century*. AEI Press, Washington, DC, 2001.

Central Intelligence Agency. *The World Factbook*. (Accessed through www.cia.gov/publications/factbook.)

Cindric, Susan J. (ed.). *Encyclopedia of Emerging Industries*. Gale Group, Farmington Hills, MI, 2000.

European Communication Council. *E-Conomics, Strategies for the Digital Marketplace*. Springer, 2000.

Encyclopedia Brittanica. 15th Edition, Encyclopedia Brittanica, Inc., Chicago, 2002.

Famighetti, Robert (editorial director). *The World Almanac and Book of Facts 2001*. Primedia Reference, Mahwah, NJ, 2000.

Kane, Joseph Nathan. *Famous First Facts*. H. W. Wilson, New York, 1981.

Moore, Stephen, and Julian L. Simon. *It's Getting Better All the Time—100 Greatest Trends of the Last 100 Years*. Cato Institute, 2000.

U.S. Census Bureau, Statistical Abstract of the United States: 2000 (120th Edition), Washington, DC, 2000.

U.S. Industry and Trade Outlook 2000. U.S. DOC/ITA and McGraw-Hill, New York, 1999.

www.bls.gov.

www.census.gov.

www.mapquest.com.

www.worldbank.org.

Chapter 2: The Trendmeister Hall of Fame

Binkley, Christina. "Hotelier Schrager plans to start chain of 'lifestyle' outlets called 'Shop.' " *Wall Street Journal,* 25 August 2000.

Current Biography: Madonna. H. W. Wilson (WilsonWeb), 1998.

Morrisey, Janet. "Boutique hotel chain avoids the Manhattan blues." *Wall Street Journal,* 4 December 2001.

Prendergast, Mark. *Uncommon Grounds, The History of Coffee and How It Transformed Our World.* Basic Books, New York, 1999.

Regalado, Antonio. "Tiny company wields patents against giants." *Wall Street Journal,* 9 March 2001.

Schultz, Howard, and Dori Jones Yang. *Pour Your Heart into It, How Starbucks Built a Company One Cup at a Time.* Hyperion, New York, 1997.

Varcharver, Nicholas. "The Patent King." *Fortune,* 14 May 2001.

Walker, Rob. "Not Much Room at the Inn." *FSB,* October 2001.

www.Zebra.com.

Wysocki, Bernard, Jr. "Royalty rewards: How patent lawsuits make a quiet engineer rich and controversial—Jerome Lemelson drums up ideas and amends them, the moves to cash in." *Wall Street Journal,* 9 April 1997.

Chapter 3: Fads, Fashion, and History

Davis, Jim. "Apple scraps Newton." *CNET News.com,* 27 February 1998.

Chapter 4: Economic and Geo-Political Trends

Interconnectedness

Abernathy, Frederick H., John T. Dunlop, Janice H. Hammond, and David Weil. "Retailing and supply chains in the Information Age." Harvard Center for Textile and Apparel Research, October 1999.

Cox, W. Michael, and Richard Alm. "Time Well Spent—The Declining Real Cost of Living in America." *Annual Report of the Federal Reserve Bank of Dallas,* 1997.

Millman, Joel. "Aerospace Suppliers Gravitate to Mexico." *Wall Street Journal,* 23 January 2002.

Oxford Atlas of Exploration, Reed International, London, United Kingdom, 1997.

World Air Transport Statistics, IATA, 1998–2001.

www.geographia.com/papua-newguinea.

www.publicpurpose.com/ic-airrailhist (Wendell Cox Consultancy).

Little India Is Coming! Little India Is Coming!

Belzer, S. A. "Ethnic markets, now a click away." *New York Times,* 29 September 1999.

Frank, Robert. "For a Philippine town, monthly allowances pave road to riches." *Wall Street Journal,* 22 May 2001.

Giordano, Tom. "The Expatriate Experience." *Hartford Courant,* 7 September 1998.

Mehta, Monica. "The Imminent Indian Influx." 206.20.14.67/achal/archive/dec98.

Ross, John. "Cross-border Bracero blues." *Latinamerica Press* (*Lima*), 16 July 2001.

Sykes, Debbi. "Indian dance, music in spotlight." *The News & Observer* (*Raleigh*), 1997.

My oh My, Megapoli

Deen, Thalif. "Growth declines, but numbers rise in poor nations." *International Press Service,* 10 April 2001.

Holmberg, Ben. "The world's 200 largest cities." *United Nations Publications,* 14 October 2000.

Statistics Canada.

Barbarians at the Gated Community

Fram, Alan. "Top incomes grew 157% from 1979–1997, CBO reports." *Portsmouth Herald* (*NH*), 31 May 2001.

Francis, David R. "Tax cut widens U.S. income gap." *Christian Science Monitor,* 23 May 2001.

Lardner, James. "What happens to American society when the gap in wealth and income grows larger?" *US News & World Report*, 12 February 2000.

Margolis, Mac. "The bulletproof lifestyle." *Newsweek*, 5 June 2000.

"Numbers." *Time*, 10 July 2000, 17 July 2000.

Peron, Jim. "Crime stoppers." *Reason*, June 1999.

Sheridan, Martha. "Ironclad isolation." *Dallas Morning News*, 20 September 1998.

"Toward a More Equitable World." *Rockefeller Foundation Annual Report*, March 2001.

"World's Richest People 2001." www.forbes.com.

Comrade Adam Smith

Holson, Laura M. "Dirty laundry keeps flying at Calpers." *New York Times*, 27 November 2001.

Houget, George R. "Forces for stabilization." *International Economy*, January/February 2001.

Jacobius, Arlene. "Change in fortune: Good times may be over for 401(k)'s." *Pensions & Investments, Crain*, 30 April 2001.

Smith, Anne Kates. "Roads to riches." *U.S. News & World Report*, 28 June 1999.

"The employee ownership 100." *Business Ethics*, September/October 2000.

Wilkus, Malon. "Employee buyouts of corporations, subsidiaries, divisions or product lines." In *Expanding the Role of ESOPs in Public Companies*. Quorum, Westport, CT, 1990, 1999.

www.nyse.com.

www.socialinvest.org/1997-trends.

The Incredible Growing Government

DeMott, John S. "Privatization puzzlement." *Nation's Business*, September 1995.

Drury, Tracey. "Globalquest Solutions finds growth formula." *Business First of Buffalo*, 6 August 2001.

"Federal contracts going to large businesses." *Business First of Columbus*, 22 June 2001.

Mukherjee, Sougata. "Federal contractors get bigger at small business's expense." *Tampa Bay Business Journal*, 7 March 1997.

www.access.gpo.gov/usbudget/fy2001/guide01.
www.congresslink.org/workloadstats.

Balkanization/Babelization

Anthony, Ted. "The English Explosion." *Albuquerque Journal,* 9 April 2000.

Downie, Andrew. "Brazil considers linguistic barricade." *Christian Science Monitor,* 6 September 2000.

Hotz, Robert Lee. "The struggle to save dying languages." *LA Times,* 25 January 2000.

Johnson, Maureen. "Scotland votes to be 'a nation again'." *San Francisco Examiner,* 12 September 1997.

LaFranchi, Howard. "Will bilingual trend make US 'habla espanol'?" *Christian Science Monitor,* 30 June 1999.

Komarow, Steven. "Some Germans fear language is being infected by English." *USA Today,* 15 May 2001.

Yavuz, M. H., and Michael M. Gunter. "The Kurdish nation." *Current History,* January 2001.

Company States

Alsop, Stewart. "The monopoly has just begun." *Fortune,* 23 July 2001.

Anderson, Sarah, and John Cavanagh. "The rise of global corporate power." *Third World Resurgence.* Penang, Malaysia, September 1998. (*Note:* Authors are with the Institute for Policy Studies in Washington, DC.)

www.undp.org

Chapter 5: Technological Trends

Instant Obsolescence

Akst, Daniel. "The new Stock Market." *The Industry Standard,* 16–23 August 1999.

Barboza, David. "Iridium, bankrupt, is planning a fiery ending for its 88 satellites." *New York Times,* 11 April 2000.

Berry, Lyn. "Recycle, don't throw old computers away." *Denver Business Journal,* 2 March 2001.

Cox and Alm, op cit. See also *Annual Report of the Federal Reserve Bank of Dallas,* 1996.

Henricks, Mark. "Old—But not out: Some timeworn products and services still find a market." *Wall Street Journal,* 19 March 2001.

Morris, Michael. "The technology of tools." *Popular Science,* September 1993.

Naim, Gautum. "Biotech firms bypass journals to make news." *Wall Street Journal,* 28 January 2002.

Porter, M. E. Data taken from a chart in the *MIT Sloan Management Review,* Summer 2001, p. 32.

Romero, Simon. "Once proudly carried, and now mere carrion." *New York Times,* 22 November 2001.

Russell, John. "Tiremakers change patterns of production." *Chicago Tribune,* 12 August 2001.

Tam, Pui-Wing, and Mahvish Khan. "Hand-held makers slash prices and rev up promotions as sales slow." *Wall Street Journal,* 2 August 2001.

Infinite Reach

Alsop, Stewart. "A handful of convergence." *Fortune,* 12 November 2001.

Genzlinger, Neil. "Area codes irking you?" *New York Times,* 28 November 1999.

Harmon, Amy. "E-mail you can't outrun." *New York Times,* 21 September 2000.

Kilgannon, Corey. "Fancy cars and gadgets help keep road rage at bay." *New York Times,* 15 August 2000.

Kirkpatrick, David. "Beyond buzzwords." *Fortune,* 18 March 2002.

Lidsky, David. "Pervasive stupidity: Computers are going to be everywhere, but keep them off me." *FSB,* February 2002.

Miller, Matthew. "Chandra and the chip." *Tribune Media Services,* 16 July 2001.

Miscellaneous reports from IDC and the Gartner Group.

Swarm to Warm

Bodipo-Memba, Alejandro. "Cities: Best place to live? Follow the moving van." *Wall Street Journal,* 23 June 1999.

Crossen, Cynthia. "Braving the elements in battery-heated jackets, antibacterial fabrics." *Wall Street Journal,* 1 March 2002.

"Evolution of Automotive Air Conditioning." *ASHRAE Journal,* September 1999. (Accessed through www.ashraejournal.org/features/archives.)

"Home Sweet Home—America's Housing, 1973 to 1993." Bureau of the Census Statistical Brief (SB/95-18), July 1995.

Patlak, Margie. "Book reopened on infectious diseases." *FDA Consumer,* April 1996.

Pills 'R' Us

"Americans Popping More Pills Than Ever." *Pharmacy Times,* February 2002.

Anand, Geeta, and Thomas Burton. "Lilly, Bayer ready drugs to take on Pfizer's Viagra." *Wall Street Journal,* 24 July 2001.

Attkinson, Sharyl. "Some drugs approved too soon." *CBS Evening News,* 28 February 2000. (Accessed through www.cbsnews.com.)

Binder, Gordon. Keynote address, PhRMA Annual Meeting, 14 April 2000. (Accessed through www.phrma.org.)

Burton, Thomas M. "Reining in drug advertising." *Wall Street Journal,* 13 March 2002.

Hamilton, David P. "A hair-raising battle in Japan—Tonics, creams try to head off Rogaine hoopla." *Wall Street Journal,* 2 August, 1999.

Hitt, Jack. "The second sexual revolution." *New York Times Magazine,* 20 February 2000.

Jenkins, Holman, Jr. "Onward and upward with self-medication." *Wall Street Journal,* 23 May 2001.

Lewis, Peter H. "Smart phone invasion. . . ." *Fortune,* 28 May 2001.

Morrow, David J. "A medicine chest or a grocery shelf?" *New York Times,* 12 December 1999.

O'Connell, Vanessa, and Rachel Zimmerman. "Drug pitches resonate with edgy public." *Wall Street Journal* (advertising column).

"R&D Expenditures by Industry Category." www.nsf.gov/sbe/srs/nsf00301/expendit.htm.

Rohzon, Tracie. "The medicine chest pumps up." *New York Times,* 1 February 2001.

Itsy, Bitsy Machines

Drexler, K. Eric. "Molecular engineering: An approach to the development of general capabilities for molecular manipulation." In

Proceedings of the National Academy of Science, September 1981. (Accessed through www.imm.org.)

Fleischman, John. "Researchers build brave new nano world." *Focus: News from Harvard Medical, Dental and Public Health Schools,* 15 September 2000. (Accessed through www.med .harvard.edu.)

"Molecular machines." *MIT Media Lab,* 4 February 2002. (www .media.mit.edu.)

"Nanotechnology and Complexity: Consequences for Computing." University of Aston, January 1996. (This was a talk prepared for gifted teens in the United Kingdom. It's very interesting. You can access it through public.logica.com/~stepneys/complex/nanotalk .htm.)

"Tiny technologies." *Open Door: Ideas and Voices from MIT,* February 2002. (Accessed through alumweb.mit.edu.)

Bionicism

"Abiomed artificial heart's fourth recipient dies." *Boston Business Journal,* 14 December 2001.

Brownlee, Shannon. "Refurbishing the body." *U.S. News & World Report,* 12 November 1990.

Bryant, Meg. "Man and machine." *New Physician,* January/February 1993.

Collins, Sarah. "To cure pets' maladies some spare no expense." *Wall Street Journal,* 1 February 2002.

Dunn, Ashley. "Merging man and machine." *LA Times,* 27 October 1998.

Fackelmann, Kathleen. "Tiny chip might restore vision in blind patients." *USA Today,* 1 August 2001.

Grady, Denise. "A new transplant frontier: Intestines." *New York Times,* 31 October 2000.

Kaufman, Leslie. "And now, a few more words about breasts." *New York Times,* 17 September 2000.

Killborn, Peter T. "Dad, what's a clutch? Well, at one time. . . ." *New York Times,* 28 May 2001.

Nagourney, Eric. "Pacemakers can harbor staph infections." *New York Times,* 4 September 2001.

Shahin, Jim. "Eyes wide cut." *Texas Monthly,* November 1999.

Wald, Matthew L. "High-voltage benefits of improved batteries." *New York Times*, 26 March 1999.

www.sixmilliondollarsite.co.uk.

Yost, Mark. "When cars had style (and muscles)." *Wall Street Journal*, 1 June 2000.

It Ain't Heavy

"Gizmo's and gadgets." *Fortune*, 23 July 2001.

Austen, Ian. "Shrinking the cellular phone." *New York Times*, 31 January 2002.

DeMeis, Rick. "Miniaturization: Not just electronics anymore." *Design News*, 17 April 2000.

Hakim, Danny. "Bush White House starts own high-mileage car program." *New York Times*, 10 January 2002.

Hamilton, Anita. "Toys for techies." *Time*, 10 July 2000.

Jantz, Richard. "Smallest projectors now down to 2 pounds." *PC World*, December 2001.

Phipps, Jennie L. "Videophones answer the call." *Electronic Media*, 5 November 2001.

Pogue, David. "Card-size cameras that (mostly) measure up." *New York Times*, 13 September 2001.

Putman, Peter H. "Is the VCR an endangered species?" *Sound & Video Contractor*, February 2000.

Rabinovitch, Eyal. "Life in the fast lane." *FSB*, February 2002.

Rodie, Janet. "Performance lite." *Textile Industries*, May 2001.

Sherman, Erik. "Time to get the lead out." *Newsweek*, 18 September 2001.

"With the right hardware, even a business trip can feel like an escape." *New York Times*, 15 November 2001.

www.vke.de.

Down in the Data Mine

Adams, Larry. "Data in the palm of your hand." *Quality*, January 2001.

Bransten, Lisa. "Technology: Looking for patterns: Data mining enables companies to better manage the reams of statistics they collect." *Wall Street Journal*, 21 July 1999.

Chopoorian, John A., Robert Witherell, and Omar E. M. Khalil. "Mind your business by mining your data." *Advanced Management Journal,* Spring 2001.

Jason, Leigh. "Apigent keeps fast-food managers in the know." *Wall Street Journal,* 30 August 2001.

Regalado, Antonio, et al. "Emerging technologies that will change. . . ." *Technology Review,* January/February 2001.

Rundle, Rhonda. "In the drive to mine medical data, VHA is the unlikely leader." *Wall Street Journal,* 10 December 2001.

Weber, Thomas E. "The new way to shop: Why marketers covet spots on your key ring." *Wall Street Journal,* 26 February 2001.

Weber, Thomas E. "To find security risks, company sifts data seeking obscure links." *Wall Street Journal,* 14 January 2002.

One Extra Lifetime per Person, Please

Altman, Lawrence K. "For surviving octuplets, progress comes in ounces." *New York Times,* 17 October 1999.

Cimons, Marlene. "Life expectancy has risen in U.S. experts say." *LA Times,* 11 October 2001.

Hunt, Albert. "Fundamental shift in what it means to be a senior." *Wall Street Journal,* 11 March 1999.

Nelson, Roxanne. "Premature babies do better than many doctors believe." *Lycos Health,* 8 May 2000. (Accessed through webmd .lycos.com.)

Ridge, Pamela. "Taking away the keys: Who is to say Dad is too old to drive?" *Wall Street Journal,* 21 June 2001.

Sherrid, Pamela. "Retired? Fine. Now get back to work." *U.S. News & World Report,* 5 June 2000.

Travers, Bridget, and F. L. Freiman (eds.). *Medical Discoveries, Medical Breakthroughs and the People Who Made Them.* U-X-L, Gale, Farmington Hills, MI, 1997.

Valeo, Tom. "The Age Limit." *Chicago Magazine,* August 2000.

Helpless in Seattle

Knestout, Brian P. "Tandy wants to program your VCR for you." *Kiplinger's Personal Finance Magazine,* August 1999.

Macht, Joshua. "An electronic field day. Chicago Auto's use of ALL-DATA CD-Rom program." *Inc Special Technology Issue,* 1995.

Mullen, William. "Techno-phobia." *Florida Times-Union* (*Jacksonville*), 20 May 1990.

Slatalla, Michelle. "Web at your back, wrench in your hand." *New York Times,* 17 May 2001.

White, Joseph B. "Auto mechanics struggle to cope with technology in today's cars." *Wall Street Journal,* 26 July 1988.

Chapter 6: Societal Trends

Polytheism

"Alternative Religions." newage.about.com. Accessed 16 November 2001.

"Dharma down under." *Chicago Tribune,* 22 November 2001.

Hadaway, C. Kirk, and Penny Long Marler. "Did you really go to church this week?" *Christian Century,* 6 May 1998.

Hargrove, Thomas, and Guido H. Stempel, III. "Poll:Religion is regional." *Rocky Mountain News* (*Denver*), 28 September 1997.

Interview with Jim Rome, *American Way,* 15 August, 2001.

Powers, Ann. "Tuning in to the chant master of American Yoga." *New York Times,* 4 June 2000.

Sheler, Jeffery L. "Spiritual America." *U.S. News & World Report,* 4 April 1994.

Shafer, Parker. "It's 50 B.C. all over again." *Report Newsmagazine* (*Edmonton, Canada*), 20 December 1999.

Strand, Clark. "Cyber spirituality." *New Age Journal,* July/August 2000.

"The Empty Church Syndrome." *Psychology Today,* November 1988.

Postnuclear Families

Fields, Robin. "U.S. decline continues for traditional families." *LA Times,* 15 May 2001. (Accessed through www.latimes.com, 7 January 2002.)

Gallagher, Maggie. "Why Murphy Brown is winning." *Wall Street Journal,* 3 June 1996.

Irvine, Martha. "So much for tradition." *Associated Press,* 24 August 2000.

Lewin, Tamar. "Americans attached to traditional roles for sexes, poll finds." *New York Times,* 27 March 1996.

Lombardi, Kate Stone. " 'The Brady Bunch' no more: Families grow less traditional." *New York Times,* 5 October 1997.

O'Connell, Vanessa, and Jon E. Hilsenrath. "Census 2000: The new demographics: Advertisers are cautious as household makeup shifts—Number of traditional families drops, but Madison Avenue is slow to change." *Wall Street Journal,* 15 May 2001.

Shellenbarger, Sue. "The heralded return of traditional families is not what it seems." *Wall Street Journal,* 31 May 2000.

"The Brady Bunch Theme Song." www.tripletsrus.com. Accessed 8 January 2002.

Retribing

Arnold, Martin. "For readers, online clubs." *New York Times,* 28 June 2001.

Cantor, Paul A. "Pro wrestling and the end of history." *Weekly Standard,* 4 October 1999.

Cashel, Jim. "Top ten trends for online communities." *Online Community Report,* 2001. (Accessed through www.onlinecommunityreport.com on 13 January 2002.)

Cothrel, Joseph, and Ruth Williams. "Online communities: Helping them form and grow." *Journal of Knowledge Management,* March 1999. (Accessed through www.participate.com)

Kanfer, Alaina. "What are communities doing online?" 7 December 1995. www.ncsa.uiuc.edu. (Accessed 3 January 2002.)

Petersen, Andrea. "Some places to go when you want to feel right at home—Communities focus on people who need people." *Wall Street Journal,* 6 January 1999.

Stille, Alexander. "With the Internet, his ideas again seem ahead of their time." *New York Times,* 14 October 2000.

"The case for on-line communities." *McKinsey Quarterly.* Accessed 12 January 2002.

www.celticnationsworld.com.

www.culteducation.com.

www.burningman.com.

Trust Deficit

"Attorney General to investigate 'David Manning' movie reviews." *Associated Press,* 5 June 2001. www.bostonherald.com, 5 June 2001.

"Did Ford cover up defective tires?" www.thedenverchannel.com. (2 September 2000.)

Arena, Kelli, and Art Harris. "FBI arrests 8 in fraud scheme targeting McDonalds game." www.cnn.com, 22 August 2001.

Donovan, Aaron. "Customers will retaliate for slights, study says." *New York Times,* 3 June 2001.

Elliot, Stuart. "Fast food marketers worry about contests after a rigging scandal." *New York Times,* 24 August 2001.

Holden, Jake. "The ring of truth." *American Demographics,* vol. 20, no. 10, October 1998.

Mulligan, Thomas S. "Texaco executives try to save face as charges of racist plot mount." *Los Angeles Times,* 5 November 1996.

Roberts, Bari-Ellen, and Jack E. White. "Portrait of a company behaving badly." *Time,* 16 March 1998.

Russell, Cheryl. "Growing distrust affects media impact." www .raveresults.com. (Accessed 27 December 2001.)

"Tough audience." *Adweek,* 29 August 1994.

South China Morning Post, 19 December 2000.

"Unconventional Wisdom." *Washington Post,* 25 July 1999.

Contradictory Consumption

Biddle, David. "Climbing the wall to boost recycling rates." *BioCycle,* September 1999.

Boerner, Christopher, and Kenneth Chilton. "False economy: The folly of demand-side recycling." *Environmental,* vol. 36, no. 1, January/February 1994.

Breslow, Mark. "I want my Ford Explorer!" *Dollars and Sense,* July/August 1998.

Brown, Lester, et al. "Population growth and . . . energy." *Beyond Malthus,* 10 April 1999.

Calian, Sara, and Tamzin Booth. "Ethical investing grows in the United Kingdom." *Wall Street Journal,* 19 June 2000.

Ford, Peter. "Organic farmers hear a call: If you grow it, they will buy." *Christian Science Monitor,* 24 March 1999.

Grier, Peter, and Liz Marlantes. "A tankful of data: Study adds fuel to debate over car efficiency." *Christian Science Monitor,* 1 August 2001.

Mitchener, Brandon. "Europe's beef farmers discover that it isn't easy going green." *Wall Street Journal,* 27 February 2001.

Pollan, Michael. "How organic became a marketing niche and a multibillion dollar industry." *New York Times Magazine,* 13 May 2001.

Puzzanghera, Jim. "Conservation not a solution, Cheney says." *San Jose Mercury News,* 1 May 2001.

Stranahan, Susan Q. "Marketing: Born free-range." *Fortune,* 29 October 2001.

Tonning, Barry. "Nuclear power—On a roll or on the ropes?" *State and Government News,* April 1999.

Transportation Statistics Annual Report, USDOT, 1999, pp. 103–117.

"White House rejects call for energy price controls." www.cnn.com. (Accessed 20 December 2001.)

www.essential.org.

www.populationaction.org. (Accessed 27 December 2001.)

Neverending Traffic Jam

Allen, Jodie T. "Sprawl, from here to eternity." *U.S. News & World Report,* 6 September 1999.

"Decentralization and downtowns." *Wall Street Journal,* 25 October 2001.

Downs, Anthony. "How America's cities are growing." *Brookings Review,* Fall 1998.

El Nasser, Haya. "Big 'burbs rival central cities." *USA Today,* 22 June 2001.

El Nasser, Haya. "Survey favors controlling sprawl." *USA Today,* 17 October 2000.

"Taking your car high tech." *Wall Street Journal,* 4 January 2002.

"Traffic: Jams cost area drivers $570 per year." *Chicago Tribune,* 2001.

You Talking to Me?

"British economics during the Middle Ages and Reformation." www.usu.edu/history. (Accessed 13 January 2002.)

Johnson, Robert. "Ad-packed TV's may soon be boarding city buses." *Wall Street Journal,* 21 February 2001.

"The peasant life." library.thinkquest.org/10949/hipeasant.html. (Accessed 13 January 2002.)

Weinstein, Elizabeth. "Some e-mail users devise tricks that keep them afloat." *Wall Street Journal,* 10 January 2002.
www.callcenter.com

Instant Polling

Bolland, Ed, Jr. "And how do you feel about being polled?" *New York Times,* 18 April 2001.

Harwood, John, and Cynthia Crossen. "Head counting: Why many new polls put different spins on presidential race—A close contest and plunge in public response rates tax an inexact science—Applying the 'sanity test'." *Wall Street Journal,* 29 September 2000.

White, Erin. "Market research on the Internet has its drawbacks—Many client companies have concerns about the accuracy of the online polls." *Wall Street Journal,* 2 March 2000.

Lawyers, Guns and Money

August, Ray. "America doesn't have 70% of the earth's lawyers." *ABA Journal,* September 1992.

Brown, Michael. "Stop 'strike suits' before they strike again." *Wall Street Journal,* 28 July 1998.

"Caseload highlights." www.ncsc.dni.us. (Accessed 15 March 2001.)

Goodman, Cindy. "Stockholders stampeding to courthouse." *Charlotte Observer,* 9 January 2000.

Jehl, Douglas. "Moratorium asked on suits that seek to protect species." *New York Times,* 12 April 2001.

Lloyd, Jillian. "Litigation explosion: Churches seeking shield from lawsuits." *Christian Science Monitor,* 28 October 1999.

Shaheena, Ahmad. "Get your sex insurance now." *U.S. News & World Report,* 2 March 1998.

Silverstein, Stuart. "Fear of lawsuits spurs the birth of new industry." *LA Times,* 27 June 1998.

Thornburgh, Dick. "Just say no to tort blackmail." *Wall Street Journal,* 21 January 2002.

www.davemcnally.com.

Screw You Very Much

"Are good manners a thing of the past?" *Yomiuri Shimbun/Daily Yomiuri,* 2 January 2001.

Calnan, Christopher. "Good manners are still key to doing business." *Knight-Ridder/Tribune Business News,* 7 October 2001.

Carpenter, Dave. "New hang-up: Cell phone rudeness." *Associated Press,* 1 August 2000.

Eder, Richard. "Picking apart manners, morals and misbehavior." *New York Times,* 13 July 1999.

Elias, Marilyn. "Study: Rudeness is poisoning U.S. workplace." *USA Today,* 14 June 2001.

Faison, Seth. "Service with some bile." *New York Times Current Events Edition,* 22 October 1995.

Jeffrey, Nancy Ann. "A rude awakening." *Wall Street Journal,* 12 May 2001.

Lueck, Thomas J. "Police have not improved enough on courtesy, survey finds." *New York Times,* 26 July 2001.

Marks, John. "The American uncivil wars; how crude, rude and obnoxious has replaced good manners and why that hurts our politics and our power." *U.S. News & World Report,* 22 April 1996.

"The matter of manners." *U.S. News & World Report,* 26 February 2001.

Shalit, Ruth. "FieldNotes: Polite society." www.linguafranca.com. (Accessed 3 January 2002.)

"The matter of manners." *U.S. News & World Report,* 26 February 2001.

Chapter 7: Consumer Trends

Peter Pan-ism

Anderton, Frances. "An electric razor, and maybe even a few close shaves." *New York Times,* 8 February 2001.

Brock, Fred. "Talking back is good medicine." *New York Times,* 4 February 2001.

Helliker, Kevin. "Health and medicine (a special report): Living with change: Start sweating: The elderly, looking to stave off the inevitable are descending on gyms, and the big rush is yet to come." *Wall Street Journal,* 18 October 1999.

Leland, John. "Riding a fad, hitting a bump." *New York Times,* 20 August 2000.

Merrick, Amy. "Stuffed animals—for adults—are holiday gift hit." *Wall Street Journal,* 24 December 2001.

Morrow, David J. "A medicine chest or a grocery shelf?" *New York Times,* 12 December 1999.

Rundle, Rhonda. "Health and medicine (a special report): Cashing in—Cutting edge: Baby boomers, refusing to give up exercise, are demanding surgical treatments that will keep them active. And surgeons are reaping the benefits." *Wall Street Journal,* 1 May 2000.

Siwolop, Sana. "Trying to roll back the clock, for a price." *New York Times,* 21 October 2001.

Stipp, David. "The executive body." *Fortune,* 7 January, 2002.

Prematurity

Argetsinger, Amy. "Earlier schooling urged, preschool for all 4-year-olds also backed." *Washington Post,* 27 January 2000.

Auerbach, Jon G. "ABC drives: Software firms coddle a growing market." *Wall Street Journal,* 2 April 1998.

Blake, Judith. "Building babies' brain power." *Seattle Times,* 5 January 1999.

Costello, Daniel. " 'Hi Mom, I'm OK'—Worried parents buy tech gear to keep tabs on their kids: What's cool, what works." *Wall Street Journal,* 28 September 2001.

Hansell, Saul. "Sparing, or spoiling, the child?" *New York Times,* 1 July 2001.

Hays, Constance L. "Technology takes over the Nursery." *New York Times,* 17 February 2000.

Petersen, Andrea. "IBM turns playful with a PC, unveiling 'Young Explorer' model." *Wall Street Journal,* 23 April 1998.

Raspberry, William. "Miracles not required." *Washington Post,* 14 May 2001.

Stanley, Alessandra. "French and Italian preschools: Models for U.S.?" *New York Times,* 25 April 2001.

Waldman, Peter. "Better behave, child, Ms. Fenstermaker is watching you—Kindergarten admission derby gets so hot, schools spy on tots at playgrounds." *Wall Street Journal,* 8 March 2000.

Zerknike, Kate. "Caps, gowns, diplomas: On graduates, to kindergarten!" *New York Times,* 29 June 2000.

Escalating Expectations

Alessandra, Tony. "Moments of magic." www.alessandra.com. (Accessed 27 January 2002.)

Barta, Patrick. "Winter of consumer discontent could worsen slowdown." *Wall Street Journal,* 20 February 2001.

Customer Service Management World Conference, 14–17 November 1999.

"Does wealth produce happiness?" *Wall Street Journal,* 2 January 2002.

Goode, Erica. "The online consumer? Tough, impatient, and gone in a blink." *New York Times,* 22 September 1999.

Hilsenrath, Jon E., and Joe Flint. "Consumers find fault with products of new economy." *Wall Street Journal,* 20 August 2001.

Millman, Joel. "Here's what happens to many lovely gifts after Santa rides off." *Wall Street Journal,* 26 December 2001.

Richtel, Matt. "24/7 service, but who's counting?" *New York Times,* 9 December 2001.

Trottman, Melanie. "Satisfaction with retail, financial companies slips." *Wall Street Journal,* 22 February 2000.

www.nbs.ac.uk.

Concrete Consumers

Bond, Jonathan, and Richard Kirschenbaum. *Under the Radar: Talking to Today's Cynical Consumer.* Wiley, New York, 1998.

Coleman, Calmetta. "Credit card offers get record low in response rate." *Wall Street Journal,* 19 March 2001.

Hays, Constance L. "Guerrilla marketing is going mainstream." *New York Times,* 7 October 1999.

McFarland, Jennifer. "Branding from the inside out." *Harvard Management Update,* February 2002.

McLean, Bethany. "Duck and coverage." *Fortune,* 13 August 2001.

Rasberry, Salli. "Advertising doesn't work—the way you think it does." *Whole Earth Review,* Spring 1987.

Shenk, Joshua Wolf. "The new anti-ad." *U.S. News & World Report,* 20 October 1997.

Slatalla, Michelle. "Mourning the magic of markdowns past." *New York Times,* 3 January 2002.

Takahashi, Corey. "Selling to Gen Y." *New York Times,* 8 April 2001.

Tedeschi, Bob. "For internet retailers, personalized E-mail advertising offers relatively low costs and a high response rate." *New York Times*, 9 August 1999.

Underhill, Paco. *Why We Buy: The Science of Shopping*. Simon and Schuster, New York, 1999.

www.ana.net.

Faux Authenticity

Costello, Daniel. "Here come . . . the '60s—Crockpots, spider-man make a comeback next year, watch for hidden fees." *Wall Street Journal*, 28 December 2001.

Merrick, Amy. "The rivalry behind retro chic." *Wall Street Journal*, 23 November 2001.

Moonan, Wendy. "A teddy bear celebrating a real teddy." *New York Times*, 14 December 2001.

Moonan, Wendy. "A trove of wheeled treasures." *New York Times*, 17 August 2001.

Siano, Joseph. "Ready for their comeback?" *New York Times*, 10 October 2001.

Sloane, Julie. "The B&B your way." *Fortune Small Business*, October 2000.

White, Gregory L. "Jeep's challenge: Stay rugged but add room for golf clubs." *Wall Street Journal*, 26 August 1998.

Born to Be Wired

Gleick, James. "Theories of connectivity." *New York Times*, 22 April 2001.

Grimes, Ann. "Technology (a special report)—The right look: You can have the greatest product imaginable. But if it isn't designed well, forget it." *Wall Street Journal*, 15 October 2001.

Romero, Simon. "Once proudly carried, now mere carrion." *New York Times*, 22 November 2001.

Selingo, Jeffrey. "Keeping up in class with software for a handheld." *New York Times*, 23 August 2001.

Sheth, Jagdish N., and Rajendra Sisodia. "Manager's journal: Why cell phones succeeded where iridium failed." *Wall Street Journal*, 23 August 1999.

Stellin, Susan. "The wired teenager." *New York Times,* 3 December 2001.

"3% of drivers are on phone, U.S. finds." *New York Times,* 24 July 2001.

Warren, Susan. "Ready-to-wear watchdogs." *Wall Street Journal,* 10 August 2001.

Nibble and Nap

Brody, Jane E. "Paying the price for cheating on sleep." *New York Times,* 28 December 1999.

Flaherty, Julie. "Perk du Jour: A well-stocked kitchen." *New York Times,* 12 January 2000.

Johnson, Dirk. "Snacking today: Any time and anywhere." *New York Times,* 30 July 1999.

"Less fun, less sleep, more work: An American portrait." *National Sleep Foundation Executive Summary,* 27 March 2001.

Miller, Martha. "Men, middle age and sleep." *Better Homes and Gardens,* vol. 79, no. 1, January 2001.

Nagourney, Eric. "Some snacks putting on a few calories." *New York Times,* 24 April 2001.

Neff, Jack, and Stephanie Thompson. "Snacking to prove more filling for TV, category expanding as on-the-go consumers nibble more often." *Advertising Age,* vol. 72, 14 May 2001.

O'Brien, Kathleen. "Fighting sleep on the job? Join the crowd." *New York Times,* 7 February 2001.

Sullivan, Allanna. "Health and medicine (a special report)—Food & fitness—Fill 'er up: To understand why Americans eat so poorly these days, keep this in mind: So little time, so much money." *Wall Street Journal,* 1 May 2000.

Thompson, Stephanie. "Snacks to go, Frito-Lay's single-serve canisters makes snacking easier—at a price." *Advertising Age,* vol. 72, 1 October 2001.

Buy Now, Pay Never

Atlas, Riva D. "Bankruptcies by individuals rise sharply so far in 2001." *New York Times,* 24 May 2001.

Bernasek, Anna. "Honey, can we afford it?" *Fortune Magazine,* 3 September 2001.

Fitch, Stephanie. "Busted." *Forbes Magazine,* 2 October 2000.

"Consumer credit rises at 1.7% rate." *New York Times,* 6 October 2001.

"Credit card payments steady in September, S&P reports." *New York Times,* 22 November 2001.

Healy, Patrick. "Credit cards a growth business with students." *Providence Business News,* 23 July 2001.

Leonhardt, David, and Riva D. Atlas. "Many Americans cut back on high interest debt." *New York Times,* 18 October 2001.

Leonhardt, David. "Easy money, harder times and the road in between." *New York Times,* 17 December 2001.

Marino, Vivian. "Resolving to pay off debt." *New York Times,* 30 December 2001.

Paul, Peralte C. "Debt counselors busy this year." *Knight-Ridder/ Tribune Business News,* 21 December 2001.

Reich, Robert B. "How long can consumers keep spending?" *New York Times,* 2 September 2001.

Sapsford, J., and Patrick Barta. "Precarious balances: Despite the recession . . ." *Wall Street Journal,* 2 January 2002.

Simpson, Burney. "Credit counselors brace for an influx." *Credit Card Management,* vol. 14, no. 7, pp. 17–24, September 2001.

Stowers, Andrea, and Steve Holiga. "Disturbing trends in bankruptcy." *Credit World,* November/December 1997.

www.hollywood.com/bankruptcies. (Accessed 17 January 2002.)

www.nfcc.org. (Accessed 3 January 2002.)

Wysocki, Bernard Jr. "Chapter 11 is becoming a more popular read." *Wall Street Journal,* 8 October 2001.

Upscaling

Lardner, James. "The urge to splurge." *U.S. News & World Report,* 24 May 1999.

Rohzon, Tracie. "Be it ever less humble: American homes get bigger." *New York Times,* 22 October 2000.

Taylor, Alex, III. "Road kill." *Fortune,* 12 November 2001.

Frugal Rich

Day, Sherri. "Wal-Mart and Home Depot are able to increase profits." *New York Times,* 15 August 2001.

Erikson, Chris. "The pursuit of less." *New York Times,* 3 September 2000.

Fairclough, Gordon. "Tobacco titans bid for organic cigarette maker." *Wall Street Journal,* 10 December 2001.

La Ferla, Ruth. " 'Cheap chic' draws crowds on 5th Ave." *New York Times,* 11 April 2000.

La Ferla, Ruth. "Jewels on a shoestring, at the pawnshop." *New York Times,* 6 January 2002.

La Ferla, Ruth. "Living the edited life: The materialism of scaling back." *New York Times,* 21 January 2001.

Marin, Rick. "Confessions of a frugal spendthrift." *New York Times,* 15 August 1999.

Murray, Kathleen. "Frugal shoppers worry retailers." *New York Times,* 17 December 2001.

Reese, Shelly. "The many faces." *Marketing Tools,* November/December 1997.

Walker, Sam. "The cheapest athletes in the world." *Wall Street Journal,* 18 June 1999.

Plumposity

Coleman, Calmetta Y. "Can't be too thin, but plus-size models get more work now—Some skinny women 'pad up,' others don't need to, Michelle Griffin's 2 lives." *Wall Street Journal,* 3 May 1999.

Creswell, Julie. "Resetting the fat thermostat." *Fortune,* 7 January 2002.

"Dining out = pigging out?" *Prepared Foods,* vol. 170, no. 10, October 2001.

Dolliver, Mark. "We can always start dieting next month." *Adweek,* vol. 42, no. 3, 15 January 2001.

Gahr, Evan. "Taste: What's the big idea?—Our correspondent visits the 'fat acceptance' convention: He weighs in." *Wall Street Journal,* 17 August 2001.

Henderson, C. W. "Over two-thirds of U.S. adults are obese or overweight." *Obesity, Fitness and Wellness Weekly,* 3 February 2001.

Jackson, Derrick Z. "The other epidemic: Deadly obesity." *Chicago Tribune,* 19 December 2001.

Kolos, Walter Douglas. "Boon times and their waistlines." *New York Times,* 11 February 2001.

Kuczynski, Alex. "Charting the outer limits of inner beauty." *New York Times,* 11 November 2001.

"Obesity alarm." *New York Times,* 16 December 2001.

Postrel, Virginia. "Americans' waistlines have become the victims of economic progress." *New York Times,* 22 March 2001.

Saltmarsh, N. R. "Greater food insecurity leads to greater obesity." *Obesity, Fitness & Wellness Week,* 14 July 2001.

Wadler, Joyce. "Turning a corner: A model at size 12." *New York Times,* 12 August 2001.

White, Erin. "Charming shoppes turns bigger sizes into bigger business." *Wall Street Journal,* 5 September 2001.

Chapter 8: Business Trends

Death of Demographics

Bulkeley, William M. "Verbind monitors customers to predict their next move." *Wall Street Journal,* 1 July 1999.

Bulkeley, William M. "E-commerce: Up and running—We're watching you." *Wall Street Journal,* 22 November 1999.

Heath, Rebecca. "The frontiers of psychographics." *American Demographics,* July 1996.

Karmin, Craig. "Spending it, investing it: Companies to watch: What demographics does—and doesn't—tell us about stock picking." *Wall Street Journal,* 29 November 1999.

Merrick, Amy. "Counting on the census—New data will let Starbucks plan store openings, help Blockbuster stock its videos." *Wall Street Journal,* 14 February 2001.

"Reversing the digital slide." *McKinsey Quarterly,* no. 4, p. 67, 2001.

Robinovitz, Karen. "Boys' night out at the Boutique." *New York Times,* 23 December 2001.

Von Bergen, Jane M. "Should stores tell what you bought?" *Philadelphia Inquirer,* 9 April 1998.

Weber, Thomas E. "Why those companies are so eager to get your e-mail address." *Wall Street Journal,* 12 February 2001.

www.dma.com. (Accessed 15 February 2002.)

Niche Picking

"Superbrands: Beer, Wine & Liquor." *Brandweek,* 19 June 2000.

Dreazen, Yochi J., Greg Ip, and Nicholas Kulish. "Why the sudden rise in the urge to merge and form oligopolies?" *Wall Street Journal,* 25 February 2002.

Gill, Dee. "Rolling into trouble: Consolidating firms promise sellers rewards—and even independence—but what they deliver is often quite different." *Wall Street Journal,* 27 November 2000.

Klein, Sarah A. "Lawyer seeks profit in pathology business." *Crain's Chicago Business,* 9 April 2001.

Maletz, Mark C., and Nitin Nohria. "Managing in the whitespace." *Harvard Business Review,* no. 2, 2001.

Maloney, Janice. "Goliath.com still winning, but David has an on-line sling." *New York Times,* 22 September 1999.

Matthews, Anna Wilde. "A giant radio chain is perfecting the art of seeming local." *Wall Street Journal,* 25 February 2002.

"Microsoft begins to muscle in on its rivals' home turf." *Wall Street Journal,* p. A10, 20 November 2001.

Experience This!

Hill, Sam. "Thirty trends in thirty minutes." *FSB,* 2 April 2001.

Pine, B. Joseph, III, and James H. Gilmore. "How to profit from experience." *Wall Street Journal,* 4 August 1997.

Pine, B. Joseph, III, and James H. Gilmore. *The Experience Economy.* Harvard Business School Press, Boston, 1999.

On the Brandwagon

Hill, Sam, and Chris Lederer. *The Infinite Asset: Managing Brands to Build New Value.* Harvard Business School Press, Boston, 2001.

Leung, Shirley. "Companies revive has-beens instead of creating brands." *Wall Street Journal,* 2001.

O'Donnell, Jayne. "Custody fight over Doughboy could burn General Mills." *USA Today,* 2001.

Vranica, Suzanne. "Ford buys Beanstalk for licensing magic." *Wall Street Journal,* 11 June 2001.

"What's in a name?" *Enterprise IG,* 2000.

A la Carte Business Models

"All yours." *Economist,* 1 April 2000.

Atkinson, William. "Supply chain management: Get more from contract manufacturers." *Purchasing,* 15 November 2001.

Doig, Stephen J., Ronald C. Ritter, Kurt Speckhals, and Daniel Woolson. "Has outsourcing gone too far?" *McKinsey Quarterly,* no. 4, 2001.

Fox, Sandra. "Business models: Contract biopharmaceutical manufacturing." *Chemical Market Reporter,* 29 October 2001.

Guth, Robert A., and Terho Uimonen. "Japan chipmakers suffer . . ." *Wall Street Journal,* 13 November 2001.

Maxwell, Jill Hecht. "The innovator's dilemma." *Inc,* October 2001.

Nelson, Emily. "Procter & Gamble considers changes in its back office." *Wall Street Journal,* 25 February 2002.

Reintermediation

Atkinson, Robert D. "Middlemen fight consumer choice." *Consumers Research Magazine,* April 2001.

Barta, Patrick. "Land grab? Why big lenders are so frightened by Fannie and Freddie." *Wall Street Journal,* 5 April 2001.

Chase, Martyn. "Metamediaries' seen as next step in services." *American Metal Market,* 22 March 2000.

Field, Graham. "Stuck in the middle." *Global Investor,* June 2001.

Hannon, David. "B2B software firms jockey for position in early 2001." *Purchasing,* 17 May 2001.

Hershey, Robert D., Jr. "Death of the fund salesman has been greatly exaggerated," *New York Times,* 8 October 2000.

Meehan, Michael. "B2B vendors take more hits as sales drop." *Computerworld,* 22 October 2001.

Stuart, Anne. "Not dead yet." *Inc,* vol. 3, no. 4, 2001.

White, Joseph B. "What works? Enough time has passed—and enough ventures have succeeded and failed—to start answering that question." *Wall Street Journal,* 23 October 2000.

www.mohansawney.com

Strange Bedfellows

Binkley, Christina. "Marriott to launch a publication using articles of top magazines." *Wall Street Journal,* 27 June 2001.

Carns, Ann, and Rebecca Buckman. "Pfizer to form tech venture with Microsoft, IBM." *Wall Street Journal,* 29 March 2001.

"Coca-Cola, AOL form $64 million alliance in marketing support." *Wall Street Journal,* 4 May 2000.

Metge, Bruce, and Andrew Nathanson. "Strategic alliances under the antitrust laws." *Mintz Levin (Boston),* 2001. (Accessed online.)

Michaelides, Stephen. "Strange bedfellows. Segment leaders forming new alliances." *Restaurant Hospitality,* September 2000.

"Poachers Are Out to Plunder Your Intellectual Property—Can You Do Anything?" Inc.com, 27 February 2002.

Schifrin, Matthew. "Partner or Perish." Forbes.com, 21 May 2001.

Thibodeau, Patrick. "DOJ investigates Microsoft's $135M investment in Corel." *Computerworld,* 19 February 2001.

Warner, Fran. "Ford, Microsoft forge alliance to create online build-to-order car-sales system." *Wall Street Journal,* 21 September 1999.

Waters, C. Dickinson. "Starbucks, Microsoft, MobileStar to create wireless environment." *Nation's Restaurant News,* 15 January 2001.

The Price Is Wrong

Abbott, John. "Lesson 11. Price management. (Yield management)." campusconnection.net. (Accessed 24 February 2002.)

Davis, Paul. "Airline ties profitability yield to management." *SIAM News,* May/June 1994.

"E-tailers catch on to personalized haggling." *Marketing Week,* 25 May 2000.

Interview with "Vinton Cerf, the father of the internet." www.alcatel.com, 1999. (Accessed 24 February 2002.)

Sharkey, Joe. "Hotels take a lesson from airline pricing." *New York Times,* 17 December 2000.

Slatalla, Michelle. "Haggling on the web interface to interface." *New York Times,* 28 September 2000.

Templin, Neal. "Your room costs $250 . . . No! $200 . . . No. . . ." *Wall Street Journal,* 2000.

Tierney, John. "A new toll? No, it's just value pricing." *New York Times,* 19 February 2002.

Trucco, Terry. "Hotel discounts: Be sure to ask." *New York Times,* 12 August 2001.

www.stanford.edu/~tammira/future.html. (Accessed 24 February 2002.)

Gotcha Tactics

"Citibank will pay $1.6 million to settle consumer complaints." *Wall Street Journal,* 28 February 2002.

Connecticut Attorney General's Office, "KB Toy Stores agree to end 'tying arrangement' in sale of Sony Playstation 2." www.cslib .org, 6 April 2001.

Ibid, "Attorney General files suit against AT&T." 20 December 2000.

Ibid, "State settles 'slamming' charges with Qwest Communications." 29 August 2001.

Ibid, "Law in plain language: Auto leasing." Accessed 24 February 2002.

"Connecticut Attorney General says even reputable telecom companies cheat consumers, on *60 Minutes,* Sunday, 16 December." CBS Television Network, 13 December 2001.

Evans, M. Stanton. "How telephone wars affect consumers." *Consumers' Research Magazine,* August 2001.

Langford, Danielle. "Real estates horrors." *Black Enterprise,* January 2002.

National Association of Attorneys General. "Travel scams: Don't get taken for a ride." www.naag.org, 2001. (Accessed 24 February 2002.)

Spagat, Elliot. "The rules—fraud: Walking the Internet beat." *Wall Street Journal,* 24 September 2001.

Zielbauer, Paul. "Car rental agency is ordered to stop charging speeders fines." *New York Times,* 21 February 2002.

Mass Personalization

Boyd, Jade. "Customer service turns practical—Businesses will look to analytical software to make better sense of raw customer data." *InternetWeek,* 17 December 2001.

Gaither, Chris. "Software to track customers' needs helped firms react." *New York Times*, 1 October 2001.

Gilmore, James H., and B. Joseph Pine, III. "The four faces of mass customization." *Harvard Business Review*, January–February 1997.

"Growing Interest in CRM." *VARbusiness*, 7 January 2002.

Kwak, Mary. "Web sites learn to make smarter suggestions." *MIT Sloan Management Review*, Summer 2001.

NATSS, "Employment change in selected industries, 1996–2006." *Contemporary Times*, Spring 1998.

Nee, Eric. "Going for rapid returns." *Fortune*, 19 March 2001.

Pound of Risk to Go

Allen, Franklin. "Financial Analysis (601) Lecture Notes." 4 December 2001.

"Designated contract markets registered with the CFTC." www .cftc.gov. (Accessed 25 February 2002.)

"Nobel Prize in Economic Sciences Winners 2001-1969," Nobel Prize Internet Archive. Accessed on Feb 25, 2002 through www.almaz.com/nobel/economics.

Perlman, Ellen. "The gambling glut," Governing, May, 1996.

"World's Futures & Options Exchanges." Accessed online on Feb 25, 2002.

Chapter 9: Workplace Trends

D-I-V-E-R-S-E

Belsie, Laurent. "Ethnic diversity grows, but not integration." *Christian Science Monitor*, 14 March 2001.

Belsie, Laurent. "Scholars unearth new field: White studies." *Christian Science Monitor*, 14 August 2001.

Dunham, Kemba J. "Career journal—The jungle: Diversity moves." *Wall Street Journal*, 1 May 2001.

Glazer, Nathan. "American diversity and the 2000 Census." *Public Interest*, Summer 2001.

Hillman, Amy. "Diversity and the bottom line: A study finds that many corporations would likely profit from diversity among their directors." *Knight-Ridder/Tribune News Service, East Lansing, Michigan,* 14 September 1998.

Maher, Kris. "Career journal: The jungle," *Wall Street Journal,* 4 December 2001.

Munk, Cheryl Winokur. "Deals and deal makers: Wall Street firms are moving towards staff of greater diversity." *Wall Street Journal,* 9 November 2001.

Wynter, Leonard. "Business and race." *Wall Street Journal,* 6 January 1999.

Paraprofessionalism

Fried, Joseph P. "Paralegal jobs surge as law firms seek to cut costs." *New York Times,* 12 March 2000.

HRSA Registered Nurse Survey.

Kelley, Tina. "Like a doctor's office, with a little more time." *New York Times,* 25 April 2000.

Kravetz, Stacy. "A special news report about life on the job—and trends taking place there." *Wall Street Journal,* 11 May 1999.

Robert Wood Johnson Foundation—Institute for the Future National Hospice and Palliative Care Office.

What, Me Work?

"Cash remains the best perk." *New York Times,* 25 June 2000.

Chorlton, Windsor. "Work: The daily grind we just can't do without." *Focus,* June 1995.

Fischer, Anne. "Is your business taking over your life?" *Fortune Small Business,* November 2001.

Greenhouse, Steven. "American's international lead in hours worked grew in 90's, report shows." *New York Times,* 1 September 2001.

Harpaz, Itzak. "The transformation of work values in Israel." *Monthly Labor Review,* May 1999.

Harrison, Chase, and Kenneth Dautrich. "The modern American worker." *Public Perspective,* August/September 1999.

Lambert, Bruce. "Booming prices for housing make for creative job perks." *New York Times,* 4 November 2000.

Messenger, Christian K. "The leisure ethic (book review)." *Studies in the Novel,* Fall 2000.

Todd, Richard. "All work, no ethic." *Worth,* December 1995/January 1996.

"Working by numbers." *Fortune,* 9 July 2001.

Last Job Review

Abelson, Reed. "Companies turn to grades, and employees go to court." *New York Times,* 19 March 2001.

Boyle, Matthew. "Performance reviews: Perilous curves ahead." *Fortune,* 28 May 2001.

Gorman, Elizabeth. "Moving away from "up or out," determinants of permanent employment in law firms." *Law & Society Review,* 1999.

Jenkins, Holman W., Jr. "Business world: How to execute 10%, nicely." *Wall Street Journal,* 18 July 2001.

Meier, Barry. "Ford is changing the way it rates work of managers." *New York Times,* 12 July 2001.

Shirouzu, Norihiko. "Documents suggest Ford policies kept white males from certain promotions." *Wall Street Journal,* 10 October 2001.

White, Joseph B. "Ford's Jacques Nasser is ousted as CEO." *Wall Street Journal,* 30 October 2001.

Celebrity CEOs

Collins, Jim. "Manager's journal: Beware the self-promoting CEO." *Wall Street Journal,* 26 November 2001.

Koudsi, Suzanne. "Beat it: Why CEOs are paid so much too." *Fortune Magazine,* 29 May 2000.

La Sage, John D. "For CEO's, image-making is going beyond blue suits. *Crain's Chicago Business,* 22 January 2001.

Lobe, Jim. "Despite 'boom,' income inequality worse than ever." *Inter Press Service,* 3 September 2000.

Nee, Eric. "Open season on Carly Fiorina: The CEO of Hewlett-Packard has had a brutal ride as her promises outpaced performance. But frankly, any CEO would have a hard time driving this company." *Fortune Magazine,* 23 July 2001.

Pollack, Ellen Joan. "Falling stars—Twilight of the gods: CEO as American icon slips into down cycle." *Wall Street Journal,* 5 January 1999.

"What the boss made." *Forbes,* 15 May 2000.

Willis, Clint. "The 100 highest rollers." *Forbes,* 2 April 2001.

www.mtv.com/news/articles/1451882/20020123/story.

Zachary, G. Pascal. "Faces of the '90s: CEOs are stars now, but why? And would Alfred Sloan approve?" *Wall Street Journal,* 3 September 1997.

Mercenary Management

Abelson, Reed. "Turning to the former chief for help in troubled times." *New York Times,* 29 October 2000.

Andrews, Fred. "Not holding a job is new work system." *New York Times,* 27 May 2001.

Ball, Susan. "Part-time executives: A new wave." *New York Times,* 10 October 1993.

Bryant, Adam. "New breed of chiefs rides to the rescue, then rides on." *New York Times,* 24 June 1998.

De Lisser, Ellen. "Executives for rent: Part-time, no benefits and happy to disappear—temporary help can be the answer." *Wall Street Journal,* 17 April 2000.

Dunham, Kemba J. "Career journal: The jungle." *Wall Street Journal,* 23 January 2001.

Ellin, Abby. "A generation of freelancers," *New York Times,* 15 August 1999.

Ho, Rodney. "Update on small business: Congress advances several bills to help small business." *Wall Street Journal,* 23 February 1999.

Jorgensen, Helene, and Hans Reimer. "Permatemps." *American Prospect,* 14 August 2000.

Leonhardt, David. "Entrepreneur's 'Golden Age' is fading in economic boom." *New York Times,* 1 December 2000.

O'Brien, Kathleen. "Calling the shots: Not just athletes are free agents." *New York Times,* 18 October 2000.

Roth, Daniel. "The question authority: Pink-slipped (sort of)." *Fortune,* 23 July 2001.

Silverman, Rachel Emma. "Career journal: CEO turnover slows as boards seem tolerant in a cool economy." *Wall Street Journal,* 24 April 2001.

Silverman, Rachel Emma. "Pay gaps: Interim CEOs require companies to ask themselves unusual questions—and come up with unusual compensation plans." *Wall Street Journal,* 12 April 2001.

Wessel, David. "Capital: Temp workers have lasting effect." *Wall Street Journal,* 1 February 2001.

24/7/365

Carton, Barbara. "Bedtime stories: In 24-hour workplace, day care is moving to the night shift." *Wall Street Journal,* 6 July 2001.

Kanabayashi, Masayoshi. "Japan moves toward 24-hour ports." *Wall Street Journal,* 11 September 2001.

Maher, Kris. "The new 24/7 work cycle." *Wall Street Journal,* 20 September 2000.

Schwadron, Terry. "They stay up late so your site does, too." *New York Times,* 20 September 2000.

Shellenbarger, Sue. "Families find ways to offset the effect of night-shift work." *Wall Street Journal,* 21 March 2001.

Shellenbarger, Sue. "Some employers begin to find what helps shift-worker families." *Wall Street Journal,* 20 September 2000.

Retooling

Bennett, Johanna. "The best way to . . . take classes." *Wall Street Journal,* 27 November 2000.

Eure, Rob. "E-commerce (a special report): The classroom—On the job: Corporate e-learning makes training available anytime, anywhere." *Wall Street Journal,* 12 March 2001.

Grimes, Ann. "E-commerce (a special report): Overview—The hope . . . and the reality—Big money is pouring into the business of education, but it's too soon to tell whether there will be any payoff." *Wall Street Journal,* 12 March 2001.

Lalonde, Robert. "The returns of going back to school for displaced workers." Center for Human Potential and Public Policy. (Accessed through www.harisschool.uchicago.edu, 22 February 2002.)

Schellenbarger, Sue. "New training methods allow jobs to intrude further into off hours." *Wall Street Journal,* 11 July 2001.

Silverman, Rachel Emma. "Career journal: CEO turnover slows as boards seem tolerant." *Wall Street Journal,* 24 April 2001.

"White collar lay-offs." *Fortune,* 23 July 2001.

Wilgoren, Jodi. "Golden years now bring new emphasis on learning." *New York Times,* 26 December 1999.

In a Land Far, Far Away

Glater, Jonathan D. "Telecommuting's big experiment." *New York Times,* 9 May 2001.

Hafner, Katie. "Working at home today?" *New York Times,* 2 November 2000.

Marino, Vivian. "Telecommuting as a workplace carrot." *New York Times,* 9 July 2000.

Siwolop, Sana. "Offices without walls, or borderlines." *New York Times,* 23 August 2000.

"Some workers swap cubicles for exotic locations." *Wall Street Journal,* 31 January 2001.

Chapter 10: Trendblasting

Bas (Ed.). *Air Conditioning, Heating & Refrigeration News,* 14 September 1998, p. 12.

Gilbert, John. "Dodge pickup's big and bold. Love it loathe it." *Star-Tribune (Minneapolis-St. Paul),* 13 October 1993.

Heber, Mark, et al. of Daimler-Chrysler prepared a white paper describing the evolution of their strategy, which was used as a basis for much of the discussion.

Hovelson, Jack. "Revamped Dodge rams rivals." *USA Today,* 4 November 1993.

Jones, Parnelli. "The artful Dodge." *Forbes FYI,* 14 March 1994.

Author's Note

Every statistic and factoid in this book comes from a reputable source. Great care has been taken to quote them accurately and in context. This book has been fact-checked, edited, reedited, copy-edited, proofread, and reviewed for accuracy (in whole and in part) by six different people. Still, somewhere in here is a mistake, and it's probably a whopper, like "Pasadena is the capital of Poland," or some such. *When* you find it, please send me an e-mail and we'll try to fix it for the next printing.

Every anecdote and personal story is true as well; however, in some circumstances I have slightly changed the names of the people involved and some details of timing and location to avoid unintended embarrassment.